The Silent Church

Human Rights and Adventist Social Ethics

Zdravko Plantak

Foreword by Sakae Kubo

First published in Great Britain 1998 by
MACMILLAN PRESS LTD
Houndmills, Basingstoke, Hampshire RG21 6XS and London
Companies and representatives throughout the world

A catalogue record for this book is available from the British Library.

ISBN 0–333–71558–6 hardcover
ISBN 0–333–72448–8 paperback

First published in the United States of America 1998 by
ST. MARTIN'S PRESS, INC.,
Scholarly and Reference Division,
175 Fifth Avenue, New York, N.Y. 10010

ISBN 0–312–21621–1

Library of Congress Cataloging-in-Publication Data
Plantak, Zdravko.
The silent church : human rights and Adventist social ethics /
Zdravko Plantak ; foreword by Sakae Kubo.
p. cm.
Includes bibliographical references and index.
ISBN 0–312–21621–1
1. Human rights—Religious aspects—Seventh-Day Adventists.
2. Seventh-Day Adventists—Doctrines. I. Title.
BX6154.P57 1998
261.7'088'267—dc21 98–18586
CIP

This book is printed on paper suitable for recycling and made from fully managed and sustained forest sources.

10 9 8 7 6 5 4 3 2 1
07 06 05 04 03 02 01 00 99 98

Printed and bound in Great Britain by
Antony Rowe Ltd, Chippenham, Wiltshire

To my best friend, companion and wife Lidija for her encouragement, intellectual integrity and support in my academic pursuit in search of knowledge and wisdom throughout this and any other study her husband undertook. Also, to our delightful daughters, Natasha Stephanie and Roberta Lara, who could not comprehend why their father had to spend so much time at a computer, in his study or libraries, reading books.

Contents

Acknowledgements ix

Foreword by Sakae Kubo xi

Introduction 1

Part I Seventh-day Adventists and Human Rights 9

1. Adventist Attitudes to Human Rights: An Historical Perspective 11

2. Emergence of Concern for Human Rights 38

Part II Seventh-day Adventist Responses to Some Issues in Human Rights 51

3. Wealth Divide: The Seventh-day Adventist Church and the Poor 53

4. Racial Divide: Discrimination and Adventism – Theological and Hermeneutical Considerations 74

5. Gender Divide: The Role of Women in the Seventh-day Adventist Church 92

Part III Social Theology in Seventh-day Adventist Scholarship 123

6. Reasons for Social Concern in Modern Adventism 125

7. Adventism's 'New Theology' 137

Part IV Theology and Ethics of Human Rights: The Seventh-day Adventist Perspective 151

8. Philosophical Basis for Human Rights 153

9. A Common Theological Basis for Human Rights 163

10. Adventist Basis for Human Rights 187

Conclusion 208

Notes 214

Further Reading 255

Index 269

Acknowledgements

I would like to acknowledge a number of people without whom this book would never have seen its completion. Many people influenced me in various ways to search for social and individual justice and to study the central theme of this book. However, several individuals and institutions deserve my special gratitude and recognition.

I would like to thank *imprimis* my academic adviser, Professor Jack Mahoney for his gentle and clear lead, for his tremendous support especially in times when my academic and pastoral duties clashed, and for his professionalism and efficiency in returning my work always within three days, even when he had to sacrifice his weekends.

I would also like to thank Dr Hugh Dunton, the then director of the Ellen G. White Research Centre, Europe, and His Honour Judge Dr Peter Jackson, one of Her Majesty's Judges in England, for taking time to read this dissertation in their already busy schedules. Their comments and suggestions were very valuable in the last stages of this research.

I am grateful to Dr Michael Pearson for initiating some ideas during his lectures and, especially, in the early days of the research when we met with a desire to establish a Seventh-day Adventist Ethics Centre for Europe.

I cannot forget the kindness and understanding of many of my parishioners at Central London Church, Eastbourne, Hastings, Bromley and Chatham, whose support and positive attitude towards my studies allowed me to spend time with books, even when it was not sermon preparation. The administration of the South England Conference of the Seventh-day Adventist Church not only allowed me to pursue part-time study, but also allocated a ten-week study-leave, so I could finish the research. This flexibility and desire for the church's ministers to continue their further education are greatly appreciated.

Finally, without the influences of my truly Christian father and mother, who taught me never to accept injustice and always to stand on the side of the oppressed, I would probably never have desired to write about social theology, ethics and human rights. I am most grateful for their example, in word and deed, of being the followers of Christ at all times.

Foreword

It is a pleasure for me to write the Foreword to this significant book. A little over ten years before he completed his dissertation and obtained his doctorate from King's College, University of London, Dr Plantak came to Newbold College (Bracknell, England) where I was principal. He came from the old Yugoslavia as a student to learn English before completing his theological studies. At best his English was elementary. In this short time he has mastered the English language to the extent that he serves as one of the leading pastors of the Seventh-day Adventist Church in Great Britain and was able to complete a doctorate in a British university. And considering the fact that he was able to do the research and complete 400-page dissertation while carrying on his pastoral duties, this is nothing short of phenomenal. Indispensable to these achievements are the wholehearted support, encouragement and understanding of his family, his two daughters, Natasha and Roberta, and especially his loving, devoted and equally talented wife, Lidija. It is thus with justifiable pride that I contribute this Foreword.

Seventh-day Adventists arose out of the Millerite movement expecting the end of the world on 22 October 1844. Even after the disappointment, though no longer setting any specific date for the coming of the Lord, that event loomed dominant in their living and thinking. Understandably in that kind of context they were little concerned about improving social conditions in this world. However, as certain social issues arose they had to decide how to respond. They decided to help runaway slaves through the underground railroad. Other issues arose that touched more specifically their own beliefs and practices. They would use their influence against alcohol. They would fight fiercely those who would establish Sunday laws. But these efforts at social reform were few and concerned their own particular self-interest. This was due to the residual effect of the sense of imminence connected with the 1844 movement. With the end so near, they could not spend their limited time and finances on anything except that which contributed to the preparation of the world for the end.

Max Warren's charge, that Adventists because of their fixation upon the second advent and their belief that this world is totally under the control of Devil forsook all responsibility for this world, was in fact being confirmed. And if this continued beyond the early years of Adventism, the failure of the church would be assured since it would be so otherworldly that it would have no present relevance.

As time went on, however, their Christian concern made them feel the need to direct themselves beyond their self-interests. They would help the poor and unfortunate of society; they would alleviate suffering by establishing hospitals. They could justify these activities because they were done for soul-winning purposes, not altruistic ones. Therefore, if the results were not commensurate with their expenses, should they be continued? After all, was not the winning of souls the overriding priority and, therefore, should their efforts and finances be diluted into helping the unfortunates? Of course, they would help the poor and sick if it served as a means of winning them to Christ. But helping the poor and sick simply to alleviate their condition and suffering was not enough. They would do good, but calculatingly not spontaneously. While this accomplished some earthly good, such goodness evaporated because of the ulterior motive.

Self-interest continued to predominate. Adventists must continue to attack alcohol and tobacco and likewise Sunday laws. But many within the church felt that ulterior motives and self-interest were not adequate reasons for Christians to do good. But there has never been a clear-cut statement regarding Adventists' response to social ethics by the church. What Dr Plantak has done in this book by bringing together the thinking of the church's theologians on this matter is to show how the church should move in this direction. Many Adventist theologians have written in this area, but this is the first time that all of their thoughts have been put together in a systematic and organised way.

Obviously no single church can deal with the vast social problems that exist in the world, not to speak of the Adventist church alone. Even with the help of governments, this is an impossible task. Adventists must move away from the idea that they should do good only if it helps to convert. They must also move away from helping only where it serves their self-interest. Yet they must not try to do everything and everywhere. As much as possible they should concentrate on areas that logically flow out of their theology, without renouncing their participation in other areas as it becomes appropriate. The Adventist Development and Relief Agency may not be particularly Adventistic in terms of Adventists' unique theology, but it is in harmony with their basic Christian concern and the world-wide organisation of the Adventist church lends itself to this kind of organisation that concerns itself with disaster and catastrophe throughout the whole world. This book should help Adventists to know where their efforts would be most appropriate since no one group can do everything.

The book should also go a long way towards helping Adventists be comfortable with the expectation of an imminent return of their Lord and a present Christian concern for the whole man. In fact they should not only feel comfortable with this dual interest, but be impelled by the first to do the second, so that the second becomes a necessity because of the first.

SAKAE KUBO

Introduction

GENERAL CONTEXT OF THE RESEARCH

The question of human rights has attracted attention since the beginning of human society. The expression 'human rights' is, however, relatively new, having come into everyday usage only with the founding of the United Nations in 1945. Although most students of human rights trace the historical development of the concept back to ancient Greece and Rome,[1] there is no reason why it should not be taken further back into antiquity to the time of creation. As Thomas Paine remarked:

> The error of those who reason by precedents drawn from antiquity, respecting the rights of man, is that they do not go far enough into antiquity. They do not go the whole way. They stop in some of the intermediate stages of an hundred or a thousand years. ... But if we proceed on, we shall at last come out right; we shall come to the time when man came from the hand of his Maker.[2]

In contemporary international usage 'human rights' has been understood in the context of the Enlightenment of the seventeenth and eighteenth centuries,[3] and especially in the light of the United Nations Charter and the Universal Declaration of Human Rights of 1948.[4]

Ironically, while the twentieth century has seen the greatest growth in the recognition of human rights and concern for their safeguarding, it has also experienced a corresponding violation of human rights.[5] Many millions of people were killed and tortured in the holocaust of Hitler's concentration camps and gas chambers, by Stalin in Siberian labour camps, in Idi Amin's reign of terror in Uganda, through the ruthless killings of the Khmer Rouge in the late 1970s, and in revolutions of countries such as Argentina, Uruguay, Chile, Salvador and South Africa. Most recently, Croatia, Bosnia-Herzegovina and Rwanda have not escaped the horrors of human right violations in the campaigns that became known as 'ethnic cleansing'.

Because of these and similar human rights violations the need to investigate further the concept of human rights is felt in the hope that a Christian perspective will throw some additional light on the debate and, at least in theory, will provide a basis for preventing further social injustice and human rights violations.

This study is concerned with investigating one church's response to the concept of human rights in the context of its history and in the scope of its theology, namely the Seventh-day Adventist church. While many treatises have been written about human rights in the second half of the twentieth century, none so far has emerged from the perspective of a relatively modern church entity such as Seventh-day Adventism. The findings of this research, therefore, may be important in wider Protestant circles and in the context of general Christian social ethics.

THE SEVENTH-DAY ADVENTIST CONTEXT

The Seventh-day Adventist church, as an international denomination, has encountered in different countries and at different times social unrest, tension and, on occasions, injustice. This research seeks to investigate Adventists' socio-ethical consciousness in different socio-political contexts in different parts of the world through its history. An endeavour to systematise or limit this investigation to one particular country has not been made, as this would limit the ability to view the church's sensitivity to socio-ethical issues in different situations at different historical periods of its brief existence. Instead, an attempt has been made to look at various socio-political situations where and when certain human rights violations occurred and what the Adventist response to them was. The main focus, however, is on Seventh-day Adventism in the United States, where the movement originated and from where it still influences its worldwide community of believers.

While Adventist socio-ethical consciousness has been raised somewhat in the last two decades, especially among its more liberally inclined scholars, as will be argued in Part III, no undertaking has been made to address the issue of human rights in a systematic way. This study strives to break new ground by analysing and filtering Adventist social theology with special reference to the theology and ethics of human rights.

THE PURPOSE OF THE RESEARCH

The purpose of this research is to examine Seventh-day Adventist history, theology and ethics in order to discover reasons for certain inconsistencies in the church's approach to human rights. A number of pragmatic and theological reasons will be identified, which arguably led Adventists into a discrepant and, at times, questionable approach to human rights.

In order to contribute to a much needed consistency in the theology and ethics of human rights, sample issues of social ethics are examined to discover the pattern of Adventist social ethics in practice. Also, a link is made, and the reasons explored, between the church's lack of interest in social thought at the beginning of the twentieth century and its social concern at the end of the twentieth century.

The Organisation of the Research

Part I seeks to provide a detailed chronology, from the beginnings of the church in the mid-nineteenth century to the present day, of the socio-ethical responses of Seventh-day Adventist to certain problems connected with human rights. Chapter 1 examines Adventist attitudes to human rights by means of an historical perspective. The problem of certain theological themes and philosophical influences recurring in the development of Adventist theology, the subject of Chapter 2, has been the primary reason for the church's reluctance to engage more often and wholeheartedly in the socio-political and socio-economic struggle for the betterment of this world.

Part II examines in more detail three major social issues in Seventh-day Adventism as related to the theory of human rights. Each of the three chapters treats an issue which is in some way connected with the struggle for human rights. Chapter 3 deals with the church's attitude to the poor. It focuses on Adventist struggles against poverty. Racial and gender division, i.e. issues relating to race relations in the church, and the understanding of the role of women are examined in Chapters 4 and 5 respectively. Lack of consistency in dealing with these three aspects of social ethics is identified and the need to find reasons for this inconsistency is established. The latter is what is attempted in Part III.

Part III deals with the question of social theology in Adventism. The reasons for social concern in modern Adventism are identified through theological themes in Chapter 6, while Chapter 7 examines why social theology became an Adventist concern in and after the 1950s. The evidence seems to suggests that the Adventist 'New Theology' can be identified as the main reason why a number of contemporary Adventist scholars are writing on issues of moral and social theology.

In Part IV an attempt is made to evaluate and synthesise a contemporary Adventist theology which could contribute to a more comprehensive theology and ethics of human rights. A general philosophical basis and wider perspective of the origins of human rights is discussed in Chapter 8. Chapter 9 examines aspects of creation, theological anthropology and the place of the Kingdom of God in the debate on human rights. Since these are theological categories common to all Christians and not only Adventists, Chapter 10 extends the discussion to several distinctive, or what Adventist sometimes call *peculiar*, features of Seventh-day Adventist theology which contribute to a theory of human rights. Such theological perspectives as the moral law, the Sabbath, the role of the prophetic community and the second coming seem to build further a basis for social involvement and give strong support to a theology and ethics of human rights.

The conclusion summarises the findings of the previous four parts, notes the reactive nature of the Adventist pragmatic approach to human rights issues and suggests that the Seventh-day Adventist church should be more proactive when faced with evils in society. The radical element of their pioneers needs to be employed again in the modern social dilemmas which Adventist encounter at the end of the twentieth century.

THE SCOPE AND SOURCES OF THE RESEARCH

Research of this kind can never be accomplished in a scholarly vacuum. Numerous people and articles influenced the direction of this study. Dr Michael Pearson, Vice-Principal of Newbold College, Bracknell, originally initiated interest in this field through his lectures and numerous discussions. Later, in the middle of this research, his book *Millennial Dreams and Moral Dilemmas* was published. Its influence is apparent on several occasions through this research. Pearson's study, although the first to investigate the ethics of the Seventh-day Adventist church, deals with moral decisions Adventists have made in the area of human sexuality, and is more, but not exclusively, concerned with personal ethics. The focus of his work are such issues as abortion, homosexuality, contraception, divorce and the role of women. This research attempts to continue Pearson's work by extending the study further to Adventist social ethics.

In addition to that, several valuable works became available at the beginning of this research which influenced parts of the study. A provocative sociological interpretation of the history of the church by Malcolm Bull and Keith Lockhart, *Seeking a Sanctuary*, was especially helpful in studies on race relations and the role of women. Also, Charles Teel's unpublished study 'Withdrawing the Sect, Accommodating the Church, Prophesying the Remnant' influenced ideas on general social ethics. However, beside a few discrete articles no major study has been undertaken on the church's attitudes to human rights.

At times it has been difficult to find the 'official' position of the church on a given issue. This is because the church, with its pragmatic approach, and in order to avoid controversy and preserve its unity, has avoided committing itself on socio-ethical dilemmas. The major primary source of information for the purposes of this research were found in Adventist periodicals: *Adventist Review*, a general paper of the Seventh-day Adventist church; *Ministry*, a magazine for clergy; *Adventist Heritage*, a journal of Adventist history; *The Adventist Women*, a publication of the Association of Adventist Women; *Liberty*, a magazine upholding religious liberty; *Light*, *Insight* and *Communicator*, papers issued in the United Kingdom. For the work of Adventist Development and Relief Agency (ADRA) newsletters such as *ADRA – TED Update*, *ADRA Advertiser* and *Bulletin of the Humanitarian Agency ADRA* were helpful. For a specific field of study of German Adventism *Der Adventbote* and *Aller Diener* were helpful. A valuable source of information about the situation in Yugoslavia was found in *Adventpress*, *Adventisticki Pregled* (Advent Review) and *Bilten Humanitarne Organizacije ADRA*.

A more self-critical analysis of Seventh-day Adventism with numerous entries on issues of social ethics has been *Spectrum*, a journal produced by Adventist intellectuals since 1969. Many articles considering issues that this inquiry undertook can be found in this publication.

A recurring feature of this research is the contribution made to Adventist social ethics, both implicitly and explicitly, by the church's prominent pioneer and co-founder, Ellen G. White. Regarded as a prophetess, her influence is still profoundly felt some 80 years after her death in 1915. Her letters, manuscripts and published works in books and articles have been drawn on throughout this study, since she helped shape both the theology and policy of the church.

There are obviously limitations to an undertaking of this kind. In chapters examining the history of the church's social involvement no new information is provided. Its value is, rather, in analysing significant developments of Seventh-day Adventist socio-moral thinking.

The issues of poverty, racism and gender inequality could each be a study on its own. All three are sufficiently important to the church that more space should be dedicated to each in a separate study. Since they serve the purpose of illustrations of the need for social theology, their value is therefore limited.

TERMINOLOGY

Some terminological points need to be made at the outset. The term 'Seventh-day Adventist church' has been abbreviated in places to 'SDA church' or 'the church' for the purposes of relieving the text of a certain heaviness and to make it easier to read. Similarly, the term 'Seventh-day Adventist' has on occasions been abbreviated to 'Adventist', describing a Seventh-day Adventist believer after the church's organisation in 1863. Also, 'Seventh-day Adventists' has been at times shortened to 'SDAs'. The terms 'advent believer' and 'Sabbatarian adventist' describe more precisely Millerite adventists before 1844 and advent believers who accepted the doctrine of the Sabbath between 1844 and the organisation of the church respectively.

American influence has been felt in Adventism from its birth to the present time. A number of publications mentioned in this study will inevitably be from Adventist American literature. No attempt has been made to change or even indicate Americanisms in quotes and original phrases and spellings which are different from UK English.

The major publishing houses which are mentioned on numerous occasions in footnotes have been abbreviated after the first entry. So, for example, 'Review and Herald Publishing Association' has been shortened to 'Review and Herald', 'Pacific Press Publishing Association' to 'Pacific Press' and 'William B. Eerdmans Publishing Company' to 'Wm. B. Eerdmans'.

THE MAIN CONTRIBUTIONS OF THE RESEARCH

A systematic analysis of significant developments in Seventh-day Adventist socio-moral thinking has not been attempted before. In this probably lies the first contribution of the book. Furthermore, as this chronicling suggests, the need for a more positive, proactive and comprehensive social ethics is firmly established. The leading factors in the church's theology and history in the direction of social consciousness are identified. Finally, an attempt towards an Adventist social theology and ethics, with a special focus on human rights, is developed. This theology and ethics of human rights, a preoccupation of Part IV, does not claim to be either comprehensive or final. It does, however, imply that Seventh-day Adventists have a contribution to make to Christian social ethics in general with their emphasis on God's moral law, the liberating influences of the Sabbath, the importance of a prophetic role which Adventists assume, and the aspects of the certainty of the second coming of Christ.

In general, the intention of the study is to sharpen Seventh-day Adventist social thought and, in this way, to influence Adventists to employ principles of social justice and equality in their own ecclesiological sphere and extend this influence outside their own circles through a selfless application of the same principles. This study calls for a balance between individual and social ethics, theology and ethics, eschatology and the present life, evangelistic proclamation and influence in the present world. As with many issues at other of its history, the church is at something of a crossroads. Depending upon the direction it takes now, its destination will be determined.

Beyond the sphere of Seventh-day Adventism, the research could be taken as a contribution to wider Christian social theology.

Especially with the implications of the weekly and annual Sabbatical concept other Christian bodies might benefit in their understanding of ethics of human rights. This research also has a socio-historical importance as the Seventh-day Adventist church could be viewed as a representative of an expanding conservative Christian denomination, an example to other such groups in its sociological and theological self-understanding and growth.

Part I
Seventh-day Adventists and Human Rights

1

Adventist Attitudes to Human Rights: An Historical Perspective

EARLY ADVENTISM IN THE FIRST HALF OF THE NINETEENTH CENTURY

The Revival Movement of William Miller

Seventh-day Adventism emerged, as an indigenous American denomination, out of the social and religious upheaval of mid-nineteenth century America. Its immediate roots are in the revivalism which swept the north-eastern States in the late 1830s and early 1840s.[1] Yet it would be wrong to perceive the revival of 1830, 'which has been hailed as the greatest in modern times',[2] as all of one piece. At least two groups can be detected by examining both sociological patterns and theological or doctrinal differences. Of the latter, Michael Pearson rightly observes that 'a major source of disagreement was the millennium'.[3] For the postmillennial group, whose representative was Charles G. Finney, America's eschatological role was of 'the last, best hope of earth'. For them, the millennium was to be the climax of the American dream, and it was to come about by human achievement; hence the wrong reason for development and reform on both a personal and a social level. For believers in the advent, accepting the premillennial apocalyptical view, this American optimism was at best a deception and certainly not in accordance with their understanding of the biblical prophecies. They believed that the millennium would follow the second advent of Christ, and hence their pessimistic view of any kind of human-initiated progress in social or moral reforms.

During the period before the expected advent the followers of William Miller,[4] the leading exponent of this view, concentrated on preaching the soon coming of Christ and preparing intensively for it. After their first disappointment on 21 March 1844, they revised the date to 22 October 1844 as the time of the Christ's second coming.[5] They found neither time nor energy to 'waste' on matters of earthly existence. Many neglected their farms and left their shops unattended as they awaited the arrival of the Lord.[6] Even less were the Millerites concerned with such issues as human rights or social welfare. Joseph Bates, a prominent abolitionist before accepting the advent message, described the attitude of Advent believers in the following way:

> Some of my good friends that were engaged in the temperance and abolition cause, came to know why I could not attend stated meetings as formerly, and argued that my belief in the coming of the Saviour should make me more ardent in endeavouring to suppress these growing evils. My reply was, that in embracing the doctrine of the second coming of the Saviour, I found enough to engage my whole time in getting ready for such an event, and aiding others to do the same... .[7]

One can easily see, therefore, that in Millerite-Adventist history, the involvement of advent believers in humanitarian and social aspects of life was minimal, if it existed at all.

Post-Disappointment Period

After the Great Disappointment in the autumn of 1844 a small group of Adventists continued to believe that the previously proposed date was correct; however, they now interpreted the event differently. By linking the prophecy of Daniel 8 with Leviticus 16 and Hebrews 9, they understood that Christ had begun the second phase of his ministry in the heavenly sanctuary instead of coming to earth to destroy sin in 1844. From that small group (which later discovered the Sabbath doctrine) a movement grew which finally, in 1863, approved a formal organisation – the General Conference of Seventh-day Adventists.[8] In the 19-year period between the Disappointment and organisation, the process of discovering its identity and the desire for survival and integrity were the group's primary concerns. Many years later the church would learn lessons about human rights and the dignity of human beings (regardless of religion, race or any other division), as it looked back at the very traumatic and tense period of its early history.[9] However, as some of the most recent examples of the role of the church in the disintegration of the former Yugoslavia arguably demonstrate, it may take time for the church to give practical effect to the lessons it has learned.[10]

SABBATARIAN ADVENTISM AFTER THE CHURCH'S ORGANISATION IN 1863

Doctrinal Discovery with Emphasis on the Prophecies of Daniel and Revelation

During the first two decades of Sabbatarian Adventism, its leading believers were predominantly concerned with the process of clarifying and redefining their doctrinal position with special interest in the prophecies of Daniel and Revelation. For the first time in Adventist thinking, the issue of religious liberty and the separation of church and state emerged within the context of prophetic studies. John N. Andrews, for example, in his 'Thoughts on Revelation XIII and XIV' identified the 'two horns like a lamb' (Rev 13: 11) as civil and religious liberty.[11] Yet, such theorising accomplished very little on the practical level of involvement in the fight for religious or any other human rights.

Godfrey Anderson, a contemporary Adventist historian, has rightly argued that Adventists' 'prophetic interpretation and their distinction from the larger society brought about by their emphasis on Sabbath, which sometimes took them into conflict with Sunday laws, led the Sabbatarian Adventists to expect nothing good from their nation'.[12] Although Adventists pursued political neutrality in the 1850s and 1860s, nevertheless, when pressed with Sunday laws and persecuted for their Sabbath observance or Sunday work, they started using political means to achieve their religious freedom guaranteed in the First Amendment of the Constitution. It began in 1878 in Georgia when the vengeful spirit was first manifested against Samuel Mitchell of Quitman. He was convicted of Sunday work and sentenced to 30 days in jail where filthy conditions ruined his health and caused his death a year and a half later.[13] This case was followed by many more, not only in Georgia but in Arkansas, Tennessee and other Southern states, as well as New Hampshire and Maine.

Sunday Laws – Reasons for Establishment of the Religious Liberty Association

The attempt to introduce legislation which would regulate public activity on Sundays (promoted by the radical Protestant organisation, the National Reform Association) was strongly opposed by Seventh Day Baptists and Seventh-day Adventists – who saw this as a threat to their religious liberty – and by other liberal-minded representatives of labour and secular bodies. However, the first time that Seventh-day Adventists appeared in legislative halls to defend their rights was on 21 May 1888, when Senator H. W. Blair of New Hampshire introduced 'a bill in the Fiftieth Congress, designed to enforce Sunday, nation wide, as "a day of religious worship"'.[14] Adventist arguments, alongside the reasoning of other small groups, were effective, the bill was successfully opposed and the Congressional committee turned down the legislation despite the efforts of Senator Blair, who was its chairman.

Adventists had been represented by A. T. Jones and J. O. Corliss, who belonged to the General Conference Committee on Religious Liberty organised in 1887. On 21 July 1889, this committee was merged into the organisation of the National Religious Liberty Association, which continued until its reorganisation in 1903, when it was renamed the Religious Liberty Department of the General Conference of the Seventh-day Adventists. At the time of organising the Religious Liberty Association, the Pacific Press, publishers of the *Sabbath Sentinel*, began the *Sentinel Library* (from 1893 known as the *International Religious Liberty Library*).[15] Its purpose, together with other publications on religious liberty, was that of '"sounding the alarm" on the "true bearing of uniting church and State" in the agitation for religious legislation'.[16] From 1886 the magazine carried different names – *Sentinel, Southern Sentinel, The American Sentinel, The Sentinel of Liberty* – but all under the umbrella of *Sentinel of Christian Liberty*. The primary objectives of the magazine were devoted to the 'defence of the principles of religious liberty in the United States. It was intended to educate the public in the principles and advantages of religious freedom for all citizens, to review the historical background of the American Constitution ... and to disclose the discriminatory nature of religious ordinances whenever and wherever introduced and enforced.'[17]

Adventist understanding of religious liberty was spelled out in four points in 1889 as the 'Declaration of Principles' of the National Religious Liberty Association organised in Battle Creek, Michigan:

> We believe in supporting the civil government, and submitting to its authority.
> We deny the right of any civil government to legislate on religious questions.
> We believe it is the right, and should be the privilege, of every man to worship according to the dictates of his own conscience.
> We also believe it to be our duty to use every lawful and honorable means to prevent religious legislation by the civil government; that we and our fellow citizens may enjoy the inestimable blessings of both civil and religious liberty.[18]

Even though these principles might sound all-embracing, nineteenth-century Adventists were basically interested in defeating the Sunday laws, which were creating great problems for the Adventist community. In other words, while the wording of the 'Declaration of Principles' was broad enough to take into consideration different types of religious liberty and other rights that all people should enjoy, Adventist involvement on a practical level can be narrowed down to only one issue – the Sabbath/Sunday problem.[19]

In the eyes of more than one Adventist historian and ethicist, this desire to protect the church's interests only has been seen as selfish and unethical.[20] It is suggested that 'Adventists have been politically active insofar as they wanted to protect the interests of organisation and members'. On the other hand, 'other worthy but non-sectarian causes have sometimes failed to attract Adventist support, and the church, it is felt, has thereby been morally compromised.'[21] The church's silence on the issue of human rights in the 1960s, for example, has been pointed to as a prime example.[22] While criticism of early Adventist non-involvement in the broader spectrum of human rights was fair and correct, more recently Adventists have become involved on a personal level and through organising independent bodies in order to fight social evils such as poverty, natural disasters and inhumane treatment of others.[23]

However, this type of involvement is still in its infancy and, unfortunately, attracts a relatively small proportion of Adventists.

Adventists have always been keen on evangelism. Their evangelistic interests and efforts can be illustrated by the growth of the church from about 300 members in 1863, when the General Conference of the Seventh-day Adventist Church was organised, to over 8 million at its last session in 1995. Nevertheless, their social involvement has become more active and acceptable to a wider membership only in the last two decades.

THEOLOGICAL PURIFICATION AT THE BEGINNING OF THE TWENTIETH CENTURY

In 1903 the church's headquarters were moved from the small town of Battle Creek to the capital, Washington, D.C. The reasons for this were numerous. One of them, suggested by Ellen G. White, was that from Washington Adventists would be better able to pursue the cause of religious liberty. However, very little was done in this direction until the early 1970s. The reasons for this are both intra-denominational and external.

At the beginning of the twentieth century Adventism faced an internal schism. The best and most outspoken Adventist physician and the leader of an enormous medical institution, John Harvey Kellogg, had been battling with the Adventist administrators for some time. Finally, in 1907, he was disfellowshipped from the Battle Creek Seventh-day Adventist Church.[24] The conflict was based on a personality clash between Kellogg and Daniels, the serving President of the General Conference, and on the theological grounds of Kellogg's pantheistic views, expressed in his book, *The Living Temple*.[25] This theological controversy entirely occupied Adventist theologians, administrators and laity in the first decade of the twentieth century. Besides the theological purification of fundamental beliefs, their attention was focused on reorganisation of the General Conference in 1903 and on evangelistic efforts both in America and abroad. In addition, external circumstances between the two world wars prevented Adventist involvement in socio-political activity.

BETWEEN THE TWO WORLD WARS

With World War I and especially with the economic and political crises of the 1920s and 1930s, the priority of Seventh-day Adventists, just like that of most people at that time, was survival. Their main concern was to endure the hardships and stay faithful to their belief in the early literal second coming of Christ and the relevance of the doctrine of Sabbath.

However, the problem by that time for the international Adventist community arose when, without any guidance or direction from the organisation and its American leadership, European Adventists had to deal for example with the delicate situation of Europe's most totalitarian states of the first half of the twentieth century – Russia and Germany.

Adventists in the Totalitarian Regimes

The notion of American Adventism in the area of church-state relations – mainly the separation of church and state and believers' submission to civil authority (based on Romans 13: 1–6) – created difficulties in countries that had not been operating on the basis of liberal democracy. While the church's chosen position may have assured stable relations with governments such as the United States and other democracies, it had not worked out in the most desirable way in totalitarian regimes such as Communist Russia and Nazi Germany.

A typical comment, which does not take into consideration the differences in governments' leadership styles, is found in the otherwise remarkable *Origins and History of Seventh-day Adventists*:

> In Europe there arose, between the first and second world wars, a new political creed, Communism ... With the political affairs of nations, Seventh-day Adventists have nothing to do! They submit themselves, save in matters of conscience, to whatever government is in power, and with all loyalty perform the duties of citizens. Their sole purpose is to promulgate the gospel of Jesus Christ.[26]

The consequences of this type of thinking can be observed in the reactions of Adventists in extraordinarily difficult moral circumstances in Nazi Germany and in a long and sometimes bitter schism among Adventists in the Soviet Union and some other East European countries.

Adventists in Germany

The German Adventists seem to have fallen short of their proclamation of religious liberty at the time of World War I, between the two wars and during World War II. In imperial Germany, most Adventists espoused extreme nationalism and active military collaboration. An Adventist author argued in December 1915 that 'the Bible teaches first, that participation in war is not against the sixth commandment; second, that fighting on the Sabbath is no transgression of the fourth law'.[27] The German church leaders, however, recognised the error of their policies after the war and confessed their loyalty to the worldwide Adventist community at the European Division meeting at Gland, Switzerland on 2 January 1923.[28]

This declaration, however, was weakened by an additional pronouncement which recognised that each member possessed 'absolute liberty to serve his country, at all times and in all places, in accord with the dictates of his personal conscientious conviction'.[29] This statement allowed German Adventists to repeat the mistake from the First World War during Hitler's regime under the Third Reich.

As Erwin Sicher has rightly observed in 'Seventh-day Adventist Publications and the Nazi Temptation', Adventists failed in numerous ways in regard to the Nazi regime. As early as 1928, before Adolf Hitler came to power, Adventists were calling for a strong *Führer*. Article after article dealt with this *Führer* ideal in German writings as well as in Adventist publications.[30]

Later, Adventist writers welcomed the apparent rebirth of Germany in their publications and also by vote. The Adventist town of Friedensau had voted by 99.9 per cent for the Nazi parliamentary state. When some Adventists refused to salute the Swastika flag and to use the Hitler greeting, the President of the East German Conference, W. Mueller, argued that it was bad for the church's image. He concluded that 'under no circumstances did any Adventist have the right to resist the government, even if the government prevented him from exercising his faith. The resistance would be unfortunate because it would mark Adventists as opponents of the new state, a situation that should be prevented.[31] Another prominent Adventist writer and the editor of various Adventist church papers, Kurt Sinz, saw Hitler's strong command at the beginning of National Social rule as designed by God.[32] Otto Bronzio went a step further, saying in the official Adventist paper, *Der Adventbote*, that 'the National Socialist Revolution was the greatest of all time, because it made the maintenance of a pure inheritance the basis of its ethnic life'.[33] Some suggest that what he meant may be gleaned from a boxed quotation from Hitler – on the question of blood – which appeared on the same page.[34]

This idea of a 'pure inheritance', instigated by Hitler and carried throughout the German nation, also afflicted German Adventists. Although blatant racism seldom appeared in Adventist publications, Adventists did frequently print negative comments about the Jews,[35] they tacitly supported sterilisation of the mentally disabled, and many were caught in the quickened pride of German nationalism.[36] The same doctrine of German superiority to other nations was carried into Adventist education in Germany where students were encouraged to learn to 'will and to think in German'. To will in German was a mystical Nazi concept; for, the Party taught, Germans 'will' differently from any other nationals. Educator W. Eberhardt insisted, in addition, that Adventist schools nurtured 'the National Socialist Spirit' between class periods, when they reviewed the news, studied Nazi ideals and sang German national songs.[37]

With growing pressure for greater collaboration, many Adventists of all age groups joined Nazi organisations such as the Hitler Youth, the BDM (Association of German Girls), the Labour Service and the German Red Cross. All these clubs were designed for the purpose of Nazi indoctrination, and although Adventists knew that a significant percentage of the Labour Service participants were members of the SA, SS and Stanhelm, the most fanatical Nazi groups who indoctrinated and militarised the youth, they approved of participation in the clubs. Johannes Langholf strongly supported the Labour Service. He wrote in *Aller Diener*, 'We expect every member to follow the divine command, "pray and work". It would be absolutely contrary to our understanding if we refuse the Labour Service.'[38] Patt suggested that the principal reason for Adventists joining the Nazi Labour Front was unemployment and other economic hardships and that 'most Adventist workingmen succumbed to the pressure and became members of the labor service to save their families.'[39] Yet, joining a party organisation was not obligatory, and some joined the party as well.

In Germany Adventists supported Nazi foreign policy and, eventually, the war. Possible lack of access to reliable information and, as a result, a misconception of the real situation led them to believe that their *Führer* was 'a man of peace'.[40] When Austria was incorporated into the Reich, German Adventists 'shared in the happiness over Austrians' return home to the motherland'.[41] They believed that by God's help and through 'God's assistance our capable Führer Adolf Hitler became the liberator of Austria'.[42] After the liquidation of Czechoslovakia on 16 March 1939, Adventists still raised no objections. Even for this act of cruelty and oppression they found some justification. Then came the attack on Poland which the whole of Europe recognised as an act of aggression. Nevertheless, in an editorial Sinz could write that in view of the 'inhuman tortures our Volkskomrads have suffered among this foreign people', the German attack was probably justified.[43] Adventists continued to support Hitler and celebrated his 51st birthday 11 days after war had escalated in the West with the German invasion of Denmark and Norway on 9 April 1940. The Adventist *Morning Watch Calendar* although printed four months earlier stated:

> Trust in his people has given the Führer the strength to carry through the fight for freedom and honour of Germany. The unshakable faith of Adolf Hitler allowed him to do great deeds, which decorate him today before the whole world. Selflessly and faithfully he has struggled for his people; courageously and proudly he has defended the honour of his nation. In Christian humility, at important times when he could celebrate with his people, he gave God in Heaven honour and recognised his dependence upon God's blessings. This humility has made him great, and this greatness was the source of blessing, from which he always gave for his people. Only very few statesmen stand so brilliantly in the sun of a blessed life, and are so praised by their own people as our Führer. He has sacrificed much in the years of his struggle and has thought little about himself in the difficult work for his people. We compare the unnumbered words, which he has issued to the people from a warm heart, with seeds which have ripened and now carry wonderful fruit.[44]

It is ironic that while Adventists had insisted upon religious liberty, they did not raise a voice against the persecution of countless Jews. Instead, they even disfellowshipped those of Jewish background.[45] At a time when German Adventists were publishing the religious liberty magazine *Kirche und Staat* (an outside observer noticed its primary purpose as being the opposition to the Sunday laws),[46] they kept quiet about the 1933 purges when hundred were murdered, and they said nothing against the persecution of Jews or about the occupied territories. Although some individual Adventists apparently resisted the Nazi temptation,[47] Sicher has shown from contemporary publications that 'no active official opposition to the inhuman Nazi regime seemed to have existed nor even to have been permitted among Adventists'.[48] Sicher's is an unfortunate but honest portrayal of German Adventism in the first half of the twentieth century.

Adventists in the Soviet Union

The split between the official Adventists and the True and Free Adventists in the Soviet Union is rooted in the conscription issue which developed during World War I in Germany. After the Bolshevik Revolution the Russian government wanted all young men to bear arms and participate fully in military service. The Adventists learned about the German pronouncement allowing young men to participate in military life, including the bearing of arms,[49] and took this policy to be a representative statement of the church. They therefore demanded that young Russian Adventists do the same in Communist Russia. In 1924 the Russian authorities asked the church to send delegates to Moscow for a meeting on church-state relations. While travelling to the conference, according to one author, many delegates were intimidated by government agents and instructed in the way they should vote on certain issues.[50] At that convention a split occurred between the two Adventist groups: one group signed the document, thinking it would be best to cooperate; the other refused to sign and subsequently became an underground church, identified as the True and Free Adventists.

In the view of the latter group, the church registered with government agencies and recognised by the Adventist central church administration at Washington abandoned the official Adventist 'truth'.[51] They went as far as to say that the registered Adventist church became Babylon when it surrendered its autonomy and became a pawn of the state.[52] They did not agree with the quiet diplomatic route which the official church was taking. They believed that one cannot be silent about such basic issues of human rights and religious freedom; that one must not compromise. Instead, one should be confrontational, challenging the authority of the government about any issue that might be contrary to the conscience of people.[53]

The leader of the unregistered Adventists, V. A. Shelkov, died in a Soviet labour camp at the age of 84.[54] Like his predecessors,

G. Ostvald and P. I. Manzura, he died in prison 'cheerful and unbowed in spirit', though 'exhausted and tormented'. He served three sentences (totalling 23 years) in 'conditions of violence, barbarity and horror, which cannot be described in words': 1931–4 in the Urals, 1945–54 in Karaganda, and 1957–67 in the camps of the Far East, Siberia and Mordovia.[55] Shelkov's only crime was his pacifism and insistence on Saturday observance. After his release from prison in 1967 – serving as leader of the All-Union Church of True and Free Seventh-Day Adventists for 13 years – Shelkov organised the Adventist *samizdat*, the publishing activity which caused such annoyance to the Soviet authorities.

It is essential to note that the True and Free Adventists established a close relationship with the Soviet human rights movement. They had been sending reports of the arrests and persecutions of Adventists to the *Chronicle of Current Events* and making contacts with secular 'dissidents' such as the academic Andrei Sakharov, and the writers Alexander Solzhenitsyn, Yuri Orlov, Alexander Ginzburg, Grigorenko and others. Shelkov himself had written to the then US President, Jimmy Carter, appealing for help on behalf of Orlov and Ginzburg defending their 'true justice and morality'. Sakharov 'attended' Shelkov's trial from outside the closed courtroom, and then appealed to heads of states which were signatories to the Helsinki agreements and to world public opinion in general. He condemned the sentence (five years in a strict regime camp) as 'cruelty surpassing all norms of decency'.[56] However, Sakharov's intervention was too late to save the 84-year-old's life; Shelkov died behind bars on 27 January 1980.

Shelkov's trial is by no means an isolated case within the 'unrecognised' Adventist church. Many suffered under the Soviet regime.[57] Two of Shelkov's closest associates, I. S. Lepshin and R. A. Spalin, were imprisoned, and others had to go into hiding. When Amnesty International brought Spalin's case before the Adventist organisation in the West, asking the General Conference of the SDAs to 'enlist their help in mobilizing the American Adventist community to remonstrate on the behalf of Mr. Spalin',[58] the response was unexpectedly negative. Amnesty International was informed that 'the General Conference does not recognise the True and Free Church as legitimate, and therefore will do nothing on [Spalin's] behalf'.[59]

Western Adventist leaders, while on a visit to the Soviet Union, did not attempt to establish any contact with the True and Free Adventists. They were of the opinion, as Sapiets has observed,[60] that the True and Free Adventists in the USSR were an offshoot of a German reformist group that had separated from the main Adventist Church in the first half of the century, primarily over the issue of military service. There is no doubt that it was difficult for Western Adventists to form a clear view of the situation in the Soviet Union, and although it is understandable that their primary concern was to preserve 'existing lines of communication and even existing freedoms'[61] of the registered Adventists, justification for the complete rejection of the True and Free Adventist Church cannot be established. The opinion of and judgement passed on the True and Free Adventists were based on official Adventist spokesmen from the USSR, rather than on the documents which have reached the West.[62] Yet, the situation in another Eastern European country shows that official Adventist spokesmen's accounts were not totally reliable.

A Romanian Example

The most blatant example of a sanitised 'official' spokesman's account of state-church relations in the East is a speech made by Dumitru Popa, President of the Romanian Union Conference of Seventh-day Adventist Church. On 30 April 1987 Popa joined eight other religious leaders in a press conference at the Romanian Embassy in Washington, D.C. These religious leaders had been sent to America for the purpose of assuring members of the Congress and the American press that not a single person was in prison in Romania for his faith. However, Popa failed to mention the struggle of his own Adventist members to preserve the largest church building, which was demolished by the government.[63] Nor did he refer to one of the most celebrated cases of any imprisoned Christian in Romania, who happened to be an Adventist. Yet, Sidney Reiners suggested that

> how Dorel Catarama was imprisoned, held by Romanian authorities, and then finally released provides a case study of what the official Adventist church is not doing and what others are able to accomplish in protecting religious and human rights in eastern Europe.[64]

In short, because of his religious beliefs, Dorel Catarama was arrested by 50 policemen on 9 April 1982. The secret police came early in the morning and ransacked his house for 12 hours, 'knocked holes in the walls, interrogated family members, dug in the ground around the house, and even looked in the tomato juice'.[65] They never revealed what they were looking for. But they apparently hoped to find incriminating evidence to use against Dorel in court. Finally, he was charged with the only offence the police could find – hoarding food. Although without any evidence, 'Romanian justice' found Catarama guilty and sentenced him to 10 years' imprisonment. His house, car, furniture and money were confiscated, leaving his wife Veronica and his seven-year-old son homeless. When he appealed against the verdict, the sentence was increased to 14 years. A third trial a year later resulted in Dorel's sentence being lengthened again.

After a long and painful struggle and harsh conditions of imprisonment, the case became known in the West. Dorel's father Valeru and his brother Viorel, who had gone to the United States before Dorel's imprisonment, protested against his sentence. Viorel began a hunger strike in front of the Cannon House of Representatives Office Building by day and the Romanian embassy by night. It finished in his hospitalisation after he collapsed 12 days later. Virel's actions caused sufficient embarrassment to the Romanian government that they granted exit visas to his mother, sister and nephew.

At the same time Keston College in Britain and Amnesty International began making known the facts of this case in the West. Press conferences and panel discussions involving the Cataramas, as well as Shultz's plea on Dorel's behalf while visiting Romania in 1986 and a demonstration in Washington on 19 May 1986, resulted in Dorel's release. But only after several months of perseverance and determination were he and his family free to go to America. Eventually, they received an emotional welcome from many supporters at Chicago's O'Hare Airport on 14 September 1986.

Despite this and many similar cases, it is ironic to note that the President of the Romanian Adventists could come to the United States and testify to religious freedom in Romania only seven months later. While there may be some reasons for Popa's attendance at the press conference in Washington, D.C.,[66] for Western Adventists there was no justifiable reason to be passive and accept the official church's accounts of the situation in Eastern Europe.[67]

Suggestions for Adventist Churches within the Totalitarian Regimes

On a practical level, Adventists could do much more for religious freedom and various human rights in countries where these are restricted. First, on an organisational level. If the church felt that it would be a mistake to single out the plight of the unofficial Adventists (i.e. True and Free Adventists in the Soviet Union or Hungarian underground Adventists) because it might damage existing lines of communication and freedom of the registered church, it could at least speak out on behalf of all people persecuted in restricted and controlled societies. It would benefit Adventists living in totalitarian regimes if the Seventh-day Adventist Church were to establish a high profile on the issue of freedom of conscience and published studies and statements on human rights, which would embrace a wider field beside narrow sectarian interests.

Second, on an independent level. The church leaders and members individually could establish, support and encourage organisations that were independent of the church administration. An example of such an establishment is the Association of Adventist Forums, which has helped the oppressed by publishing data, informing the public about human rights restrictions and by assisting Amnesty International and other human rights organisations.

Third, on an individual level. If Adventists were to recognise that it is *their* business to care for others, to plead on behalf of the oppressed, to be involved in human rights movements, to be more outspoken in voicing their support for people such as members of True and Free Adventist Churches and other underground groups, they would join in demonstrations for greater human rights and write letters to government officials and embassies of totalitarian governments to create more pressure. Alternatively, they could write to individuals who are persecuted for their religion or any other basic human right. In this way Adventists would show the oppressed our appreciation of their stand and our Christian care and support.

HUMAN RIGHTS AND MODERN ADVENTISM

In the Soviet Union

The Seventh-day Adventist church is slowly moving towards the above goals. The President of the Trans-European Division[68] of

Seventh-day Adventists, Jan Paulsen, and the former President of the General Conference of the Seventh-day Adventist Church, Neal Wilson, participated in the Soviet-sponsored International Forum for a Non-Nuclear World and the Survival of Humanity held in mid-February 1987, in Moscow. It was the first time that top Adventist officials had taken part in such a conference. In an interview which he gave on his return to England, Paulsen expressed a desire for more involvement of this kind and he underlined the importance of addressing issues of 'liberty and peace, not only peace world-wide but also on an individual basis, such as that related to certain human rights issues'. He continued by stating that this was an occasion when the church had something to say, something 'to identify ourselves with'.[69] It was important, they considered, not only for their listeners in the USSR, 'but also for the rest of the world to understand that these matters concern us'. These matters referred to were the 'need to relax tensions and hostility between nations, *the release of the prisoners of conscience*, and *the right of a Christian Church to express in public its Christian witness*'[70] (emphasis added).

The world leader of the Seventh-day Adventist Church challenged the leaders of the Soviet Union on these points. He called on the Soviet leaders to release all 'prisoners of conscience' before 1 May 1988, 'a gesture that would arrest and grip the attention of the world'.[71] He also urged a new commitment to the United Nations Declaration on the Elimination of all Forms of Intolerance and of Discrimination Based on Religion or Belief, and added that such a commitment would include a respect for religious holy days and freedom to witness. Finally, he offered to explore ways in which Adventists could cooperate with the Soviet government in science, education, medicine, prevention of alcoholism and other dependencies, and in a variety of other humanitarian activities.

This is a type of involvement that we should hope to see initiated more frequently from the Adventist leadership in future.

Spectrum's Cooperation with Amnesty International

On the other side of the Atlantic, the Association of Adventist Forum's publication, *Spectrum*, organised a meeting to which they invited national leaders of Amnesty International to address 60 student association leaders from 13 Adventist colleges in North America. Amnesty International representatives challenged the

Adventist student officers 'to become involved in the struggle for human rights'.[72] Then information was distributed about how to help Sabbath-keeping Adventist prisoners of conscience. It was in line with what *Spectrum* has been trying to do for almost two decades through its articles and appeals geared towards the Adventist community.

Adventist Refugee Care (ARC) and the Seventh-day Adventist World Service (SAWS)

Another independent organisation, Adventist Refugee Care (ARC), has recently emerged in the Netherlands. Its sole purpose is to assist spiritually, emotionally and physically refugees from Laos, Cambodia, Vietnam and China.[73] However, ARC is not the first Adventist organisation established to help refugees from South-East Asia. The Seventh-day Adventist World Service, Incorporated (known as SAWS)[74] has probably been the avenue for the greatest number of Adventists to get involved in helping refugees. Over 320 people from Australia, Canada, Philippines and America have been able to assist refugees in Thailand through SAWS. The most conservative statistics estimated between 50,000 and 450,000 deaths of Vietnamese boat people, with 80 per cent of survivors being attacked at sea on average three to four times, and, with 15–20-year-old women facing a 60 per cent chance of being raped up to 40 or 50 times. Some Adventists have rightly wondered 'if their resources and energy should extend beyond caring for victims, to helping prevent the atrocities refugees have endured'.[75] Roy Branson's proposal is certainly worth considering. He suggested that Adventists should 'call for the United States government to issue an authoritative report informing the public concerning piracy against refugees in the Gulf of Thailand and the South China Sea'.[76] He went a step further, inviting the Adventist community to write to key people and providing the addresses of Congressman S. Solarz and Senator Alan K. Simpson, who were responsible for Immigration and Refugee Policy.

Babi Mululu Kisekka: An Example of an Adventist Politician

Some Adventists understand that human rights involvement goes far beyond immediate Adventist interests. One example is Babi Mululu Kisekka, who became Prime Minister of Uganda. He first became interested in justice and peace and basic human rights in his youth. Lack of justice and human rights in his country under Idi Amin Dada urged him to think, as an educated man, what his duty to his country and his people was. He decided to act in the most responsible way working with President Museveni to bring liberation to Uganda and restore peace and human rights. In the opinion of many, Kisekka has succeeded. Examining his example, D. Nsereko suggested that 'the Adventist church should educate members of their duty as citizens to speak out on moral issues and shape public opinion'. Nsereko concluded his thesis with the claim that Dr Kisekka has shown 'the Adventist church how members can act against injustice and right grievous wrongs'.[77]

Robert Bainum: A Layman's Vision Accomplished

Another example of what an individual can do for human rights is illustrated by a Seventh-day Adventist businessman, Robert Bainum. While listening to his car radio, Bainum heard that each month thousands of refugees were dying in the Gulf of Thailand. Immediately he made a decision to go to South-East Asia and help rescue the 'boat people'. A month later, Bainum was heading for Bangkok. He had no set plan and no organisation to back him. Nevertheless, during the next two years his achievements would far exceed anyone's dreams.

Bainum worked in Thailand on six occasions and raised over $900,000 for refugee relief. Most importantly, he founded two refugee relief organisations which sent more than 200 volunteers to Thailand. Further, he personally rescued hundreds of boat people. Back in the United States, Bainum offered SAWS headquarters $200,000 if SAWS would purchase trucks to transport food into Cambodia. The director of SAWS told him that trucks were not needed in the capital of Cambodia. Yet he wanted to accept the offer for unrestricted use. Consequently, Bainum made the same offer to the Church of the Saviour in Washington who supported the project, calling it COSIGN (Church of the Saviour – International Good Neighbours). Within a short space of time one-third of COSIGN's volunteers were Adventists.

While continuing to support COSIGN, Bainum decided to establish another organisation – Volunteers International. The idea behind this was that every volunteer should pay his own expenses for a minimum of a month (approximately $13 a day).

Then Volunteers International would arrange with US airlines to fly volunteers to Thailand free of charge. Since its inception in October 1980, Volunteers International has had an annual budget of $600,000. The majority of the foundation's board is comprised of Adventists, and many of its volunteers are also Adventists, although it welcomes any Christian and other humanitarian volunteers. Among other things, Volunteers International is concerned with assisting the boat people who continue to suffer and die in the Gulf of Thailand. Its plane alone has assisted in 339 people being spotted and rescued from the Gulf.

Bainum remains optimistic as to what still can be done by willing Christians. He challenges Adventists:

> Anytime you complain about something wrong, you usually have the power to change it. It isn't enough just to feel bad. We all have a tremendous amount of power to change things.[78]

As an individual Christian, Bainum has done everything he can to fight for people who are denied their basic human rights. However, parallel to more positive examples of Adventist social involvement such as his, ARC and SAWS work and *Spectrum*'s influence, the inconsistency of dealing with the potentially explosive situation in the former Yugoslavia during that country's disintegration crept into contemporary Adventism in the Balkans.

Disintegration of Former Yugoslavia in the 1990s

Despite the fact that the media had been at 'war' in the Socialist Federative Republic of Yugoslavia long before June 1991, hardly anybody expected the real shooting war which the world has witnessed since then. Almost everyone was taken by surprise, the Seventh-day Adventist church included. However, the situation developing from this conflict and, in particular, the church's reaction to it illustrated, just as in Germany during the Third Reich and in the Soviet Union during and immediately after the Bolshevik Revolution, the need for clearer and more comprehensive social ethics. Uniquely here one could observe a lack of consistency in dealing with the problem of war among the church's administrators in different republics of the former Yugoslavia.

Seventh-day Adventism in Yugoslavia has been in a state of disintegration since the outbreak of war in the early 1990s. The somewhat confusing view that the church should support the existing government, adopted from Romans 13: 1–7, has not been very helpful when several different governments mushroomed on the territory of the former Yugoslavia where previously there was just one. Suddenly the Serbian Adventists were loyal to the Serbian government, the Croatian Adventists to the Croatian government, and the Macedonian Adventists to the Macedonian government. How was this loyalty expressed, to what extent was it acceptable when it meant supporting the policy of a government which led to the war, and what it meant in terms of relationship between different structures of the church as it existed for many years on the territory of Yugoslavia are questions which once again, when considered carefully, illustrate the need for the more comprehensive and consistent social theology, and in particular the ethics of human rights.

Branislav Mirilov argues that nationalism flourished among Yugoslav nationalities (Croats, Macedonians, Serbs and Slovenes) within the church prior to the conflict in the 1990s.[79] When the disintegration was imminent, and especially after the war between Serbs and Croats began, Seventh-day Adventists in the two republics concerned reacted differently. While Croatian Adventists condemned the war and immediately began a humanitarian relief operation, Serbian Adventists tacitly approved the Serbian government's effort to 'liberate' their people who lived outside of the Serbian territory, even when it meant occupying these territories both in Croatia and later in Bosnia-Herzegovina.[80]

The awkwardness of the position of the Yugoslavian Adventists towards military service came to the forefront at this time as well. The West conference leadership unequivocally advised its members 'not to join voluntarily the fighting squads because of the commandment "Do not kill", and the commandment about Sabbath'. The article, 'In the War Conditions', continued,

> Due to the fact that the children of God are found in every nation they can be mobilised in any army, any warring side. We do not want to be murderers of our brothers, neither of the potential candidates for the Kingdom of God.[81]

At the same time, the Union leadership remained ambiguously silent and, as a result, a number of Adventists joined the armed forces.

While the higher organisation of the Yugoslav Union in Belgrade responded with an ambiguous silence and lack of any real support for the Adventists in Croatia during the first few months of the war between the Serbian government-controlled forces and Croatian police and people, the Croatian Conference (at that time still under the umbrella of the Yugoslav Union) responded immediately to pleas for humanitarian aid. ADRA's (Adventist Development and Relief Agency's) work became the top priority of every local congregation, and church buildings became ADRA's depots and centres of distribution of humanitarian aid. Pastors and lay members together worked day and night to satisfy the demand and needs of refugees, whether Adventists or from the public at large 'regardless of his/her religious, national, racial or political identity'.[83] Beside the distribution of food, clothing and medicines, members of the church were reported building and 'repairing destroyed houses, rebuilding damaged infrastructure and sheltering refugees'.[84]

The work of ADRA in Belgrade and throughout Serbia and Montenegro, however slow in the initial stages during the war in Croatia, picked up somewhat in the later stages in the Bosnian conflict. In November 1992, only after a ten-month blockade of Sarajevo, an ADRA truck from Belgrade reached the capital with '30 tonnes of food, medical supplies and plastic sheeting'.[85] Since then, this involvement of ADRA-Yugoslavia has developed into a steady flow of material help from different parts of the world chanelled through Belgrade, just as was done through Croatia for many months before.

But the greatest difference between the attitude of the church leaders in Belgrade and Zagreb towards the conflict in Croatia and later in Bosnia can be observed in written documents and in published material. While the Belgrade leadership kept quiet for two years in its regular church publications about the war in its Union, and gave no counsel or advice to its members on how to deal with the war and its consequences, the Zagreb leadership established the *Adventist Press Service*, which served Adventists and the national and international public in informing them about the situation in Croatia, about ADRA's needs, and any other matter relating to the problems of the war. In its various publications such as the youth magazine *Odjek*, *Bulletin of the Humanitarian Agency ADRA*, regular publication *Adventpress* and most recently in its official paper, *Adventisticki Pregled* (Advent Review), Conference leaders and ministers wrote about the church's attitude towards the war, about the need for peace, about individual and group efforts in humanitarian and other areas in different parts of the Conference, and about the needs of people in Bosnia. Through the publications they appealed for more humanitarian aid, and for calm and trust in the Lord who is always the greatest help in times of trouble.[86]

The rift within the leadership of the church in the former Yugoslavia became by far the most obvious division. As Mirilov observed,

> The leadership of the West Conference blamed the Union leaders for their inefficiency in administrative and financial matters, their failure to see the real causes of war, and for holding back the aid that was to go to Croatia … [The Union leadership] blamed the leadership of the West Conference for their quick shift of loyalties and their adaptability to the new regime, for failing to co-operate with the Union officials, and for attempting to build up a good reputation for themselves by generously giving out aid through ADRA.[87]

But the rift went to the heart of understanding and interpreting the war and its causes. As the editor of *Adventist Press Service* in Croatia, Tihomir Kukolja, put it, 'the Union has not been up to the situation which the recent circumstances demanded. We [the West Conference] are having a pretty hard time with the Union officials because they would rather believe Serbian media, than leaders and pastors of the church in Croatia'.[88] Yet, accusations went the other way too. Jovan Lorencin, the President of the Union in Belgrade, expressed the understanding of the church in Belgrade when he wrote that the West Conference presented 'the view of the present Croatian government'.[89] So, the church in the midst of the war has proved not to be 'completely immune to what is happening around it: the situation in the country has left its imprint.'[90]

Following the division between the Union and the West Conference, the result of the breakdown of communications internally and externally as a consequence of the war, and especially because in Croatia the church could not be officially led from Belgrade which was considered to be the seat of the Serbian enemy state,[91] the Trans-European Division decided to rename the former West Yugoslavian Conference the Croatian-Slovenian Conference and to make it an entity attached directly to the Trans-European Division.[92] A month earlier, the Yugoslav Union also changed its name to the South-East European Union.[93]

Adventists in Croatia not only wrote for Adventist publications at home but also sent regular press releases to non-Adventist sources, such as national newspapers and TV stations and to international Adventist press groups. As a result, many articles about the work of ADRA or about destruction of Adventist church buildings and deaths of its members appeared in the two leading national newspapers in Croatia – *Vecernji List* and *Vjesnik*,[94] and in other international journals.[95] In this way, Adventists in Croatia have been informed about their leaders' attitude towards the war, encouraged in times of difficulty and destruction, and directed towards the Christian striving for peace, justice and human rights. Furthermore, information shared in this way prompted greater international humanitarian effort.

At the same time, the Serbian Adventist leadership's apparent lack of interest in addressing the issue of war has resulted in ignorance of what has happened to members, friends and churches in Croatia and Bosnia and what the needs are in the war-torn parts of the former Yugoslavia.[96] However, as one outside observer remarked about the statement of the then President of the Yugoslav Union, as early in the conflict as September 1991: 'It is now far too late, to shut the eyes, and keep silence'.[97] But that seems to be what the President did.

In an open letter[98] to the Yugoslav Adventists in Australia, in describing the situation in the territory of the former Yugoslavia, the President did not mention 12 Adventists killed in Croatia or hundreds of refugees many of whom have been taken care of by the churches in Croatia. However, he did manage to mention the broken telephone lines, difficulties and confusion in money changing between different republics, and 'what hurt them [the administration in Belgrade] the most [was] that ADRA's mini-bus was stolen'.[99] Then he wrote about administrative changes and the new organisation of the theological school in Belgrade. Sadly, nowhere in his circular did the President of the Yugoslav union call for peace; nowhere did he condemn the war; nowhere did he invite Adventists outside the former Yugoslavia to pray for Croatia or Bosnia or for the Adventist families which have been shattered because of the war; nowhere did he call for unity which was so much needed at a time when Adventist churches were beginning to split in Australia along ethnic lines. Ironically, and some would say providentially, all this much-needed counsel came in an open letter to the same churches in Australia from Jovan Slankamenac, a retired minister from Croatia, who was the President's predecessor as the leader of the Yugoslav Union. Furthermore, Zdenko Hlisc-Bladt, the President of the then Western Conference in Zagreb, responded to the Union's circular with a letter to all ministers of Adventist churches in Australia in which he disassociated his Conference from Union's statement that

> the loss of a mini-bus in Sarajevo was the greatest blow to the church. For us the greatest hurt are deaths of twelve of our brothers and sisters, and unclear situation with as many others, hurt, tragedy and horror through which our ministerial colleagues pass in Sarajevo, Banja Luka as well as our members in Bosnia and Hercegovina for some of whom we know and for others that we don't. We are also hurt by the enormous distraction (sic.) of churches and houses of our believers in Croatia and Bosnia which amount to millions of German marks… .[101]

One can only conclude that, as Hlisc-Bladt observed, 'the present misunderstanding between the Union and the West Conference, only resembles much deeper differences that we have, that steam [sic] out of the two opposing attitudes towards the present conflict in our country'.[102] And this misunderstanding[103] 'has been a cause of slowness and unreadiness to act appropriately to the extent of tragedy and suffering that many in our republic [Croatia] are going through at the moment'.[104]

With conflict growing in the Adventist churches with mixed nationalities abroad, the competition and sometimes seeming rivalry of ADRA's work in different parts of the former Yugoslavia, and the violent split of the Macedonian Adventist community from the Union at the end of 1992, it was obvious that parts of the church on the territory of the former Yugoslavia were growing rapidly apart, and that there was little chance of union in the foreseeable future.

Socio-political factors and rapid changes in society during the break-up of Yugoslavia affected the unity of the Yugoslav Adventists. As one observer rightly recognised, this suggests 'that the activity, role, and attitudes of the Adventist church were not immune to the socio-political changes but, on the contrary, were often determined by these factors'.[105] One can only guess whether the church would have acted differently had it *a priori* adopted a comprehensive attitude towards certain socio-ethical issues. However, one thing is certain, namely that it might have had a greater chance of surviving the tensions which the war brought to the country, which had for decades preached brotherhood and equality based on the communist Utopia rather on the basis of Christian values. It seems that the church also built its message of peace, non-violence, equality, justice and brotherhood on the basis of the secular philosophy popular at the time of the socialist regime. However, when the government's tactics changed, the church's basic message and values lost their strength and flavour – a lesson which could have been learned from the Adventists' existence under earlier totalitarian regimes.[106]

Although the account of the work of the church in the former Yugoslavia attempted to make the church's effort appear very united,[107] there was little cooperation and communication between the various organisational structures of the church in different parts of the Balkans. Sometimes, the work of ADRA, instead of being of one accord, looked more like rivalry and competition between the church in Belgrade and Zagreb.[108] Even the ADRA headquarters in St Albans, England has not shown itself to be above criticism concerning the situation in Croatia and Bosnia and Herzegovina,[109] as they took on a project in Albania just before the war started in Croatia. The Albanian project might well have looked to some more like a PR exercise. It was carried through with considerable enthusiasm, perhaps because it received considerable publicity from the BBC. The help needed in Croatia and Bosnia, however, was much more urgent than the good and necessary work which ADRA has done for the people of Albania.

Unfortunately, while working for human rights on the level of alleviating the suffering of the people who became refugees in parts of the former Yugoslavia, the church has been slow to condemn evil, injustice and torture of civilians and to reject war as a legitimate means of resolving differences. In the cause of the change of social and political structures in different republics of the former Yugoslavia, the church has found itself yet again in a dilemma. There is little doubt that the Adventist church has been a leading force in the humanitarian efforts in both Croatia and Bosnia-Herzegovina,[110] during the war. However, the lack of trust in Adventist leaders from different parts of the country, and the misrepresentation and deliberate or possibly accidental misunderstanding between some church workers and leaders have all contributed to the need for a more concerted approach to human rights and questions of social responsibility within the church.

CONCLUSION

While there are obvious signs that the Adventist community worldwide is becoming involved in some areas of human rights, undoubtedly more so today than at any other time in the church's history, there is still much room for improvement. On the institutional level, one would hope to see specific steps towards clarifying issues of religious freedom, even in the sectarian areas where Adventists have always been involved.[111] The leaders of the church should encourage and educate members on their duty as citizens to speak out on moral issues (even when they embrace the socio-political sphere) and to shape public opinion. The need for a clearer theological anthropology from within Adventist circles is essential, with a strong connection demonstrated between the well-established theology of creation and human rights. It is questionable whether American pragmatism is always the best philosophy to follow when one considers state–church issues. The church would do well to re-examine the common notion: 'Look for what is best for the survival and growth of the church'. Joe Mesar has rightly observed that this is a limited outlook which dulls our senses to the evils a state can inflict in another context, as in Nazi Germany, the Soviet Union, Hungary, Romania and most recently in the former Yugoslavia.[112]

More publicity and finances are required for independent Adventist groups which struggle for human rights in different countries. More of such organisations should be encouraged to emerge from the Adventist laity. Individual members of the SDA Church should be expected to support such organisations and to demonstrate personal involvement in their community to generate support for the church's human rights effort. Letters of comfort and consolation could be sent to those deprived of religious and other basic human rights. Pressure on totalitarian governments could be stepped up by individuals lobbying politicians in their home countries. Concern for fellow human beings can be expressed at every level of social structure in most countries where Adventists live.

The primary goal is not effectiveness (although it should never be excluded), but faithfulness. Adventists have to become involved, because the God in whom they believe cares about human rights. The only way for Christians to identify themselves with Jesus is to identify themselves with the oppressed and those who are denied their basic human rights (Matt 25: 31–46). It is not enough to possess a social conscience. There is a definitive need for social action too. 'Too many of us evangelicals', observes John Stott, 'have been, or maybe still are, irresponsible escapists'.[113] There are social issues, most of which are related to human rights, which the church must address without being too careful, non-controversial and socially acceptable. In that respect the call to all evangelicals should ring in ears of every Seventh-day Adventist around the world.

> There are occasions of moral principle in which the church must take its stand, whatever the cost. For the church is the community of the Suffering Servant who is also the Lord, and it is called to serve and suffer with him. It is not popularity which is the authentic mark of the church, but prophetic suffering, even martyrdom. 'Indeed all who desire to live a godly life in Christ Jesus will be persecuted' (2 Tim. 3: 14). May we be given grace to stand firm.[114]

2

Emergence of Concern for Human Rights in Adventism

INTRODUCTION

In a review of the historical development of Seventh-day Adventism, an early interest and somewhat superficial involvement in protection of religious liberty can be detected. However, this interest was mostly initiated and acted upon in response to events which directly involved the members of the Adventist community. In other words, there was no apparent interest in religious liberty or other human rights for their own sake nor, for instance, in cases which involved non-Adventists. This was especially the situation with Adventists in America in the second half of the nineteenth century.[1]

Despite numerous references to particular instances of Adventist believers being ill-treated because of their seventh-day Sabbath keeping, neither the leaders of the church in its formative stages in the mid-nineteenth century nor its theologians at the turn of the century developed a basis for their religious liberty and human rights standpoint. This might be understood, if not justified, by the fact that their assumptions were commonly based on the 'American democracy' of their time, which at least professed, if not practised, freedom, justice and equality. However, this Adventist assumption, taken for granted in the United States, created confusion and difficulty, both in principle and in application, for the Adventist community elsewhere.[2] It is, therefore, essential to examine closely the doctrines that prompted Seventh-day Adventists to action or withdrawal on human rights issues and to look at the underlying philosophical assumptions leading the Adventist community in decision-making regarding social ethics.

URGENCY OF THE SECOND COMING OF JESUS CHRIST

Growing out of the Advent Movement of William Miller, Seventh-day Adventism has inevitably inherited some of the beliefs of the early Advent believers of the mid-nineteenth century. The first and foremost of these doctrines was the imminence of the second coming of Christ. According to William Miller's understanding of prophecy, especially as recorded in the book of Daniel, Christ was supposed to come in about 1843 (this was later adjusted to 1844).[3] After the Great Disappointment on 22 October 1844,[4] the Adventist community was disillusioned and discouraged, and many believers left the faith. However, several groups re-examined the biblical prophecies and interpreted them in a new way.[5] One such group, which was later to become the Seventh-day Adventist Church, understood the imminent return of Christ to be an inescapable fact to which the prophetic books of Daniel and Revelation, as well as the rest of the Bible, directly pointed.[6]

This belief in the imminence of the physical and universally visible second coming of Jesus unavoidably influenced Adventist attitudes towards and interest in social matters. Human rights were not thought to be a believer's concern at a time when Christ's return was so near that they had to think about ultimate salvation from this corrupt and sinful world. An example from the life of one of the pioneers of Adventism is apt: Joseph Bates' change of heart towards social involvement illustrates vividly how acceptance of the belief in the 'soon' second coming[7] determined his priorities. According to Bates the social injustice of his time was only a symptom of a much larger disease, namely sin, which would be eradicated only at the second coming of Christ, in the near future. Hence, the proclamation of the overall cure was certainly a higher priority than treating individual symptoms of sin. Bates concluded that, 'When Christ comes liquor will be forgotten and the slave will be free. The lesser causes are swallowed in the greater.'[8] In this task of proclaiming the Second Advent he found enough to engage his whole time and energy in getting ready and helping others to do the same.[9]

EVANGELISM – THE HIGHEST PRIORITY

Expectation of the very near second coming of Jesus Christ made evangelism and self-examination immediate and dominant priorities.

And even after the Great Disappointment of 1844, this strong belief in the imminent coming of the Lord did not disappear from Adventist circles. Thus many former Millerites remained Advent believers, some eventually becoming Seventh-day Adventists.[10]

As a consequence of this urgency to prepare for the coming of Christ and owing to the self-awareness of being a movement raised by God to proclaim the three angels' messages of Revelation 14,[11] the greatest task of Adventism in the 1880s became evangelism. This is the period of Adventist history when missions emerged and missionary programmes and endeavours developed; the time when the first missionaries were sent from North America to other parts of the world.[12] It was the time of Adventist history when, despite their primary emphasis on evangelism and mission expansion, Adventists were becoming aware of social structures and relationships and when, as the modern historian Emmett Vandevere rightly observed, 'their approach began to take on more positive dimensions'[13] when compared to the social alienation before the church's organization in 1863. The reason for their social awareness rose primarily because of the problems and persecution Adventists faced for their strong belief in and strict observance of Saturday as a day of rest.

SABBATH/SUNDAY ISSUE

By far the most influential doctrine that brought Seventh-day Adventists into conflict with the local authorities and with society at large in the United States was the doctrine of the Sabbath.[14] Early in the 1880s, Adventist individuals and groups were persecuted, imprisoned and condemned for Sunday working and Sabbath observance because it challenged other Christians from established churches. Such was the case, for example, with five members of the Springville Adventist Church, Tennessee, J. H. Dortch, W. S. Lowry, J. Moon, J. Stern and W. H. Ward,[15] who were indicted by the Grand Jury at Paris, the county seat.

After their conviction in Tennessee, and immediately after in Arkansas, the General Conference Committee on Sunday Arrests advised against paying the fines. In this way the convicted would call public attention to injustice. This and similar cases resulted in *The Sabbath Sentinel* being published for the first time in 1884. Later, its name changed to *The Sentinel of Liberty* and from 1906 to the present day it has been known as *Liberty*.[16] Its target was the non-Adventist public and had as its aim 'to awaken national concern for problems of civil and religious liberty'.[17]

At first Adventists expressed their views only by voice and pen. However, the more they were affected by the Sunday laws, the more actively involved they became. In July 1889 the National Religious Liberty Association was organised with the intention, as Jonathan Butler noted,

> to preserve the American Constitution against changes threatened by the National Reform Association, and pledged to oppose all religious legislation before Congress, and protect the rights of persecuted people of any race, color, or creed.[18]

Four years later Allen Moon, the President of the same organisation, and his co-worker, Albion Ballenger, circulated thousands of leaflets and spoke at various meetings against any Sunday closing sanctions. At the same time, Adventists sabotaged a local meeting of the American Sabbath Union in Chicago. The meeting was supposed to be a mass showing of Sabbath [Sunday] closing sentiment. Yet the closing resolution was defeated, which came as a great surprise and shock for American Sabbath Union officials. Later, the *Chicago Tribune* 'reported its defeat to be mainly the work of Adventists in attendance'.[19]

From an almost unsocial and definitely apolitical community in the middle of the nineteenth century, Seventh-day Adventists had become towards the end of the century socially aware and responsive to the point of becoming political in their action against sanctions regarding Sunday laws. Sadly, in most cases this social involvement went only as far as their own defence was concerned, and no further.

Ellen G. White, the most prominent Adventist author of the time and the person who greatly influenced and still continues to influence Seventh-day Adventists, encouraged believers to be direct and honest when presenting their views and principles. In her opinion Adventists should not be defensive and apologetic, but should act in a positive and committed way in favour of social order and equal rights for all people. In 1890 White wrote:

> We are not to cringe and beg pardon of the world for telling them the truth ... The world has a right to know what to expect

> of us, and will look upon us as dishonest, as hiding our real sentiments and principles out of policy, if we carry even the semblance of being uncommitted till the popular voice has pointed out the safe way.[20]

White's warning against calculated and overcautious treatment of issues of religious liberty, and implicitly other basic human rights, stands out still today. Nowadays White's line of thinking is partly practised by the church's magazine on religious freedom, *Liberty*, and other denominational and affiliated organisations within the church which are concerned with religious liberty.[21]

To any observer of the Adventist church it is obvious that early Sunday laws which discriminated against Adventist believers who observed the biblical Sabbath (Ex 20: 8–11) practically involved the believers in community affairs. This defensive involvement initiated large-scale concern for religious freedom which resulted in organisations such as the National Religious Liberty Association (presently Public Affairs and Religious Liberty Department of General Conference of Seventh-day Adventists) and publications such as *Sabbath Sentinel* and *American Sentinel* (presently *Liberty*).

PREMILLENNIALISM AND HUMAN RIGHTS

However, even when in need of greater religious freedom, Adventists never fully allowed social concerns to lead their religious impulses, primarily because of their eschatological views. As premillennialists, Adventist believers were always influenced by the idea that the world around them is evil and that it is declining until the point in history when Jesus will come to establish his heavenly kingdom. Then, and not before, will the millennium start, and the right and just social order will be established.

In the first half of the nineteenth century the majority of American Christians understood prophecies of the millennium as applying to their time. Many believed that God had already established a thousand-year kingdom in the promised land of America.[22] Millerites, and consequently Adventists, on the contrary, accepted a premillennial view[23] whereby God will come to this earth before establishing the Kingdom. Therefore, Seventh-day Adventists emphasised the fact that this world cannot be entirely changed, that the world in which we live is getting more evil, and that society at large will not be improved until Jesus' second coming. In other words, unlike other American believers of the early nineteenth century who believed that America is the promised land in which God had already begun his millennium, Adventist believers were of the opinion that Christ must first come visibly to earth, than take the faithful to heaven, and finally establish the millennium (Rev 20 1–6). For that reason, Adventists thought, there was no need to be involved in changing society on earth since God would change it when he came. As Robin Theobald observed in his study of 'Seventh-day Adventists and the Millennium' published in *A Sociological Yearbook of Religion in Britain*,

> The idea, therefore, of the revolutionary overthrow of existing society was viewed by the movement's leaders, not only as anathema, but as wholly irrelevant to the world's problems ... The central goal of the nascent Seventh-day Adventist movement then became that of preaching the message of the second advent.[24]

The report on *Evangelism and Social Responsibility* (1982), undertaken jointly by the World Evangelical Fellowship and Lausanne Committee for World Evangelisation, suggests that, without any doubt, one's understanding of the millennium affects the way one views the world. 'The degree of hope which we sustain seems to be proportionate to the degree to which we see the Kingdom of God as an already present reality or as a largely or exclusively future expectation.'[25] For a long time Adventists viewed the Kingdom of God primarily as a future expectation and, consequently, this view of the Kingdom influenced the church's role in society.[26]

COVENANT THEME

As Gerhard Hasel pointed out in *New Testament Theology: Basic Issues in the Current Debate*, 'the covenant concept of the Bible has come into the forefront of Biblical studies in recent years'.[27] In 1982 Hasel suggested in his Sabbath School lessons on the covenant and accompanying book *Covenant of Blood* that many Biblical scholars accept that 'the central idea of the Bible, both in the Old Testament and in the New, is the covenant'.[28]

According to some observers,[29] the covenant motif was central to Adventism from the church's beginnings. Indeed, the numerous references to the covenant theme in the early history[30] of Adventism testify to this. Although the nature of the covenant was identified with law-keeping and with the 'fulfillment of certain conditions',[3] it was also differentiated from the Ten Commandments. The Decalogue existed from eternity, asserted Adventist pioneers in an attempt to secure and guard their distinguishing belief in the importance of the Sabbath.[32] The covenant was made with Adam at the Fall, but it became fully effective only with Abraham. The 'old' covenant was formally ratified at Sinai, but the 'new' or 'everlasting' covenant was fully ratified only on the cross of Calvary. 'Essentially, the provisions, conditions and objectives of the 2 covenants are identical.'[33]

Ellen White used the concept of the covenant in a somewhat broader sense than her contemporaries.[34] Although she saw the covenant as a contract between God and his people, and consequently as a defence of Adventist identity,[35] she went beyond it to explore the ideas of the covenant of peace,[36] the covenant as a plan of salvation,[37] the covenant as a revelation of God,[38] and the conditions of the covenant.[39] Moreover, when White applied the concept of the covenant to church life, she incorporated such ideas as financial and prudence ethics,[40] family life and child care,[41] diet and general health and healing,[42] membership in secret societies [43] and use of language.[44] As Pearson rightly suggested,

> One cannot escape the conclusion that Ellen White's perspective on the covenant was broader than that of her fellow-travellers, that she recognized that in considering the covenant theme there was more to do than defend denominational identity. ... The dominant impression is of a wider understanding of the term [covenant] than was common among other Adventist writers.[45]

On the contemporary Adventist scene, very little has changed from the original narrowness of most interpreters of the covenant and one can sense only some aspects of White's vision in considering the scope of the covenant idea. Hasel, for example, has been criticised for attempting to use the covenant motif to 'reassure Adventists of their special status as God's covenant people ... [and being] more concerned with the identification of the covenant community than with a consideration of its responsibility'.[46] On the other hand Roy Branson argued that the covenant and the great controversy themes inadequately express the understanding of the relationship between God and the church. Branson consequently proposed the motif of glory in order to supplement the two. His criticism of the covenant idea as a legal concept over which many Adventist scholars have debated for decades makes sense only if the covenant is understood in its narrow sense. In its wider aspect the covenant notion can bring a new light and freshness to the already flagging discussion among Adventists about grace and law, justification and sanctification, perfection and sinfulness.[47]

This kind of concept of the covenant is explored in Pearson's article on 'Covenant and Ethics'. Pearson suggested that there are 'rich veins in the covenant theme yet to be mined', and that he had only 'scratched the surface of covenant teaching'.[48] However, he probably scratched where most Adventist unfortunately do not itch.

In 'Some Possible New Directions in Covenant Thinking',[49] Pearson proposed a number of social and human rights considerations which have not been previously connected in Adventism with the covenant theme. He talked about the spirit of the covenant in contrast to the letter. First, in addressing the question of the Ten Commandments, Pearson suggested the implicit applications as well as explicit. For example, failure to champion human rights might be implicitly 'the equivalent of breaking the sixth commandment by installments'.[50] This could be either the human rights of people persecuted under totalitarian regimes in whose plight we show little interest, if any. Or it could be a group of people in our own midst, such as women, blacks or Hispanics, whose members die a little inside every time we deny them the respect or access to opportunity which should be theirs.

Pearson also pointed to the fifth commandment and discussed it in the context of elderly people being isolated from that which is best loved and/or those whom they love best and all because of 'our compulsive addiction to work and our thoughtless commitment to social mobility'.[51] Even the church's retirement homes were questioned as a possible institutional breaking of the commandment to honour our fathers and mothers. And finally, a political dimension was introduced too. Would our care for senior citizens also mean a commitment to higher taxation, or are we truly the covenant people when we subject the elderly to the insecurity of market forces? Pearson asked.

Moreover, Pearson noticed that there are numerous other aspect to which covenant calls, but they are 'beyond the Decalogue'. The general Protestant emphasis on individual responsibility must be extended to corporate responsibility.[52] Personal piety and the private morality of self-sufficient individualism must be expanded to corporate responsibility and, with it, to the concept of structural sin. The suggestion goes that we not only perform discrete sinful acts as individuals but also incorporate sinful attitudes, values and responses and, therefore, are guilty of corporate sins of omission as well as of commission.[53]

Pearson then suggested some of the sins which are closely linked to the idea of the covenant. Consumerism and the desire for a fair share of national prosperity must be checked against the background of economic availability to poorer members.[54] The rights of stranger, respect, generosity and hospitality feature frequently within the context of the covenant. In contemporary culture these reflect not only on our attitudes towards refugees and immigrants, but also on treatment without prejudice of those of different ethnic backgrounds or those who speak with a different accent cultivating sensitivity towards our superiors or our juniors; and extending to women prerogatives hither to given only to men, even ordaining them to the gospel ministry and giving them a full share of responsibility in the leadership of the church.[55]

Within the covenant context, the regular warning against different forms of idolatry must make Adventists aware, the suggestion goes, of inclinations towards making idols of our material possessions and professional aspirations. Also nationalism and identification with American culture[56] could be dangerous areas of modern idolatry. Even the symbols and fruits of God's covenant blessing could become idols, such as in the case of the bronze serpent in the reign of Hezekiah. Pearson questioned whether such assets of Adventism as health reform, organisational structure, remnant identity or even the ministry of Ellen White have not become a hindrance and idols of which Adventists must be aware.

Lastly, Pearson suggested that 'the covenant teaches that work confers dignity on people'.[57] The vital question of unemployment, therefore, ought to receive a different consideration for the covenant people.

With all these suggestions and with 'some guiding principles' which he offered towards the end of the essay, Pearson opened another dimension of covenant thinking in Adventism. The criticism rightly offered is that 'believing ourselves to be separated for service, we have nonetheless found it easier to separate than to serve'.[58] However, 'the covenant calls us to do the truth, corporately as well as individually'.[59] The challenge for Adventists is there if they truly believe they belong to the covenant group.

REMNANT THEOLOGY

The last theological preoccupation that led Adventists astray from social involvement is 'remnant' theology.[60] As Pearson observed, 'The perception of itself as "God's remnant church" has led Adventism to seek political neutrality'.[61] This understanding of special blessing and a sense of destiny, which Adventists feel, can lead to pride and indifference. Furthermore, it can lead to triumphalism and a narrow exclusivism and the church turning its back on the cry of suffering, desperate humanity. William Johnsson recently admitted that 'at times Adventists have fallen into these traps'.[62] It remains to be seen whether SDAs can learn from their past failures and change as a result.

Edward Vick, an English Adventist theologian, has successfully established the point that we are in the world and simply cannot be isolated. The question that he left open is 'how are we to be there?'.[63] This question Adventists have to answer in the context of their self-understanding if they want to be relevant to modern society. It is of primary importance that members of the church, too often claiming exclusiveness, step out of their protected Adventist nucleus[64] and involve themselves in the society in which they live. The claim that Adventists are politically neutral is unrealistic. There is no such thing as political neutrality. By non-involvement, which is by no means always practised,[65] Adventists reveal their political stand.

Ironically, Adventists were occasionally involved in politics, but it was highly selective involvement: temperance, religious liberty and military service, for example, were always areas of Adventist concern. However, they were sectarian issues. 'They show primary concern for ourselves and our standards, rather than a concern for others,'[66] Dybdahl observed. It is an ethic of self-interest. 'Other worthy but non-sectarian causes,' it is suggested, 'have sometimes failed to attract Adventist support, and the church has been thereby morally compromised.'[67] It is this area of non-sectarian interests that SDAs need to be more involved in. The responsibility of Adventist ethicists and theologians is to call for awareness, concern and responsible action; the responsibility of Adventist administrators is to express clearly disagreement with various injustices in the world; and the responsibility of each member of the church is to stand on the side of Christ and on the side of his neighbour, regardless of the consequences.

The reason Adventists need to become involved in the world is not because they think they can turn this world into God's eternal kingdom. On the contrary, Adventists believe and preach that his eternal kingdom is still to come. Adventists must become involved because their God cares and wants them to care for each other. Identifying with Jesus means identifying with the poor, oppressed and those whose basic rights and freedoms are denied them. It is not enough to care for a person and have no concern about the laws that affect the life of that person in society. Many issues labelled 'political' have a broader human dimension. It would be hypocritical not to be involved in issues that are labelled political when they concern people, when they involve the lives and fates of human beings.

A PHILOSOPHICAL PERSPECTIVE

Pragmatism

No other philosophical approach has influenced SDAs on a practical level of moral decision making more than pragmatism.[68] Although the pragmatic approach helped Seventh-day Adventism to be flexible and not to resist change, it also disadvantaged them to the extent of becoming largely reactive to changes in the world instead of influencing them. It is true that in personal ethics Adventists called for high standards of piety and moral responsibility in such concerns as dress, eating and drinking habits, theatre-going and other forms of worldly entertainment.[69] However, on a more social level, their ethics have been linked mostly to issues which their members encountered in their contact with society at large.

This ready pragmatism helped the church to accommodate so that it could survive. Theobald rightly observed that the church was able to 'come to terms' with the world without allowing such acts of accommodation to threaten the essence of Adventism.[70] The Adventist genius for mixing otherworldly and this-worldly concerns, suggested another author, pervades most aspects of the church's work.[71] 'A pragmatic approach', Pearson argued, 'provides the flexibility necessary to an organization which is international in its membership and highly diversified in its interests.'

However, he added, 'the major disservice of such an approach has been that the church has failed to demand of its scholars and leaders, until very recently, a careful investigation of ethical concerns, with the result that Adventist moral action has sometimes lacked consistency.'[72] It is this problem of ethical inconsistency that was the greatest casualty of the pragmatic approach to policy making and even to theological adaptation in regard, for example, to issues of race relations and the role of women in leadership positions in the church.[73]

Individualism

Like most of Western culture, the SDA church has been influenced by an individualistic spirit. It is true that the roots of individualism can be found in the history of both Hellenistic and Hebrew societies, but the primary source of the emphasis on the individual for SDAs has been their Protestant heritage. Martin Luther and the Reformation placed a heightened emphasis on personal responsibility. It was maintained that repentance and faith are personal, all Christians are called to be priests, and the emphasis is on the personal nature of faith in believers' baptism.[74]

However, it is arguable whether modern individualism is a purely Christian concept. It is suggested by some that non-Christian roots of affirmation of self in the seventeenth century by Hobbes and Descartes, and its continuation with Locke, Hume, Bentham and Mill in the next two centuries, ending with existentialist philosophers of the twentieth century such as Kierkegaard, Heidegger and Sartre, have much more to do with the contemporary view of individualism than biblical or even Protestant influences.[75] The additional New Testament concept of the church, however, such as the body of Christ, a community of faith, a holy nation and the household of God, call for a more balanced view between individualism and collectivism; between the emphasis on individual and corporal or social ethics.

An individualistic spirit could be regarded as an asset for Adventists in such situations when believers have to swim against the social current, as, inevitably, members have to at times. It has been observed, on the other hand, that this commitment to the ideal of self-sufficient individualism was not most helpful when social justice was in question.[76]

Adventists hold that social change is possible only through the transformation of individuals. In Ellen White's words,

> The government under which Jesus lived was corrupt and oppressive; on every hand were crying abuses, extortion, intolerance, and grinding cruelty. Yet the Saviour attempted no civil reforms. He attacked no national abuses, nor condemned the national enemies. He did not interfere with the authority or administration of those powers. He who was our example kept aloof from earthly governments. Not because he was indifferent to the woes of men, but because the remedy did not lie in merely human and external measures. To be efficient, *the cure must reach men individually, and must regenerate the heart.*[77] (emphasis added)

As another Adventist concluded, 'Adventism clearly stands for the view that good men make good social institutions, rather than that good institutions make men good'.[78] Ironically, Adventists have expended much effort and money to create good institutions.

The essential Christian belief in the person being part of the created community needs to be carefully guarded from overemphasis whether in the direction of individualism or submergence in total collectivism. Each of these two, Roger Shinn argues, 'expresses a partial truth and a partial distortion of the Christian understanding'. He concludes, 'Individualism is the development of one aspect of the Christian understanding of the person-in-community. It needs continuous correction from those who understand that the self lives only in relation with others.'[79]

Adventists and other Christians, are called to be that force which would constantly balance individual and social understanding of the dynamics between the person and the community.

Part II
Seventh-day Adventist Responses to Some Issues in Human Rights

3

Wealth Divide: The Seventh-day Adventist Church and the Poor

Widespread popular opinion is that the millennarian movements of the mid-nineteenth century, working in conditions of intolerable discomfort and poverty, understood and interpreted sections of the Bible as the anticipation of the destruction of the present world and the early coming of Jesus Christ.[1] However, contrary to this view, the Seventh-day Adventist church emerged in the mid-nineteenth century from a relatively affluent middle-class society of farmers and other independent artisans. A recent study of the socio-economic status of early Adventist believers has shown that in the 1860s they were 'generally white, occupationally independent, distributed in a wide spectrum of economic statuses, but favouring the upper side of that spectrum'.[2] They were found to be 'a lot more wealthy' than was previously believed. Ronald Graybill, drawing on three essential studies of the economic status of Adventists,[3] noted that members have been economically upwardly mobile ever since their modest beginnings in the 1850s. However, this upward economic mobility, Graybill concluded, did not prevent them from being concerned with improving the socio-economic status of others, as can be witnessed in a number of areas of church life and its ideology. We shall look at this through an historical sketch.

EARLY ADVENTISM BEFORE WORLD WAR I

Ellen G. White

Ellen G. White had by far the greatest influence on the consciousness of the early Adventists. Believed to possess a special prophetic gift, White aroused an awareness among the then-forming church of economic and social inequality. She spoke extensively against poverty and challenged members of the church to do faithful work for the needy whether they were fellow believers or not.[4] Ellen White gave several reasons for the existence of poverty: sickness, misfortune, carelessness, social injustice, religious persecution and perhaps surprisingly, the will of God. But regardless of the reason for their condition, she regarded all classes of poor as needing the church's attention, sympathy and practical help.

The Duty of Seventh-day Adventists

In White's writings on poverty several areas of concern emerge simultaneously. First, she outlines the duty of Seventh-day Adventists to the poor and divides the work into three basic areas: (a) the church community or local congregation, (b) the local community, and (c) the world community. Seventh-day Adventists have a duty to help their less fortunate brothers and sisters as the earliest Christian community did (Acts 2: 44–6). They are to care for their widows, orphans and the poor among them. Charity begins at home, the prophetess firmly believed, but it does not end there. It must be extended to others, 'irrespective of their faith'. About this kind of work she wrote:

> The work of gathering in the needy, the oppressed, the suffering, the destitute, is the very work which every church that believes the truth for this time should long since have been doing. We are to show the tender sympathy of the Samaritan in supplying physical necessities, feeding the hungry, bringing the poor that are cast out to our homes, gathering from God every day grace and strength that will enable us to reach to the very depths of human misery and help those who cannot help themselves.[5]

But not only in the local community do Adventists have a duty to attempt to eradicate misery and poverty. It is a world-wide task too. When commenting on Jesus' parable of the Good Samaritan, Ellen White said that 'any human being who needs our sympathy and our kind offices is our neighbour. The suffering and destitute of all classes are our neighbours; and when their wants are brought to our knowledge, it is our duty to relieve them as far as possible.' In short, 'Our neighbours are the whole human family'.[6] We could, therefore, conclude that when thinking about the duty of Seventh-day Adventists, Ellen White went beyond narrow sectarianism and exclusiveness. Calvin Rock, an influential black thinker, observed that White believed that 'living sumptuously in provincial regard only for those we see, amounts to a denial of our faith – a scandal upon the name of Him who became poor for our sake and whose service among outcasts provided us an example.'[7]

The Task of the Church

The second area concerns the task of the church. There is no doubt that Ellen White regarded evangelism as the primary task of the Church. She believed that the church was raised with the specific purpose of proclaiming the everlasting gospel of the three angels of Revelation 14 (including the judgment, the Sabbath and the second coming messages). Therefore its primary resources (i.e. the 10 per cent tithe that members freely give) should be used for that particular purpose. However, as Rock argues, 'Ellen White did not relegate labor for the needy to a secondary or parallel function of the gospel. ... For her the essence of the gospel is human restoration, and the work of the gospel includes sharing both temporal and spiritual benefits.'[8] The apparent tension between the two aspects of mission, namely evangelism and welfare work, can be resolved if we look at White's pleas for balance in utilising funds essential for maintaining the church structure in order to continue work on both tasks, as Jesus did throughout his ministry.

The Principle of Stewardship

The third area of White's concern is the principle of stewardship.[9] She expanded a theology of stewardship[10] which can be simplified in a statement: everything we have is God's and we could and should use it for the good of others. God has made sufficient provisions for us all. He has made people his stewards and has given to thousands of men large supplies with which they could alleviate poverty.[11] But those who received abundantly have failed to relieve the suffering of the needy. 'To the rich, God has given wealth that they may relieve and comfort His suffering children; but too often they are indifferent to the wants.'[12]

By the same token, God allows the poor to remain with us to test our sympathies. So, in other words, wealth and poverty should balance themselves out in an ideal setting as designed by God in, for example, the Old Testament laws specified in Deuteronomy. Unfortunately, we have to realise that we do not live in an ideal world. However, Ellen White, suggests as Christians we need to work towards that ideal goal.

The Example of Jesus and the Goal of the Church

This takes us to the fourth concern: the task of Jesus should be carried out by his church on earth. She suggests that 'We shall find His footprints beside the sickbed, in the hovels of poverty, in the crowded alleys of the great city, and in every place where there are human hearts in need of consolation. In doing as Jesus did when on earth, we shall walk in His steps.'[13] White understood this 'doing as Jesus did' to be the goal of the Seventh-day Adventist Church. A contemporary theologian and the president of the Trans-European Division sees it in similar but more specific terms. Jan Paulsen's suggestion is that,

> There are certain vestiges of injustice, inequality, and deprivation in the world, expressions of the devil's work, which the church as community must expose and take part in discrediting. The evil which is alien to God's Kingdom is under God's judgment . ... *God must be able to express himself through the church. Concerns which are God's must by definition be the church's.*[14] (emphasis added)

Therefore, just as we also noticed in White's view, the church is the extended hand of God caring for the needy, providing for the deprived and working for the poor.

Benefits for the Benefactors

Fifthly, in the kind of social involvement suggested not only does the receiver benefit, but so does the giver. In demonstrating mercy, benevolence and tender pity for the hungry, homeless and jobless benefactors receive enormous blessing: 'It is more blessed to give than to receive' (Acts 20: 35). Furthermore, this type of work can have a positive effect on young people because of the fact that, in such work, the self is often forgotten in earnest work to do others good.[15]

Personal Involvement Essential

The last area of Ellen White's concern is linked to personal involvement and interest. In her private letters White showed real interest in doing her best for the poor on a one-to-one basis.[16] She also emphasised the danger of institutionalising personal responsibility to the point that Adventists shift their responsibility on to the organisation instead of relying on their own abilities to use their gifts for the benefit of those who are less fortunate. Ellen White concluded that personal responsibility cannot be substituted by corporate responsibility, but both have their place and should go hand in hand in God's plan of redemption.[17]

Early Adventist Organisations

Having had an enormous influence on Seventh-day Adventists and their policies, Ellen White directed Adventist thinking towards the poor, the homeless, the destitute and those who did not have access to basic human living conditions. Even before the organisation of the General Conference in 1863, provisions were made at Battle Creek, Michigan, for a fund to aid the poor.[18] The *Seventh-day Adventist Encyclopaedia* asserts that this task was carried our primarily by the deacons and deaconesses of the church at the time.[19] After the official organisation of the church, the need for organised welfare work was met by the establishment of the so-called Dorcas Societies.

The Dorcas Welfare Society

This organisation of Adventist women, first formed as the 'Dorcas and Benevolent Association' in October 1874, has grown from a prayer-band meeting of a few women in Battle Creek, Michigan to a group of more than 10,000 local church societies around the world a century later. Influenced by the example of Tabitha or Dorcas (Acts 9: 36), the Dorcas Welfare Society became involved in 'making garments and supplying food for needy families, caring for the fatherless and widows, and ministering to the sick.'[20] It soon spread throughout North America. Dorcas Society activities were not limited to meeting the needs of the church's poor, but reached out into the wider community. The *SDA Encyclopaedia* described the objectives and services of the organisation in the following way:

> The objective of the Dorcas Welfare Society is to help people physically and spiritually, in the name and spirit of Jesus. Its concern is for every case of need, irrespective of creed, class, nationality, or ethinic origin. The society attempts to meet emergency needs not provided by other agencies. The repair and distribution of good clothing is a speciality: surplus supplies are shipped abroad through Seventh-day Adventist World Service,

Inc. In addition to continuing services, it carries on occasional projects, such as supplying shoes for needy children and sending disadvantaged children to summer camps.[21]

Owing to the problems and difficulties of distribution, the Dorcas Welfare Society needed later in the church's history to be backed by another organisation, which had a greater world-wide picture of the needs.

Community Services

Community Services of the Seventh-day Adventist Church not only served as a vehicle for Dorcas Welfare distribution of life's necessities internationally, but it was the base for adult education also. Its primary role was to 'designate social and emergency services given by the church to individuals, families, and large groups in the community.'[22] But more importantly, Community Services was designed by the church to go a step further – *to help the poor help themselves.* Through adult education classes in such areas as dressmaking, budgeting and homemanagement, child care and home nursing, medical self-help and first aid, healthy cooking and living, mobile health screening and relief ministry to disaster victims, the Community Services' aim was to create programmes which would teach dignity and responsibility, and would help the poor to help themselves. This was initiated by Ellen White, who wrote that only this kind of thinking 'means a genuine interest in the welfare of others. ... To give thought and time and personal effort costs far more than merely to give money. But it is the truest charity.'[23]

Although the Seventh-day Adventist Community Services was pioneered in the North American Division, the other Divisions accepted the task. Notable has been the work of the two European Divisions. The earliest Adventist welfare organisation outside of America was an agency founded in Hamburg, Germany in 1897. Since the late 1920s the welfare organisation of the church has been registered with and recognised by the Fifth Union and the German Liga, the organisation of voluntary and public welfare agencies of Germany.

However, the work done by the official church organisations was thought by some Adventists to be inadequate, especially in many large cities of the United States. Such was the view of

Adventism's 'social gospel' advocate of the nineteenth century, Dr John Harvey Kellogg.

John H. Kellogg's Welfare Activities

The Chicago Medical Mission

In many respects John Harvey Kellogg was 'Adventism's social gospel advocate' a long time before 25 June 1893. On this day he finally succeeded in making his dreams a reality by opening a mission for Chicago's unfortunates, offering a free laundry, free baths, a free medical dispensary, an evening Chinese school and a visiting nurse service.

After visiting the famous Bowery Mission in New York City in which Jerry McAuley's 'goal was to clean people up on the outside while the Lord cleanses them inside'[24] and after the visit he made to Dowkontt's Mission, Dr Kellogg became fully convinced that 'this is a most blessed kind of work, and a most fruitful field of labor.'[25] As soon as he had received a gift of $40,000 from Francis and Henry Wessels of South Africa in 1893, he began work among 'Chicago's heathen'.

Before deciding where to open his mission, Kellogg had visited the Chicago Police Department and asked to be directed to the 'dirtiest and wickedest' quarters of the city. After opening the mission, in addition to the free medical dispensary, baths and laundry, a doctor from the Branch Sanatorium was on duty for at least two hours a day, free obstetric care for the neighbourhood's poor women and unemployed was provided, and a diet service with special foods supplied free by Kellogg's Sanatorium Health Food Company was offered. Hundreds of Chicago unfortunates had only the clothes they wore and no place to wash. They soon became filthy and so appreciated the service which was now available. Some mission workers thought that 'if the gospel were preached, it would lead men to clean up of their own accord'.[26] However, Kellogg believed that if they were cleaned first, they would be easier to reach with the Christian message.

Within a few months the mission was regularly employing ten nurses, and the services included 'free kindergarten for the benefit of working mothers and a series of mothers' meetings for instruction in the physical and moral training of children'.[27] Another interesting feature of the mission was the practice of offering a bowl of bean soup with 'zwieback' crackers for 1 cent at noon on Sundays.

Later, this programme was extended and was offered daily. Some 600 people took advantage of the 1 cent lunch, the figure rising some days to 1500. Even though Kellogg insisted that no meal be given free (in deference to people's dignity), he sometimes put up the cent for a person who did not have money at all. Through this kind of service some were converted. Such was the case with Tom Mackey, who after conversion became the leader of similar missions in Chicago and several other major cities.

Seeing the need for better and warmer clothing for the poor, the doctor initiated a programme by which all Adventist members could support the mission. He placed an advert in Adventist publications requesting good quality used garments. Later Kellogg reported that after four years 75,000 people had been given a new clothing as the results of church members' gifts. It was the beginning of modern Adventist welfare activities.[28]

Another facility developed a few years later, when the Chicago Medical Mission purchased an old church near the Pacific Garden Mission. It was used as the Workingmen's Home, where dormitory-style rooms accommodated up to 400 individuals a night. In order to get a bed the applicant had to agree to take a bath and have his clothing fumigated. The purpose of the Home was to help the unemployed. An unemployed person could earn his keep by weaving rugs or making brooms which church members could purchase through advertisements placed in Adventist journals. In that way it was a place where the unemployed could temporarily stay and work until they found better jobs.

For the kind of work that was being done in Chicago, Ellen White commended John Kellogg. In her letter to him dated 14 June 1895 she wrote:

> In your letter of April 18 you speak of the work that is being done in Chicago. I am in full sympathy with the work that is being done there. … Visiting the sick, comforting the poor and the sorrowful for Christ's sake, will bring beams of the Sun of Righteousness, and even the countenance will express the peace that dwells in the soul.[29]

Although she was encouraged by 'the work that is being done in Chicago, and in a few other places', she suggested that Kellogg should not invest so much money in just one medical centre such as Battle Creek, but spread it to other big cities as well.[30] White never expressed herself negatively towards what Kellogg was doing, but she always addressed the issue of the unequal spread of finances and expressed a desire to see the mission spreading more widely to many different stations, rather then deeper in one place.

The Life Boat Mission, Chicago

The Life Boat Mission was an organisation dealing with very contemporary issues at the turn of the century. *The Life Boat* magazine, edited by Dr David Paulson, reflected the purpose of the Mission. In the broad understanding of the gospel the Mission was 'not interested in saving the "soul" only, but the soul, mind, and body – the whole man.'[31] Both the mission workers and magazine writers dealt with issues such as juvenile delinquency, intolerable child labour conditions, prostitution, prison conditions and similar. Paulson wrote in 1902 that 'these social problems will not be settled in prayer meetings or in conventions, but ... by individual effort on the part of men and women in whose hearts throbs a genuine love of humanity.'[32]

The work at the Life Boat did not differ from the work in the rest of the Chicago Medical Mission. The Life Boat was just smaller. The only specific work it provided was in regard to rescuing prostitutes. Schwarz gives us an insight into the difficult and delicate task which some of the staff had to endure:

> Each evening pairs of mature nurses left the Settlement House to visit Chicago's 'red-light' district, where they attempted to persuade streetwalkers to turn from lives of prostitution. The prostitutes who responded to this 'Life Boat Rescue Service' were placed in private Christian homes for a period.[33]

Considerable courage was needed for these women to go and work from midnight to 1:30 am in the most undesirable districts of Chicago where the most desperate class of prostitutes gathered. Still, the results were encouraging. During their first year of operation they succeeded in persuading 75 girls to leave the streets and return to a better life.[34]

It was this kind of work that Ellen White recommended and the Life Boat Mission became her model for the medical missionary work in big cities. 'Those who are conducting this home are doing an important work,' wrote White and added, 'and I believe that as a result of such efforts, many souls will be saved'.[35] White highly commended the work done by the only part of Kellogg's Medical Missionary and Benevolent Association which carried a Seventh-day Adventist label, as long as it did not dig too heavily into the church's resources.[36]

Kellogg's Concern for Children

When Kellogg was just over ten years old, he found his 'life work – to help children'.[37] This mission was in his heart and mind throughout his life. He became father to 42 foster children for whom he built a big house – the Residence – and for whom he 'hired private teachers to conduct a school in his home'.[38] First, Kellogg and his wife planned to take in only children from good family backgrounds. However, since both the doctor and his wife believed in the power of environment to overcome hereditary tendencies, they put their beliefs to the test and accepted children no one else wanted. Several of children were secured when their parents died at the Sanatorium. Wherever Kellogg went, he brought children back home. From Europe he brought a five-year-old boy of a poor English Adventist family. Later he added to his family children of different races, colours, creeds and nationality.

On a wider scope, Kellogg engaged in organising kindergartens and physical training classes for children, sponsored free medical examinations for school-children and involved himself in a general welfare programme for orphans (the founding of the Haskell Home is just one example). When he saw that children in Battle Creek did not have community playgrounds and facilities, Kellogg, 'in the early summer of 1911, converted a part of the extensive grounds surrounding his home into a modern play area for the children of the neighbourhood. John Harvey Kellogg had a large swimming pool constructed here and also installed a sand-pile, swings, slides, and other equipment for the children's use.'[39] Each Monday morning free rides were offered to neighbouring children in the doctor's automobile.

In his overall social concern Kellogg's desire to improve life conditions of children, to promote in practical ways children's rights and to advance the condition of their health and environment must be specially noteworthy. There is little doubt that Kellogg was a true humanitarian.

Finances

Kellogg wanted to involve Adventists in social welfare programmes as much as possible. He personally thought that Adventists had advantages over others because of their health reform teachings, and therefore, that they should sponsor the good work done for the unbelievers. However, rarely did he succeed in his task of persuading Adventist leaders to finance projects whose sole purpose was to help others.

Most of his expenses were met by many generous gifts and contributions from outside the church and by fund-raising which he planned and initiated. By 1901 'less then one-tenth of the financial expenses of the Chicago Mission was coming from Adventist donations'.[40] When he tried raising money for social welfare activities by means of securing the proceeds of a crop planted on donated land to go exclusively to the Medical Missionary and Benevolent Association,[41] he was criticised and undermined by some Adventist local conferences. Hard-pressed financially, they found it necessary to divert money received from the Missionary Acre Fund to projects which were not approved and had nothing to do with the MMBA, which had initiated the project in the first place.

Kellogg was often forced to make 'heavy personal contributions to the MMBA'. He 'dipped into his private bank account to support projects which appealed to him in a special way'.[42] Kellogg claimed that accounts could show that during the 13 years he served as President of the Association, he had 'made personal contributions to the work amounting to as much or more than the entire denomination did, and in addition to this raised from outside parties as much and more than the entire denomination raised'.[43]

It is true that he had a generous heart, and the funds which Kellogg received personally, beyond what was needed to support his family, were soon expanded on charitable causes. While supporting the family of 29, in 1895, 'he was also paying the salaries of a Baptist and a Methodist missionary in India, meeting half of the expenses of ten boys in a mission school, and endowing two charity beds in the Seventh-day Baptist hospital in Shangai, a bed in the Adventist medical mission in Mexico, and one in the Battle Creek Sanatorium'.[44] With all his genius for invention Kellogg could have been a rich man. But he believed that money is for nothing other than 'to make the whole world better, to help people have a better life'. When challenged by a close friend in the 1920s that he had let money slip through his fingers too easily, Kellogg readily pointed out that he 'had always been interested in human service rather than money'.[45] This was not always the case with the church from which he broke away in 1907.

Although Kellogg and the church administratons differed in opinion on the scale of welfare work, this was not the main reason for their split.[46] However, among the major administrative and somewhat theological differences (i.e. the control of all SDA medical institutions and the theology of pantheism),[47] an important disagreement emerged in the understanding of the purpose of concern for the poor. The nature of welfare, Kellogg thought, was purely to help the poor out of Christian love. Therefore, the welfare work Kellogg engaged in had to stay non-sectarian and non-denominational. He believed that 'when a man helps his neighbourhood he does it as a Christian, and not as a Baptist, a Methodist, or a Seventh-day Adventist'.[48] The church leaders, on the other hand, believed that it was the goal of welfare activity to convert people to the church. Despite different views between Kellogg and the Adventist mainstream leaders, Seventh-day Adventism was greatly influenced by Kellogg's social involvement and by his unselfish welfare activity.

ADVENTISM AFTER WORLD WAR I

With the outbreak of war in Europe in 1914 and, more importantly for Adventism, with the death of its prophetess and co-founder Ellen White in 1915, the church was put through severe difficulties. 'Survival' as well as 'power struggle' are terms that could easily describe the church in that period. In spite of the fact that the church's membership increased by 27,000 between 1914 and 1919, which was more than twice the growth for any previous four-year period,[49] the SDA church had its share of difficulties and problems just as many other churches did at the time. Organisational questions, which also led to some theological debate and a redefinition of the authority and inspiration of Ellen White, were among the major internal struggles of the church. All social activity, including welfare interests, became secondary in importance.

Whereas the troubles of the 1920s were primarily internal, the ones the denomination faced in the 1930s were largely external. 'International economic depression,' commented Keld Reynolds in his well-argued article on the church history between 1931 and 1960, 'a truly world wide war, and a rapidly changing postwar world strained Seventh-day Adventism to the utmost.' And he summed up:

Although not all the problems were resolved, the events of these years broadened the Seventh-day Adventist conception of mission in a more humanitarian direction and to some degree broke down its sectarian exclusiveness. The years of stress were also years of growth – institutionally, theologically, and morally.[50]

SDA World Service, Incorporated (SAWS)

Natural disasters as well as the scale of the catastrophe of the two world wars demonstrated the need for a Christian disaster relief service which would be both efficient and immediate. In 1950 local Adventist churches were encouraged to stockpile food and clothing for emergency purposes, and to make provisions in their annual budgeting for unexpected disasters. A sense of responsibility for some kind of international relief work initiated the development of a Disaster and Famine Relief Service following World War II. As part of the growing support of Community Services by the whole church membership, Health and Welfare centres were established in the 1950s. In 1956, the need to coordinate these different relief agencies inaugurated an international relief organisation under the name Seventh-day Adventist World Service, Incorporated (SAWS).

SAWS's main purpose was to coordinate the church's international disaster and famine relief programme. Its funds were secured mainly through 'the Disaster and Famine Relief Offering received in all churches in the world field once every year'[51] (in 1973, for example, the offering in North America totalled the generous sum of $473, 647.24).

As a member of Inter-Church Medical Assistance (IMA), SAWS received donations of medicines from pharmaceutical companies for use in mission clinics, dispensaries and medical centres. This is how the work of SAWS is described in *SDA Encyclopaedia*:

> In a 12-month period ending June 30, 1974, 78 countries received aid from SAWS in North America. Supplies shipped included 1,052,975 pounds of clothing and bedding; medical supplies in dollar value amounted to $706,161. In addition, miscellaneous supplies and equipment were shipped valued at $67,388. Surplus food distributed amounted to 11,307,681 pounds. Total pounds of all supplies shipped was 12,873,602. Cash remittances made amounted to $28,496.[52]

In 1980 the SAWS budget amounted to almost $20 million, and SAWS was active in 26 countries. The total estimated value of all SAWS activities in 1980 was $28 million.[53]

'Ingathering Campaign'

The 'Ingathering Campaign' was another way to secure funds for philanthropic organisations such as SAWS and, especially, Community Services developed early in the twentieth century. This programme started flourishing after 1915 and especially after 1935 when an 'individual goal' and 'conference goal' were introduced respectively. The so-called 'Ingathering Campaign' is an annual worldwide denominational appeal to, and gathering in of funds from, the general public. It serves a double purpose: (a) to provide funds to aid a world programme which includes medical, educational, welfare and evangelistic endeavours, and (b) to introduce millions of people around the world to the work of the church by a special issue of a magazine or a leaflet describing the work of the SDA church.

About two-thirds of the money raised each year is sent to overseas missions to provide for various projects, such as clinics, dispensaries, leprosy (more recently TB) hospitals and missions schools. The rest of the money stays in the donor countries and is used for specific projects. For example, in China several hospitals have been established with funds raised locally.[54]

There are several different methods of conducting the Campaign. But usually it lasts between three and six weeks and is done by house-to-house collection, street solicitation, visits to places of business, singing bands, Christmas carolling, 'pubbing' (i.e. collecting in pubs) and correspondence. Young people are also encouraged to get involved. All participation is on a voluntary basis.

From the time the 'Ingathering Programme' was officially inaugurated in 1908 until 1992, a total of just under US$5 billion had been collected worldwide. It is suggested that the programme also has positive effects on the participants: 'At the close of an Ingathering field day the students usually return richer in Christian spirit, in unity, and in outlook after having worked together toward a humanitarian goal.'[55] However, the money that is collected is obviously of great help, especially to Adventist Community Services (ACS), which distributes about 55 per cent of the total raised for mobile units, disaster services and other related projects.

In 1987 more than 2.9 million people were helped by Adventist Community Services in the United States, Canada and Bermuda alone.[56] Disaster relief and famine relief are two major areas of concern for ACS. And beside more than 4 million volunteer-hours a year which are put into ACS work, the programme depends heavily on the 'Ingathering' money to operate effectively. 'When Ingathering dollars decline', says Monte Sahlin, the overseer of ACS in America, 'Community Services is hurt more than any other program.'[57]

Adventist Development and Relief Agency (ADRA) International

In 1983 SAWS was reorganised under the name Adventist Development and Relief Agency (ADRA) International. 'The goal was', explains Ray Tetz, a director of public relations for ADRA, 'to provide better management and administration for the agency and to address in a distinctive way developmental issues and institutional development.'[58] ADRA became a vital part of the ministry of the church around the world. Active in more than 70 countries and able to provide rapid disaster relief to more than 190 countries, some of which have no Adventist presence at all (e.g. Mali, Niger and Burkina Faso), ADRA has become a great asset to the church's service and ministry.

ADRA's major activities include not only the traditional commitment to disaster and famine relief, which are still a very important part of ADRA's work, but also development activities such as family farming and preventive and primary health, working on behalf of mothers and children, developing better water resources, training for self-sufficiency, building and equipping communities and institutions, etc.

The estimate for the total value of all ADRA's activities for 1996 is in excess of US$190 million (of which the Trans-European Division based in St Albans, England has been able to raise $41.6 million).[59] This amount comes from different sources including 'material and financial resources donated by the Adventist membership; donated materials, equipment, and food from private corporations as well as government sources; and financial grants from government and private sources for specific community development projects, institutional development, and other humanitarian activities.'[60]

ADRA remains unwavering in its Christian mission of helping the poor, the distressed, the politically and economically disadvantaged, regardless of race, creed, sex or religion. Its response is to the 'voice of need, the voice of want, the voice of humanity', the voice in which, asserted the president of ADRA, Ralph Watts, 'we almost always hear the calling of the Father'.[61] Watts added,

> We place a high value on our relationship with the poor. We regard them with respect, as partners with whom we work in a learning and sharing relationship. Listening to them helps us to discern the nature and appropriateness of our activities. Discussion of the options generally brings the best to the top.[62]

Although ADRA International and Community Services are engaged in the enormous task of helping the poor and the distressed from a corporate church perspective, some Adventists feel called to a greater personal responsibility and ability to help specific groups of those who are in need. In such a way independent non-denominational organisations such as Render Effective Aid to Children (REACH) International, Adventist Refugee Care (ARC) and others were organized.

Independent Adventist Groups

Render Effective Aid to Children (REACH)
In 1973 a group of concerned Seventh-day Adventists founded a non-profit volunteer, charitable, tax-exempt organization, REACH International, with a view to meeting the need of starving, needy children. They first concentrated on India. Up to 1979 REACH sponsors have been able to support nearly 1000 children in 13 schools and one orphanage in India, Bangladesh, Rwanda and Malaysia. REACH operates entirely on a sponsorship basis. In its report published at the end of 1988, a call for new sponsors was advertised. As a sponsor one would receive one's child's picture and personal data, and also have an opportunity to correspond with the sponsored child by name through translated letters. The sponsor would even be able to visit his child, if he chose to.[63] In such a way the sponsorship becomes more direct and personal. The president of REACH International, Jasmine Jacob, describes the structure of the organisation:

> The bylaws of the organization specify that 100 percent of the sponsorship funds will go to care for the children. Office work is done by volunteers. Special donations designated for operational expenses care for organizational needs, but every effort is made to keep these expenses to a minimum. The REACH staff is well aware of the handicaps in running a program on this basis, but feels that the benefits outweigh any drawbacks ... The program gains credibility when sponsors realize that it is not conducted for self in any way, that no one receives a salary. This approach also keeps the staff dependant on God.[64]

Although REACH's work is not comparable in size with ADRA's work, it has enormous value in that encourages personal responsibility and more direct, first-hand involvement of individual Adventists. Similar is the case with Adventist Refugee Care (ARC).

Adventist Refugee Care (ARC)

Adventist Refugee Care is a Christian organisation established in the Netherlands in the 1980s. Its main aim is to give physical and spiritual assistance to refugees from Laos, Cambodia, Vietnam and China. Most of the refugees live in the degrading conditions of refugee camps, if they were lucky enough to escape from persecution, robbery, and sexual assaults and multiple rapes on their way to the camps. Some end up committing suicide. ARC sees its task in helping to provide adequate living conditions, counselling and hope in the Christian message to many disillusioned and poor among the refugees. But ARC, as well as REACH International, do not see their role only in providing immediate help. They too would like to teach the needy how to help themselves. Their goal is expressed in a Chinese proverb cited by Jasmine Jacob: 'If you give a hungry man a fish you feed him for a day, but if you teach him how to fish you feed him for a lifetime.'[65]

Croatia Relief Organisation (CRO)

Croatia Relief Organisation (CRO) is one of the latest additions to Adventist independent humanitarian agencies. CRO was set up in Australia in order to 'organize relief support for those disadvantaged by the war in Croatia and neighbouring countries'.[66] Originally started as a one-year operation,[67] CRO sensed, at its annual meeting in Sydney on 27 June 1993, the need to continue with its humanitarian work.[68] At its founding CRO was 'determined to strive to raise funds and other forms of relief support to enable at least one container to be shipped to Zagreb each month for the next twelve months'.[69] Having reached this goal within its first year, CRO's founders and members decided to double the task and in its second year send two containers of help each month.[70]

In its first official publication *CROPaper*, CRO pledged to be 'a dynamic body which – using its influence and the contacts available through its members – should be capable of attracting enormous support from a wide range of sources'.[71] As for its philosophy, CRO adopted a statement of the well-known liberation theologian, J. Heldera Camera, 'no one is so poor that they have nothing to give, and no one is so rich that they require nothing'. CRO's stated desire is to cooperate with ADRA Australia and ADRA Croatia with a totally humanitarian purpose and with no political aspirations and no sectarian interests. For this reason, the organisation's founders believe that CRO 'can appeal to people from all sources, people who have the welfare of their less fortunate fellow men at heart'.[72] As with other independent humanitarian agencies organised and led by Adventist laymen, CRO has a limited and specific purpose for a situation which developed unexpectedly. It will operate either for a fixed time or until it is no longer needed.

CONCLUSION

It would be utopian to think that Seventh-day Adventists can significantly change the overall gap between the poor and wealthy nations with their own human or/and financial resources. With a membership of just over eight million and an annual budget of about $4 billion, Adventists are unable to provide annualy even a single meal for 'some 800 million individuals [who] continue to be trapped in ... absolute poverty'.[73] It is said that one-fifth of the world's population (predominantly in the West) live in affluence and consume four-fifths of the world's income. While they 'generously' contribute to the Third World's development the rather small sum of $20 billion, developed countries spend more than 20 times that amount (about $420 billion) on armaments.[74] But the question still remains, 'In what way can Adventists get involved in the problem of unequal distribution of wealth?'

The very imaginative way to become involved and show that theirs is a caring church is by organising such agencies as ADRA

International, or REACH. Just a few years ago ADRA International was referred to by its executive director Ralf Watts as 'the best secret in our church'.[75] Through its philanthropic and humanitarian involvement, as described in ADRA's *Annual Report*, 1983/84,

> ADRA is concerned for the very poor, the deprived, the sick and malnourished, the victims of natural and man-made disasters. ADRA works very closely with communities of the Third World countries to establish training programs that will develop local leadership in the areas of health, agriculture and literacy.[76]

The primary motive for Adventists to care for people announced by a former executive director of ADRA International, R. R. Drachenberg,[77] is realised in different ways: development programmes, in disaster relief activities, in rehabilitation, and by feeding and refugee programmes.[78]

The danger that an organisation such as ADRA brings is that individual members can sit back and feel that their representatives are involved in the fight against poverty in the world and they, therefore, do not need to do anything. This is a danger that must be avoided. It is encouraging to see church officials' appeal to the Adventist community in that respect. The statement voted at the Trans-European Division Winter Meetings in November 1985 reveals another way in which Adventists can involve themselves in the fight against world's poverty:

> Every Adventist in co-operation with others of good will should endeavour to ... urge the nations of the world to beat their 'swords into ploughshare' and channel the tremendous resources of the world into humanitarian and development projects, thus helping the hundreds of millions of poor and deprived people.[79]

This is a plea to every church member to become actively involved. As citizens with a social conscience, Seventh-day Adventists should be involved in socio-economic matters by 'voice and pen and vote', in urging the wealthy nations of the world to distribute goods equally and to use much more money in the developing countries of the Third World. And there is the third way to ensure that everybody gets involved in the fight against the evil of poverty, in particular the poverty which we face on the streets of large cities in the West.

Stott suggests in his book *Issues Facing Christians Today* that 'a grave disparity *between* wealth and poverty is to be found not only between nations, but *within* most nations as well'.[80] Poverty cannot always be described as a North–South division because it has not been eliminated from wealthy nations of Europe and North America. In Britain, for example, over six million people live on an income which is below the level of supplementary benefit, the state's definition of the boundary between poverty and subsistence.[81] Towards the end of the 1980s, a report by the charity Centrepoint Soho revealed that 50,000 teenagers in London are without a home and recognised homelessness as a nationwide problem.[82] Adventists have a great opportunity to get involved just by stepping over their doorsteps.

In an article entitled 'People Helping People', Margaret Robertson, the Community Service Director of the South England Conference, described the severity of winter 1987–8 which meant 'all hands on deck' to care for the elderly, house-bound, those at risk, the underprivileged and the homeless.[83] Practical help was offered to the homeless of London by providing food, blankets and clothing, but there was scope for much more. Robertson's bold appeal still stands: 'A call for Welfare workers comes to one and all. Workers for the needy, will you hear the call? Will you answer quickly such a challenge clear? Will you be enlisted as a Welfare volunteer?'[84]

While some church members have the opportunity to offer immediate help to those in need, others are in a position to criticise society in general and the government in particular which could do more for such deprived people. It would be desirable for Adventists, as a part of the body of Christ, to express through their publications their stand on poverty and the unequal distribution of wealth. But, on another level, each member of the body of Christ has a duty to get involved in social ministry to the poor and the deprived, whether as a donor to or volunteer of agencies such as ADRA, Red Cross, Oxfam or Band Aid; through appealing to and urging the nations of the world to channel resources into humanitarian projects; or by personal involvement with the poor neighbours whom they encounter on a daily basis.

In a candid presentation to the Conference of Secretaries of Christian Communions, William Johnsson observed:

> Adventism has made its share of mistakes. At times it has been narrow, too small in its thinking. At times it has turned its back on the cry of suffering, desperate humanity. ... [Yet] God has

> been marvellously gracious to the Seventh-day Adventist Church. Through her He has helped make know the everlasting gospel to millions; He has disseminated information about healthful living that has been a blessing to millions of others; He has set up institutions that have saved millions of lives and given others a chance to stretch their minds and to rise socially.[85]

In many respects the Seventh-day Adventist Church has done its best as an institution to care for the poor and underprivileged. But sometimes it lacked personal involvement and individual interest. Since, as was suggested at the beginning of this chapter, Adventism encourages upward social and economic mobility, its members are sometimes so preoccupied with their own middle-class life-style that they do not approbate the scale of the problem of poverty and their Christian duty in this respect. As one Adventist student recognised after travelling through Africa:

> The contrast between the two worlds is immense. While we enjoy and fellowship over large, well-prepared Sabbath potlucks with a good assortment of rich desserts, fellow human beings are surviving on just one meal every day. As we sit on our cushioned pews listening to melodies on organs costing thousands of dollars and reflecting upon beautiful stained-glass windows, fellow Christians – Seventh-day Adventists – worship in members' homes, in open fields, or if fortunate, in simple one-room churches. We must ask, What do our luxurious representative institutional buildings and expensive lifestyle represent to the poor?[86]

So, despite the fact that the Adventist community has done a considerable amount for the poor, there is still a long way to go. The personal invitation to the contemporary generation of Adventists stands:

> I sometimes wonder how God looks on this generation. Could we be profoundly immoral? We who live so well while millions starve, we who squander the earths resources while babies die (18 every minute), we who waste while multitudes comb the garbage heap for rotten food –how will we fare when God calls us to the bar of His justice? How will we Adventists fare? We love a theological argument; do we love the poor?[87]

4

Racial Divide: Discrimination and Adventism – Theological and Hermeneutical Considerations

The Seventh-day Adventist church, beginning as it did as a minority group that was discriminated against, was very careful not to discriminate against its minorities during the early history of the church. But with the developments of the structure of the church, the improvement of its organisation and the expansion in its membership, and the executive power struggle typically linked with these changes, the church has changed in its outlook and treatment of some minority groups within its domain.

In the next two chapters, two such groups will be considered: blacks and women.[1] Specific attention will be given to the theological implications offered by various influential Adventists. Assistance will be gained by considering sociological insights raised by Adventists in commenting on the changes. Lastly, reference will be made to the use of 'principles of interpretation', to which increasing importance is given within Adventist scholarship, especially in facing issues of discrimination.

RACE RELATIONS WITHIN ADVENTISM – HISTORICAL SKETCH

In order to understand better the change in attitudes and principles of race relations, and tensions that were caused by it, one needs to turn to the history of the church and its pragmatic response to the changes in society at large. Only then can one understand the theological support that was given to practical problems the church has faced in every step along its development.

Race relations in Seventh-day Adventist history have followed the history of race relations in America at large. Simultaneously with many other 'Northerners', American Adventists of the first half of the nineteenth century condemned the institution of slavery. As early as the mid-1830s Joseph Bates, a leading Millerite who later helped to form Sabbatarian Adventism, organised an anti-slavery society. Bates described his unequivocal decision: 'duty was clear that I could not be a consistent Christian if I stood on the side of the oppressor, for God was not there. Neither could I claim his promises if I stood on neutral ground. Hence my only alternative was to plead for the slave, and thus I decided.'[2]

Although his abolitionist friends thought that his newly established beliefs should initiate even greater interests in justice and equality, Bates decreased his abolitionist activity. Despite this fact, Bates' attitudes and desires against the evil of slavery remained. As soon as he found an opening to go down to the South in order to preach the gospel message, Bates accepted the challenge with enthusiasm and with true love.[3] And in 1847, Bates verbally attacked the United States as a 'slave-holding, neighbor-murdering country'.[4] However, he was not the only Adventist in the church's early history who showed the bravery and simplicity of 'early radicalism'.

As Jonathan Butler rightly points out, there were a number of Seventh-day Adventist pioneers who participated directly or indirectly in the abolition movement of the mid-nineteenth century. One could mention such men as Joshua V. Himes, Charles Fitch and George Storrs.[5] John Byington, who was to become the first General Conference president of Seventh-day Adventists, also became involved in the abolition movement. He appealed to a 'higher law' than the Federal Fugitive Slave Law, refusing to return runaway slaves. Instead Byington, with another prominent Adventist, John Preston Kellogg, engineered an underground railroad on their family properties.[6]

As the 1850s approached, the Adventist eschatology developed to the point of interpreting the two-horned beast of Revelation 13 as America. John N. Andrews, the earliest official missionary and youngest systematic theologian among Adventists, commented that despite the lamblike profession of America about freedom and equality which come from the inalienable rights to life, liberty and the pursuit of happiness, the American dragon held three million slaves in bondage. Andrews concluded that America's professed equality was a lie.[7]

Keith Lockhart argues that at that particular point of Adventist history 'race ceased to be an issue of social reform and became instead [the] means of demonstrating American hypocrisy'. He goes on to say that to early Adventists 'race was largely an abstract concept that had more to do with proving their eschatological understanding than with effecting social reform'.[8] While it is true that prophetic interpretations were the major activity of the church leaders of the time, Lockhart's analysis is an overstatement. *Review and Herald*, the official publication of the church, carried many articles against slavery during that period. M. E. Cornell, in sending his evangelistic report to the paper, referred to the Fourth of July as the celebration of 'American slavery, alias independence and liberty'.[9] Furthermore, Ellen White, by then recognised and accepted as 'God's messenger', wrote and spoke on the slavery issue.

Ellen White and the Issue of Slavery

In one instance, White told a Seventh-day Adventist that he would be disfellowshipped if he retained his pro-slavery opinions.[10] She believed slavery to be a sin and crime of one man towards another.[11] In her earliest writings White stated:

> All heaven beholds with indignation human beings, the workmanship of God, reduced by their fellow men to the lowest depths of degradation and placed on a level with the brute creation. Professed followers of that dear Saviour whose compassion was ever moved at that the sight of human woe, heartily engage in this enormous and grievous sin, and deal in slaves and souls of men.'[12]

In 1862 she wrote: 'God is punishing this nation for the high crime of slavery. He has the destiny of the nation in His hands. He will punish the South for the sin of slavery, and the North for so long suffering its overreaching and overbearing influence.'[13] Adventist understanding of race relations has followed the line of thought which Ellen White set. And as she modified her highly idealistic statements of full equality between black and white people proclaimed up to the 1890s[14] to her more pragmatic statements about segregation of blacks and whites in worship after the 1890s,[15] the praxis of the Adventist believers immediately followed.

Roy Branson rightly observes in his well-argued article 'Ellen G. White – Racist or Champion of Equality?',[16] that White's theology of race relations never changed. She never retreated from her position that all men are equal regardless of race, nationality or colour. However, when faced with practical problems of evangelism which was being jeopardised owing to the non-segregation policy of the pre-1890s, Ellen White advised that 'so far as possible, everything that will stir up the race prejudice of the white people should be avoided. There is danger of closing the door so that our white laborers will not be able to work in some places in the south'.[17]

The Separation Issue

Therefore, the reason for the change in Ellen White's attitude towards race issues and her approach towards the separation of black people was triggered by concern for the gospel being preached to everyone, even to those who cherished prejudice. With her statements on the separation of the races, White desired both to avoid offending the prejudices of the white people and to reach and win to Christ the black community.[18] For these reasons, as she pointed out, separate black and white churches were to be in operation *'until the Lord shows us a better way'*[19] (emphasis added).

The first decade of the twentieth century was especially hard for the black race in the United States. It was a time when the trend of the whole country was towards racial separation and segregation, be it by law, opinion or force. Within this historic context the proposal to separate the two races in both churches and educational institutions arose. James Edson White, a son of Ellen White who started to work on behalf of the blacks in the South in 1894, wrote in January 1901 about the deteriorating conditions of work among the black population in the South:

> During the six years of our labor in this field we have seen race prejudice and hatred spread and deepen. Work we could do at first we cannot do now. Disfranchisement in some States, mob violence, educational enactments like the above, undertaken in Tennessee and Florida, all indicate that some present methods of work will not be possible much longer.[20]

After noticing a fresh news item in the *Nashville Banner* of 21 January 1901, Edson White added: 'The bill introduced in the Senate Saturday by Senator Walter Peak of Chattanooga prohibiting the employment of White teachers in schools, colleges, and universities where colored pupils are taught, is a measure of great importance and involves large and varied interests.'[21] And he concluded, 'can you see the trend of these events? How shall we relate ourselves to the work in the light of such sentiments ...?'[22] The answer, adopted from his mother's counsel, was to continue cautiously by separating the church's work for the white and the black races.

While the church supported the separation of the races, and in the midst of racial prejudice that did not leave Adventists unaffected,[23] Ellen White continued to promote the equality of all people regardless of race, skin colour or nationality. She described Negroes as 'men standing in God's broad sunlight with mind and soul like other men, with as goodly a frame as has the best developed white men'.[24] She continued,

> Let us as Christians who accept the principle that all men, white and black, are free and equal, adhere to this principle, and not be cowards in the face of the world, and in the face of the heavenly intelligences. We should treat the colored man just as respectfully as we would treat the white man. And we can now, by precept and example, win others to this course.[25]

Perhaps most remarkably, in 1900, at the peak of her stand on the separation of the races, White wrote to an Adventist worker in South Africa, another country with troublesome racial problems:

> In regard to the question of caste and color, nothing would be gained by making a decided distinction, but the Spirit of God would be grieved. We are all supposed to be preparing for the same heaven. We have the same heavenly Father and the same Redeemer, who loved us and gave Himself for us all, without any distinction ... When the love of Christ is cherished in the heart ... there will be no caste, no pride of nationality; no difference will be made because of the color of the skin. In one place the proposition was made that a curtain be drawn between the colored people and the white people. I asked, Would Jesus do that? This grieves the heart of Christ. The color of the skin is no criterion as to the value of the soul. By the mighty cleaver of

truth we have all been quarried out from the world. God has taken us, all classes, all nations, all languages, all nationalities, and brought us into His workshop, to be prepared for His temple.[26]

It is clear from these statements that while the leaders of the church had a clear theology of equality between races, the prejudice of the society in which they lived and their inability to evangelise both sections of society, especially in the South, persuaded the leaders to accept the separation between the races as the most pragmatic and only workable solution of their desire to carry their work to the black as well as the white people of their time.

However, the practice of segregation stayed embedded in the church system long after the original reasons for its introduction had vanished. It was in the 1940s that segregation was energetically reintroduced by means of regional (black) conferences.

Regional (Black) Conferences[27]

The struggle for separate conferences was long and claimed many members on its way. In 1929 it was staunchly proposed by James K. Humphrey, a black pastor and activist who left the church with his entire congregation. The First Harlem church was expelled in January 1930 from the membership of the Seventh-day Adventist church because of the 'near-riot' and 'uncontrollable and disrespectful audience' who demanded the realisation of Humphrey's plan for black conferences in the Adventist church.[28] This and other perceived injustices within the structure, policy and relationships of the church initiated a student strike at the only black Adventist educational institution.

The 'movement for freedom and advancement',[29] started at Oakwood Junior College in October 1931, was a more successful move for the improvement of the role of blacks in the church. The students' demand to appoint a black president of Oakwood College and to have better representation on the board from Northern blacks was initiated by students who later became prominent leaders in the church. On 8 October 1931 a student, Samuel Rashford, with the support of other student activists, including Alan Anderson, Jr, W. W. Fordham, Ernest Mosely, H. R. Morphy (who were all expelled as a result) and others, declared to the student body a strike as 'the struggle for our human dignity'.[30] One may question the need for such drastic action, wrote Fordham in his autobiography,

> but I know what was in our hearts, what tensions we were living under, and the need we felt. We felt compelled to take those difficult steps if just to maintain our God-given right to human dignity, which was being denied us. There was no confrontation with the city, nor was any expected. Our problem was with our own organization.[31]

The new direction in relationships between the races was established. Two years later Oakwood College finally had its first black president, J. L. Moran. And although, as Fordham pointed out, 'equality and dignity were not ... to come without a price', all but one of the strike organisers expelled from the college in 1931 later became Adventist leaders and ministers.

The struggle for equality was by no means over with the student strike in 1931. Fordham recalled a number of instances later when, as a minister in a leadership position, he 'felt the sting of racism in our church'.[32] Yet he was never tempted to give up the battle. He experienced at first hand how humiliated the black people have been

> as a result of the attitude of many of our White leaders. We at times have had to swallow our pride. But we determined to continue the struggle, no matter how long it would take. We would not allow racism and segregation to drive us off the 'ship of hope'. Our motto was 'Stay with the ship'. Thank God, we did![33]

This racism, as Fordham pointed out, consisted in several obvious areas of church policy: separate dining areas for black and white workers,[34] unequal pay for the same job within denominational work,[35] racially explosive remarks which were often unintentional and well-meaning but very oppressive to black members,[36] and even non-admission to Adventist hospitals on the grounds of race.[37] However difficult they found it at times to fight for justice, equality and dignity, some black leaders continued to press forward. Their dream came true when, only 15 years after the 'Humphrey defection' of the First Harlem church, two black conferences were organised in the Eastern United States.[38]

Unlike in the 1890s when the whites proposed segregation within the church, in the 1930s the idea of segregation came from the black constituency. Integration might have been the initial goal, but as Lockhart rightly observed, 'if competition becomes too fierce and the white majority proves too intransigent, blacks are likely to see separation as the best way forward. Segregation is then seen as the answer to discrimination.' In Lockhart's opinion, in the Adventist case, 'blacks proposed regional conferences after they felt integration was an unobtainable goal'.[39] More recently Robert Kennedy, a black theologian and lecturer at Atlantic Union College, South Lancaster, Massachusetts, agreed with Lockhart that 'blacks and some other minorities continue to call for regional conferences whenever they become terribly frustrated at a system in which they feel disenfranchised.'[40]

Proposals for Further Segregation

Even though major changes were introduced throughout the church structure in the 1960s and the early 1970s,[41] some black leaders believed that further separation would be advisable on the grounds of evangelism and the power struggle.[42] That is why two black Adventists, E. E. Cleveland and Calvin Rock, argued for black unions, a step further on the scale of the Adventist organisation. Throughout the 1970s, black unions were debated and the level of the black consciousness was raised.[43] Finally, in 1979, the rapidly increasing black constituency received some consolation when a black administrator, Charles Bradford, was elected as a president of the North American Division, probably one of the most powerful administrative position in the church.[44]

In the mid-1980s, at the annual Professional Growth in Ministry Meetings at the Oakwood College campus, designed to promote growth in moral and professional pastoral competence within the black community in North America, some promoted further segregation as a way of establishing a black North American division.[45] The question remains in the minds of both white and some black members of the church whether this is the way to go forward. Penelope Winkler suggested that 'the size of the regional conferences may make black unions not only economically feasible, but politically necessary'.[46] Whether the reason for segregation today is due to the power struggle or genuine evangelistic concern is not certain. What is clear is that reason for the continuation of segregation is different from what was originally suggested by the pioneers of the church at the turn of the century.

While it is true that, as Tom Dybdahl remarked, 'the racism of white America has also infected the Adventist Church',[47] many non-Adventists see the Seventh-day Adventist church as a champion of racial equality, especially in its early history. Timothy Smith of Johns Hopkins University stated that

> the movement of black people converted to Adventism out of Alabama and Mississippi during the early years of this century, especially during the two World Wars, laid foundations for an indigenous black Adventist movement that was a rebuke to the racism that still gripped American Protestantism decades after the end of the Civil War.[48]

In order to comprehend better the idea of championing equality among different races, as well as to understand the reasons for racial tensions within the church, we need to turn to Adventist theology as it relates to the issues of race relations.

THEOLOGICAL INSIGHTS REGARDING RACE RELATIONS

Ellen G. White

As we have already noted, Ellen White believed all races to be equal before God. She also believed that black people have the same spiritual and intellectual potential as their fellow whites. In 1895 she wrote to her son Edson White that black people are before God with mind, soul and moral potential as any other men.[49] Probably the clearest statement asserting her belief in the full equality of white and black people comes from a manuscript written in 1896, in which she called on all Christians to adhere to this principle of equality regardless of the consequences:

> No matter what the gain or the loss, we must act nobly and courageously in the sight of God and our Saviour. Let us as Christians who accept *the principle that all men, white and black, are free and equal*, adhere to this principle, and not be cowards in the face of the world, and in the face of the heavenly intelligences. We should treat the colored man just as respectfully as we would treat white man.[50] (emphasis added)

Although in the later years of her life practical considerations of mission took precedent over her theological insights, her theological understanding always stayed firm. Three most prominent aspects of theology stand out as she speaks about race relations. Her anti-slavery statements were grounded in eschatology. In the study of the last-day events White recognised slavery as one of the 'signs of the end'. But later in her ministry, White further developed anti-slavery statements and based the idea of full equality of people on the grounds of Christology, the theology of creation and soteriology.

Equality Grounded in Christology

Adventists believe that Christ came to establish a bond between all the peoples of the earth. Christ, in White's opinion, established 'one common brotherhood' making all people within this brotherhood equal. In Christ all people can experience this common brotherhood, and this should change their relationship with others. She wrote:

> Christ came to this earth with a message of mercy and forgiveness. He laid the foundation for a religion by which Jew and Gentile, *black and white*, free and bond, *are linked together in one common brotherhood, recognized as equal* in the sight of God. The Saviour has a boundless love for every human beings.[51] (emphasis added)

For Ellen White, as Roy Branson rightly observed, 'Christ had brought men into a new relationship where each was equally related to Him. Christians, therefore must look on other Christians as equals.'[52]

Equality Grounded in Creation

One might legitimately ask then, what happens in race relations between Christians and non-Christians who do not belong to this 'common brotherhood'? In such a case the doctrine of creation prevents any inequality from taking place. White insisted on several occasions that 'man is God's property by creation and redemption'.[53] Even when people are unconverted, the doctrine of creation assures that all men belong to God. Where man's freedom and equality are violated, it is not according to God's desire or plan. She wanted whites to remember that blacks' common relationship to them is 'by creation and by redemption, and their right to the blessings of freedom'.[54] Not only are all people bound by one creation and One Creator, but they are also linked through one redemption and One Saviour. Hence soteriology accomplishes and fulfils the original intention of God the Creator, who was in both instances Jesus himself (John 1: 1–3).

Equality Grounded on Soteriology

Commenting on White's soteriology, Roy Branson asserted that 'Christ's atoning and reconciling work meant that all men were saved, and none were more saved than others.'[55] In other words, the act of salvation cannot and does not differentiate between races, cultures or nationalities. John the Baptist exclaimed when he saw Jesus, 'Behold the Lamb of God who takes away the sin of the world' (John 1: 29). This means the sins of black as well as white people. Hence, it is clear why White believed that through Jesus' redemption all people become equal before God.[56]

Moreover, in White's statement that the blacks have a 'right to the blessings of freedom',[57] one can easily discern a hint of theology of liberation. The right to freedom in Christ is an inalienable right, which all people share equally. Unfortunately, she did not elaborate on this point elsewhere in her writings.

In White's opinion, the strong ground for equality between the races comes from the common brotherhood in Christ, common creation and common redemption through Jesus. Although she never elaborated on themes of liberation in Christ and judgment when all will be judged according to their response to Christ she occasionally alluded to both these themes. Her ethics of race relations was straightforward and simple. In her practical approach, White was more pragmatic and culturally bound, and this is especially reflected in her statements from *Testimonies* 9. Yet, it was her theology which influenced the expositions of more contemporary Adventists writing on issues of race relations which sprang up in the 1970s. Our attention will, therefore, turn to the more comprehensive theology of race relations established by Talbert O. Shaw, Emory J. Tolbert and Johnson A. Adeniji. Further, we shall look at the official statements issued by the Seventh-day Adventist Church in the 1970s and 1980s.

Talbert O. Shaw

Talbert O. Shaw, a black commentator, gives the most comprehensive theology of race relations in Adventism. In his article on

'Racism and Adventist Theology', he begins with an implicit statement about 'Natural Revelation'. Shaw believes that 'the God of Creation is active in history, and that he uses varied avenues to reveal truths'.[58] In other words, he accepts what Adventists always cherished – progressive revelation. However, Shaw stops short of developing further this hermeneutical point and dealing with biblical data which apparently speak in pro-slavery terms (e.g. the apparent acceptance of slavery throughout the Old Testament and Paul's statements made in Eph 6: 5, Col 3: 22 and Tit 2: 9).

Racism, according to Shaw, does not come from God, but developed because of, what one might call, Adam's sin. 'The problem of race', asserts Shaw, 'resides in man's demonic iniquity, in his perverse will, in his worship of the finite rather than the infinite.'[59] It was not so in the beginning.

One God – One Blood

The account of the creation which Shaw analyses comes from the pen of Paul. He uses Paul's discourse with the philosophers in Athens because it provides the key to God's creative activity as it relates to the racial question: God 'hath made of one blood all nations of men for to dwell on all the face of the earth' (Acts 17: 26).

Two major points emerge from this passage: (a) there is a common source – one God, and (b) there is a common content – one blood. Shaw concludes from this passage, in conjunction with other 'creation' passages, that surely 'there can be no greater argument for racial purity than a common source and content'.[60] But he goes on to say that our theology of creation must not include only the 'original Creation' but also the 'dynamic activity of God in sustaining and remaking man in his image'.[61] So for Shaw, God has created and is creating (re-creation or 'new creation' in Jesus) an order of racial equality within racial diversity.

The Fall

While he recognises that racial unity never implies sameness but variety, Shaw is concerned that there is common ground of '*creatureliness*' and '*finitude*' which must give a good basis for race equality.

The next theological concept which Shaw neatly ties to the question of race relations is the Fall. In the Fall, man at the same time lost his innocence and gained pride. Man's pride leads to self-glorification and self-worship. Hence, as a product of sin we have racial self-worship. 'Racial life in the Fall is that of self-love and race-love rather than mutual love.'[62] Hence, since sin is at the root of racial pride; it also unbalances and disturbs social aspects of the created community.

The Judgment

Shaw explored one of the most prominent themes of Adventism – God's Judgment. The argument that Shaw develops is as follows: Since sin is at the root of racial pride, and God will deal with sin and the sinner at the Judgment ('all men must stand before the judgment bar of God'), the racist cannot escape the judgment of God. It is interesting to note that at this point Shaw applies this to both white and black racists, people of any colour with racial pride and race-love.[63]

Racial Redemption

Further, Shaw develops a soteriological point which he terms 'Grace and Racial Redemption'. He proposes that 'our soteriology envisions the healing of torn race relations, for God is the God of Creation, Judgment, and Redemption'.[64] The goal of race redemption is an open, integrated society in which all people, regardless of race, can enjoy freedom and equality which inevitably result in Christian self-fulfilment. If the goal of redemption is not similar to the goal of creation, we are left with a theological contradiction. The God of Creation and the God of Redemption are not in conflict. Rather, it is one and the same God (John 1: 1–3).

Shaw believes that Adventist epistemology is grounded in divine revelation. Nevertheless, the church's emphasis on the 'individual' rather than on corporate aspects of human experience can often result in the persistence of racism. Individualism, highly developed in the Adventist Church, with it emphasis on forgiveness of personal sins, 'feeds on the dynamics of insecurity and exclusiveness' and creates a vacuum in which people do not feel any communal responsibilities.[65]

Radical Eschatology

Another serious criticism of the church's theology that Shaw raises is its 'radical eschatology'. Adventist interests lie primarily in the 'other world' where God will take care of all social problems. 'Withdrawal from the world and preoccupation with the world to come, support the tendency toward exclusiveness'. This exclusiveness can be seen in relation to other churches and denominations, but also in relation to different races within the church. In Shaw's opinion, 'Moral insensitivity and a lack of social vigor flow from a perfectionistic ethic that does not see the will of God as relevant to the racial problems in society'.[66] Therefore, in Shaw's opinion, emphasis 'on individual salvation and a radical eschatology' prevents Adventists from understanding that the Kingdom of God is not only the future reality but also the present one. The long-term views of Adventist eschatology, coupled with individualism highly praised by Adventists, blurs the vision of the need for the community to respond to the socio-moral questions of the here and now.

Emory J. Tolbert

The Identity of Black People

In a more practical article than Shaw's, on 'Black Power and Christianity', Emory J. Tolbert raises two additional theological concerns which are worth noting. The first concerns the identity of black people. The black man's precious identity is that of a child of God. As such he is not an 'it'. By exposing racism as evil the black man engages in 'the love-act which is most relevant to oppressed blacks'.[67]

Theology of Identification

In addition, Tolbert understands Christ's action on behalf of humanity as willingness to suffer, to identify and to liberate. If Christ has done that for each human being, those who accept Christ should do likewise. 'Christianity deals with identity and with liberation and with suffering because Christ dealt with them.'[68] We could call Tolbert's proposition a theology of identification. One could only wish that he had elaborated more on theology itself and less on personal resentment, which can be felt throughout his article.

Johnson A. Adeniji

Christian Agape Love

Johnson A. Adeniji develops two different ideas as well as some already mentioned above. Adeniji finds the solution to the problems of racial tension in true Christian *agape* love. He cites Jesus' command, 'Love thy neighbour as thyself' as a biblical teaching which could transform society. While his theology of love is a powerful Christian notion, it is more abstract than one would think.

Love as a formula is one thing, its implementation is another. Adeniji's suggestion for overcoming this problem is again simplistic, yet deeply rooted in the Gospel – allowing Jesus' love to work through the process of sanctification.

Theology of Parallel

Another of his relevant theological insights concerns what one could call the theology of parallel. Adeniji works on the basis of comparison between this life and the heavenly life. He asserts,

> People of all races are going to heaven. As God's children we must all learn here how to co-exist peaceably. The Psalmist points to the need of peaceful co-existence when he says: 'Behold, how good and pleasant it is for brethren to dwell together in unity' (Psalm 133: 1).[69]

And Adeniji concludes that since 'all men and women of all races will live together in the earth made new', by the theology of parallelism, we need to 'start from here'.[70]

Adventist Statements on Race Relations

In this study on race relations two examples of statements issued by the church in two different cultural contexts must not be omitted. The first is a *Christian Declaration on Race Relations* ('Declaration')[71] which was adopted by the Southern New England Conference of Seventh-day Adventists in session in March 1970; the other is a *Statement on Human Relations* ('Statement')[72] which was voted at the Trans-European Division 1988 Winter Meetings and is an integral part of the church's Working Policy.

'Declaration'

'Declaration' begins by affirming that 'mankind is one because God called men into being by one act of creation'. God created man in his own image and of one blood (Gen 1: 26; Acts 17: 26). It affirms oneness due to one act of redemption through Jesus Christ (Gal 6: 15). Now, therefore, there are no walls of separation (Eph 2: 14) because in Christ there is no Jew nor Gentile, neither bondman nor free (Gal 3: 28). 'Declaration' goes on to make a new ecclesiological point asserting that in the fellowship of the reconciled all people belong to the Body of Christ as its members (Rom 12: 4) as a part of the household of God (Eph 2: 19). In its conclusion the 'Declaration' calls for the 'supposedly biblical basis for discrimination' to be immediately corrected.

'Statement'

'Statement' declares the Adventist belief in 'the universal fatherhood of God and the brotherhood of man'.[73] It also points out to Adventists the task of proclaiming the message of Revelation 14: 6–12 to all peoples of the earth. This dedication and the course of action which resulted from it in the past 150 years 'has made the church both multi-racial and multi-ethnic'. Hence 'the church rejects any system or philosophy which basis human relationships or social and economic structures on race or colour'.[74]

The major theological themes of creation, the Fall, redemption, sanctification, ecclesiology of the Body of Christ, judgment and the second coming have been more or less explored so far. There is a great need to elaborate on some of them owing to the fact that some authors have only implicitly hinted at them. Others have received sufficient treatment already in Adventist literature. In Part IV we shall explore further how some of these doctrines throw light on the general ethics of human rights.

CONCLUSION

A tendency exists for a large group to exploit the minorities with which it comes into contact. In the case of race relations, the black minority have been discriminated against by the white majority in the great portion of the history of mixing of races. The church has not been immune from this general trend. Seventh-day Adventists, like many other Christian denominations, have fallen into the trap both on a personal and on an institutional level on a number of occasions. As Sherwood Wirt put it in *The Social Conscience and the Evangelical*: 'Evangelical Christians have much ground to recover in the field of race relations.'[75]

On the other hand, one could look at Adventist 'radical discipleship' in the second half of the nineteenth century to see how early Adventists championed human equality, human dignity and human rights in the fight for justice and sound race relations. Such individuals as Joseph Bates, Ellen White, John Preston Kellogg and others come to mind.

However, in some instances, the direction of apparent racism can be seen as an entirely opposite trend to anti-racism. One needs only look at historical circumstance at the turn of the century to see how Adventist pioneers dealt pragmatically with problems which society imposed on them. Instead of being discouraged by the social prejudice of the white population and the religious prejudice[76] of other Christian churches and giving up on preaching to the blacks in the South, the Adventists, led by Edson White, persevered by finding a solution in separating the work for the white and the black constituencies and continuing in proclamation and nurture of both groups.

At times, again, race relations were used in an unfortunate power struggle in administrative control. This could be said of the whites controlling and administrating the blacks in the first half of the twentieth century as well as of the blacks trying to gain control and power 'to sit where the action is' in the second half.[77]

Even though the SDA church has failed on some occasions the true test of brotherhood on a practical level, at other times it has upheld the principle of brotherly love and equality of all people regardless of their race or nationality. The reason for the latter is that Adventist pioneers established, at the root level, positive theological statements about equality before God. The common creation in the image of God and the accessible redemption to all who accept Jesus as their Saviour were not only prominent themes of the church's pioneers, but became the backbone of modern Adventism. Adventists believe in one God Creator who created one blood on earth, and by the one blood of Jesus restored the human race. Such unparalleled love, it is expected, needs to be expressed by the true followers of Christ. This is a theme that strongly supports equality among races and the dignity that all people inherit from the Supreme Being. So, the right to racial equality is inalienable and therefore, as it was voted at the General Conference session in Atlantic City, New Jersey, in 1970, 'It is time for the remnant church to show her true Christian colors by revealing to a divided, polarized world that our church is capable of genuine brotherhood in Christ.'[78]

Inconsistency seems to exist between the church's theology, polity and praxis in its approach to race relations. An historical, organisational and theological examination directs our attention towards a more consistent theology and ethics of human rights in order to overcome the difficulties that come with a church that has been partially and is more and more becoming a mixture of races, nationalities, cultures and customs. Therefore, in Part IV we shall attempt to contribute towards this important, and at times absent, ethics of human rights.

5

Gender Divide: The Role of Women in the Seventh-day Adventist Church

HISTORICAL SKETCH

The Nineteenth Century

Women played an important role in the early history of the Seventh-day Adventist Church. Ellen White helped her husband, James, to establish the church in 1863.[1] She was recognised and appreciated, by that time, as the key leader and communicator of God's will to the denomination. Not only did she assume a leadership role of teaching and preaching, but she led the way in shaping the doctrines and fundamental beliefs of the church. But all this was not without opposition. Early in Ellen White's ministry, criticism came from members and non-members of the movement alike. The main objection was raised by quoting 1 Corinthians 14: 34: 'Women should remain silent in the churches. They are not allowed to speak, but must be in submission, as the Law says', and 1 Timothy 2: 12: 'I do not permit a woman to teach or to have authority over a man; she must be silent.'

It is of interest to note that Ellen White never engaged publicly in this debate. Instead her closest associates, all men, answered questions regarding the role of women within the church. In 1858 Ellen's husband argued that prophecy was a work that called for equal opportunities for both men and women.[2] He quoted Joel 2: 28–32 saying:

> Under the influence of the Holy Spirit both sons and daughters will prophesy. Some have excluded females from a share in this work, because it says, 'Your young men shall see visions.' They

> seem to forget that 'man' and 'men' in the Scriptures generally means both male and female.[3]

Just a year earlier, D. Hewitt, a Battle Creek layman, answered objections based on 1 Corinthians 14 and 2 Timothy 2 by a close exegesis of the texts. Hewitt argued:

> ... simply praying, or singing, or speaking in meeting would not be usurping authority over the man, but edifying the man, and pleasing the Lord ... A sister's telling in meeting what the Lord has done for her, and what she intends to do through grace, would not be ... usurping authority over the man.[4]

It is obvious from these two examples, and many more that were published in the early history of Adventism,[5] that while women took prominent roles in worship, showed enthusiasm and from time to time took on some leadership roles, the male pioneers of the church had to explain, justify and defend the work of their female colleagues.

Owing to the strong influence of the female prophet and radical support that Ellen White received from the men around her, the Adventist Church experienced steady progress in the participation of its women members at all levels of the church structure. Whether this was due to sociological and cultural patterns as some suggest[6] or because of the theological insight of the leaders of the church, in the nineteenth century 'women have made a significant contribution to the growth and development of this denomination'.[7]

As John Beach illustrated in his paper on 'The Role of Women in Leadership Position Within the Seventh-day Adventist Church', there are 'hundreds of women who contributed to the cause, each in her own way, down through the annals of this church's history'[8] And yet, concludes Beach,

> these women for the most part have served with little recognition, lacking equality of salary, serving obediently without petitioning for newer, higher responsibilities and almost invariably working in love and devotion. They have done virtually everything, asked for nothing, and received their rewards in knowing they have done what they could.[9]

Although Adventist women in the nineteenth century did not receive equal pay with their male counterparts, and despite the fact that, as Bull and Lockhart recognised, 'the extent of their participation has been determined by men who, from an early stage, have controlled the church's bureaucracy',[10] Beach concluded that 'women have demonstrated their capabilities, they have proven their value, they have offered their services with conviction and in a humble manner'.[11] And they were given the opportunity to do so until the turn of the century.

At the Beginning of the Twentieth Century

The new emphasis in the counsel of Ellen White became obvious around the turn of the century. Partly it was influenced by Mrs S. M. I. Henry, the former national evangelist of the Woman's Christian Temperance Union who converted to Adventism in 1896.[12] After joining the church, Mrs Henry continued her leadership role and carried enormous influence within the Adventist church. In 1898 Ellen White wrote about the great work that could be accomplished through the combined effort of men and women.[13] She believed that women could accomplish more than men in some areas of the ministry,[14] and she encouraged young women to seek the highest education to pursue that kind of work.[15] White even insisted that women be paid a fair wage for their work from tithe revenues which were reserved for the payment of ministry.[16] In one instance she went as far as threatening that she would withhold her tithe money 'to pay those women whom she felt were being exploited by male church leaders.'[17] There was no surprise that by 1905 many women had advanced to the administrative position in the church.

One research suggests that in 1910 there were 'around twenty women education department leaders in all conferences in the United States, over fifty Sabbath School leaders, and almost twenty conference treasures'.[18] The highest number of women in leading roles was in 1915. However, since the church's prophetess died in that year, and, as Bertha Dasher noted, 'the church became larger and more prestigious, men began taking over leadership position'.[19] Dasher graphically illustrates that, by the 1950s, this decline reached its lowest point with no woman in administrative or departmental leadership in any of the conferences of the North American Division. This was no pure chance, as is illustrated by the charts which Dasher included at the end of her article. The decline of women in the leadership roles followed a definite pattern:[20]

Conference Treasurers

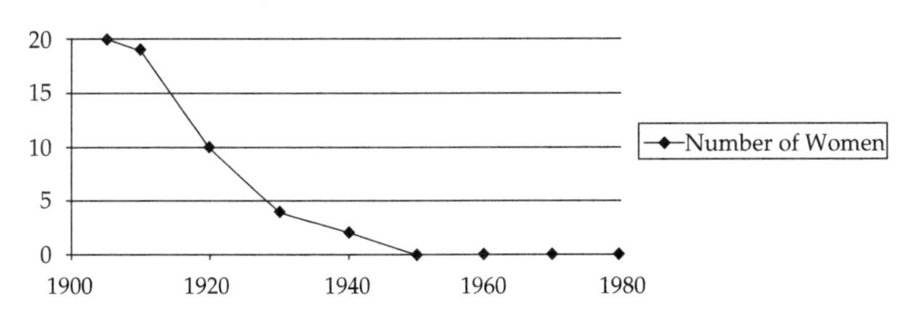

Conference Secretaries

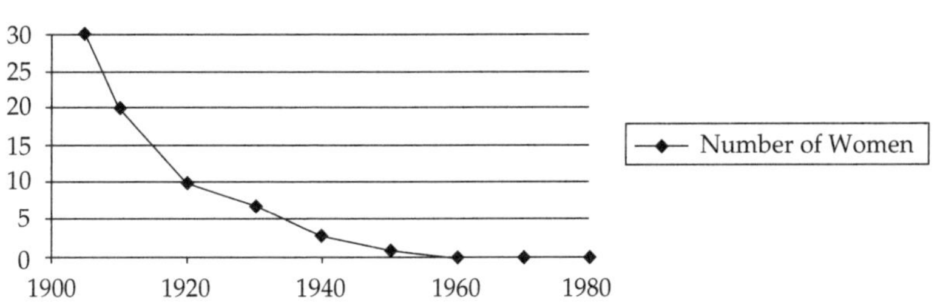

Education Department Leaders

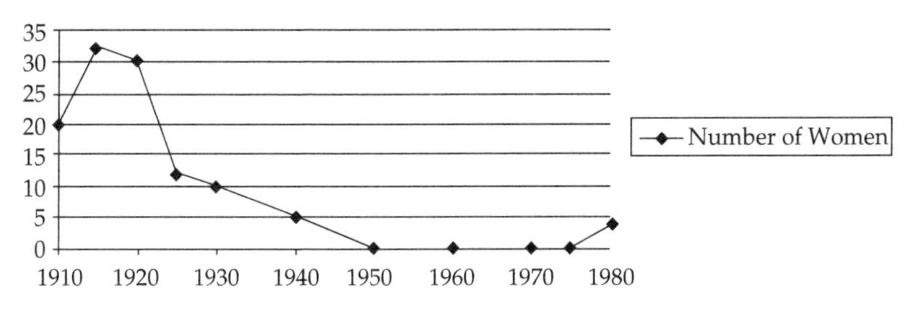

Education Departmental Secretaries

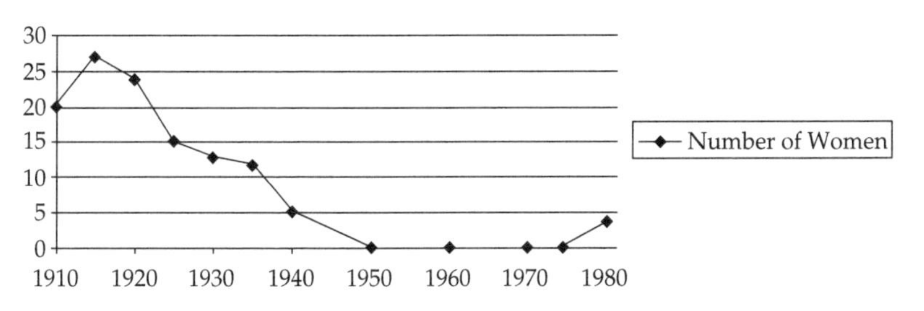

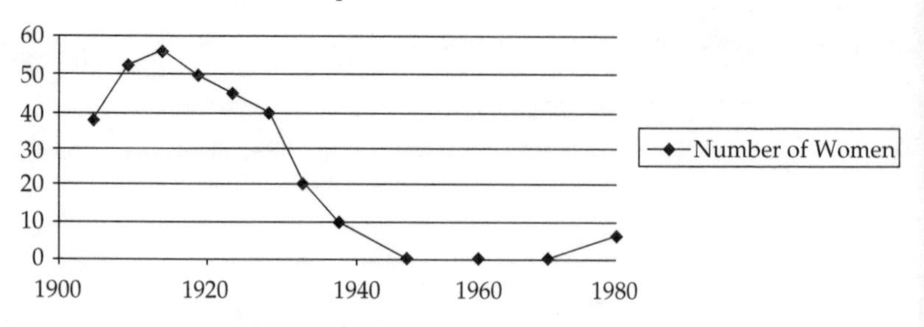

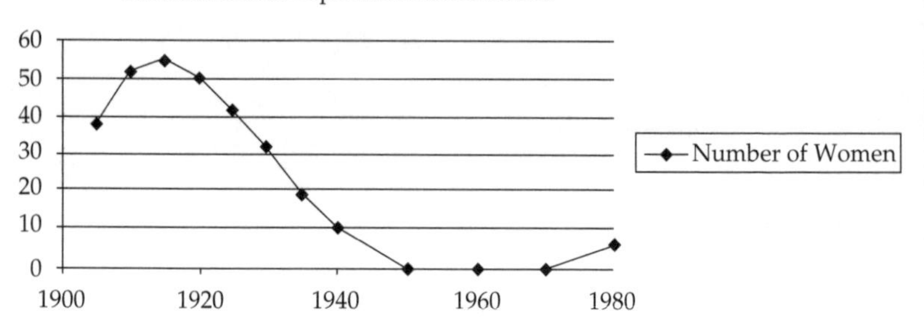

In Modern Times

These charts not only illustrate a sharp decline in women leaders in the years between 1915 and 1950, but also point to the opposite movement in the late 1970s. Just as with the modern emancipation of blacks, the church in the 1970s sought greater involvement and experienced more rapid emancipation of its women than at any previous time in its history.

Robert Pierson, the General Conference President, noted in 1971 that 'two committed women serve as associate departmental secretaries and members of the General Conference Committee'.[21] He further called 'our sisters [to] join their brethren in developing the fullest potential of their talent for a finished work and a soon return of the Saviour'.[22] And he admitted in conclusion that

> God has granted talents of leadership to both sexes. We will recognize woman's capability and her eligibility for participation in the many areas in which she is equipped to serve. We must deal justly with her, assuring her compensation in keeping with the responsibilities she carries.[23]

But the practice of the administration that Pierson led was far away from the ideals he expressed in his article. The church administration was finally challenged in 1973 in court[24] when Merikay Silver, an editorial assistant with the Pacific Press Publishing Association, sued the church on the grounds that her remuneration was less than that given to men doing the same job.

A Court Case and the Initiation of New Openness

The court decision in the case of Merikay Silver went against the church and the church decided to make an out of court settlement several years later. However, the case opened a sore wound in Adventism, and after a prolonged debate in the church's journals,[25] equal pay for equal work has now been accepted in principle.[26] Although Merikay Silver paid a high personal price for her stand, many Adventist women are indebted to her for having the temerity and courage to challenge the injustice of the church's policy.

Another women's issue became prominent around the same time: the ordination of women to the ministry. The number of women clergy in North America tripled between 1960 and 1980. This inevitably brought the issue of women's ordination to the forefront of the agenda of the Adventist Church.

The Ordination Issue

Brenda Butka openly supported the general principles of women's liberation in an article[27] appearing in *Spectrum*. Other articles about a more liberated role for women started appearing at a regular rate.[28] At the same time, in 1973, the Annual Council of the Church recorded an action entitled. 'The Role of Women in the Church'. Although the Council recognised the need for the 'priesthood of all believers and the necessity of involving the total resources of the church for the rapid completion of the gospel commission', it also believed 'that the time is not ripe nor opportune' for the ordination of women to the gospel ministry to be initiated for the sake of unity in the world-wide church.[29] However, the Council requested the Divisions to pursue their study of the question of the role of women in the church and to share it with the General Conference. For this purpose theologians and scholars of the church were commissioned to prepare studies on different topics relating to the role of women.

Some of these studies[30] were presented at Camp Mohaven (16–29 September, 1973). This period of the church's history is described as 'a high point for Adventist women of feminist persuasion'.[31] The Camp Mohaven committee 'suggested a plan leading to ordination and urged greater participation of women in the leadership of the church'.[32] But what the Camp Mohaven meeting did not achieve by the time of the 1973 Annual Council of the General Conference, which came to its participants as somewhat a surprise,[33] was a rapid change in the attitude of the male leadership and new opportunities granted to women eager to serve their church. Although the papers of the 'Mohaven group of scholars' were not published and did not receive widespread distribution, their content gradually became known to academics and administrators of the church. They had a stunning influence on many who read the church's most prominent scholars one after the other affirming the full equality of women and seeing no theological impediment to the ordination of women to the gospel ministry. Finally, in 1984, their papers were published in full in *Symposium on the Role of Women in the Church*.[34]

While the 1970s was the decade of opening up issues concerning the role of women in the church, the 1980s became 'the decade that had the most impact on the Adventist women'.[35] Women started uniting in different groups and organisations in order to maximise their resources and to support each other in the struggle for equality. Between 1982 and 1988 many women's organisations were established with similar purposes: to 'create a sense of belonging', 'to pursue actively the attainment of the full and equal participation', 'to encourage Adventist women to recognize their worth and value', 'to support and affirm the calling and gifts of women', 'to uphold, encourage and challenge Adventist women in their pilgrimage as disciples of Jesus Christ', etc. At least ten such societies were founded in this short period of time: *Adventist Women in Ministry, Adventist Women International, Association of Adventist Women, Chaplains for Women in Ministry*. Office of Human Relations Women's Commission, *Shepherdess International, TEAM* and *Women's Ministries Advisory*.[36]

The Adventist Woman, a publication of the most widespread of these organisations, The Association of Adventist Women (AAW), reports the relevant news about Adventist women and their concerns. In the June/July 1989 issue, Elwyn Planter reported that the Southeastern California Conference called for the ordination of women pastors and presented their names for approval to the Pacific Union Conference executive committee.[37] Their desire has not been carried out due to the decision of the world-wide church which, in its quinquennial meeting in 1990, voted down the ordination of women to the gospel ministry. The main reason for this decision was the concern for the world-wide *unity of the church* and the numerical advantage of the ever-growing Adventist church in South America and Africa.

Many were disappointed at the vote which denied women ordination. And yet, the Session approved the proposal that unordained women ministers might perform more of the functions of ministry: namely weddings and baptisms. This provided an escape for some North American Conferences which had recommended their women candidates for ordination before the General Conference Session. Such was the case, for example, with the Southeastern California Conference, which eventually decided not to take unilateral action to ordain women ministers. Instead, as it was reported,

> the conference will encourage higher levels of church leadership to eliminate gender discrimination from church ordination policies; request a new vote on the ordination of women at a future Annual Council; work harder to hire, educate, place, and support women in ministry; and appoint a commission on justice to fulfil the conference's goals of racial, ethnic, and gender equality.[38]

However, this attitude of 'wait and see' changed immediately after the 1995 General Conference Session. Roy Branson captured the hurt and disappointment of many North Americans and Western Europeans in the phrase put to the Potomac Conference Committee members, 'Unfortunately, *Utrecht has happened*'.[39] At Utrecht, Netherlands, the world church voted overwhelmingly (1481 to 673), for the second time in five years, to deny women the privilege of full ordination to the gospel ministry.[40] This decision provoked a storm, which resulted only 11 weeks later, on 23 September 1995, in the first three women being ordained to the gospel ministry in Sligo Seventh-day Adventist church.[41] This unilateral action was followed by La Sierra University church and, after 'Equality in Ministry service', at Walla Walla College church, the action of its board and business meetings which voted on 4 December 1995 to 'support the ordination of qualified women to the gospel ministry'.[42] Truly, as one of the first women ordinands remarked in the response following the Sligo church ordination, 'This Sabbath is a sacred moment ... for me, for Sligo, for the entire Seventh-day Adventist Church'.[43]

It remains to be seen whether the deciding factor in the issue of the role of women in the Seventh-day Adventist church, world-wide, and indeed the question of the ordination of women to the gospel ministry, will be resolved by a theology of womanhood, theology of unity of the world-wide church, cultural anthropology, or in any other way. But for any Christian church, theology is the primary source in matters relating to church policy, especially when it deals with a sensitive moral issue such as the role of women. For that reason we now turn to Adventist theology of womanhood as it relates to women's place and role in general, and in the church in particular.

THEOLOGICAL CONSIDERATIONS

Understanding of the Church's Pioneers

The early leaders of the Adventist Church did not develop a coherent theology of womanhood; nor did they establish a comprehensive study on the role of women. However, they assumed that women should take responsibilities within the church community as well as within their homes. The main concern of the leaders of the church in the nineteenth century was to defend the work of Ellen White, and with her all the women who laboured in the denomination. For that reason they primarily dealt with the 'objection' texts of the Bible which were occasionally raised: 1 Corinthians 14 and 2 Timothy 2. James White, G. C. Tenney and John N. Andrews are typical examples of the endeavour of the early leaders to defend the involvement of women in the church life.

James White

James White (1821–81) recognised that women held positions of responsibility and honour in both the Old and the New Testaments. He cited Miriam who, according to Micah 6: 3.4, occupied a 'position equal to that of Moses and Aaron'.[44] Then he noted that Deborah judged Israel, received divine instruction and taught the people (Judges 4: 4–10). White concluded that 'a higher position no man has ever occupied'.[45] He recognised Ruth's and Esther's contributions, whose books held a prominent place in the Old Testament. He then turned to the New Testament.

Both Simeon and Anna greeted the infant Saviour in the temple (Luke 2: 25–38); four of Phillip's daughters prophesied (Acts 21: 8,9); and Paul's helpers were devoted women (Phoebe, Priscilla, Tryphena and Tryphosa). But above all, James White believed that Joel's prophecy quoted in Acts 2: 17 was a direct application to the end time: 'And it shall come to pass in the last days, saith God, I will pour out my Spirit upon all flesh, and your sons and your daughters shall prophesy' (KJV). He believed that Joel's prophecy pointed to the time he and his contemporaries lived in.

George C. Tenney

Before G. C. Tenney (1847–1921) attempted to do exegesis of the text in 1 Corinthians 14: 34, 35 and 1 Timothy 2: 12, he built a picture of the importance of women throughout the Bible. He believed that the Bible should be able to explain itself and that the proper way to understand the difficult texts of Paul is to understand how the Scriptures in their entirety approach the subject of the role of women in a religious community.

Tenney argued from the start that 'the work of the Bible has been to elevate [woman]'.[46] The reason for this Tenney found in the purpose of woman's creation to be a 'help meet (not a help-meet)'. By this phrase he understood woman to be 'a fit companion' to man. He also cited Galatians 3: 28, 'there is neither Jew nor Greek, there is neither bond nor free, there is neither male nor female: for ye are all one in Christ Jesus' (KJV). He rightly understood that 'this text has a generic application: it is of universal force whenever the gospel reaches'.[47]

Looking at Christ's relationship with women, Tenney concluded that Jesus elevated women throughout his lifetime. A similar pattern emerges in Paul's ministry: Paul 'was a friend … of women in the work of the Christian church'.[48] After this sketch of the biblical attitudes towards women Tenney comes back to two Pauline texts which apparently forbid women's participation in church services.

1 Corinthians 14: 34 deals, in Tenney's view, with a particular situation in a local church. There were various disorders in place in the church in Corinth and the meetings had become a disgrace.

'Unruly' and 'obstreperous' women 'added their clatter to the general confusion, and along with the other disorders, Paul sought to rebuke this trouble, those women were out of place'.[49] Also, among three different terms for 'speaking', *ei-pon*, *le-go* and *la-le-o*. Paul uses the last one, which can be translated: '*to prattle*; to babble; *to chatter*'. Tenney concluded from this that 'the apostle was rebuking garrulity rather than prohibiting Christians from witnessing for the cause of God'.[50]

It was not only the circumstances of the Corinthian church and language that Paul used that led Tenney to conclude that these restriction were to apply to special cases of impropriety, but 1 Corinthians 11 helped him establish the same point. Verse 5 proves the point that, even within the Corinthian church, women were eligible and free to pray and prophesy publicly. And Tenney concluded, by affirming 1 Corinthians 11: 11, that in the Lord, 'neither is the man without the woman, neither the woman without the man' (KJV).

John N. Andrews

Like Tenney, John Andrews (1829–83) noted that the church in Corinth was in a state of great disorder, the women 'acting with such indecorum as to be a matter of shame'. Therefore, he added, 'what the apostle says to women in such a church as this, and in such a state of things, is not to be taken as directions to all Christian women in other churches and in other times, when and where such disorders do not exist.'[51] Andrews also used 1 Corinthians 11: 5 to prove that there were some Corinthian women who were allowed to pray and prophesy publicly. But he, unlike Tenney and White, saw 1 Timothy 2: 12 as 'Paul's general rule with regard to women as public teachers'.[52] All the work done by women in the time of Paul (such as Phoebe, Priscilla, Tryphena and Tryphosa), Andrews saw as exceptions to the general rule. Therefore, Andrews' position regarding the role of women is more ambiguous than that of the other two leaders of the early Adventist church.

Ellen G. White

Although Ellen White (1827–1915) elevated the maternal role of women ('the queen of a home') to the highest level, she also believed that women could do much in the church. 'There certainly should be', wrote White, 'a larger number of women engaged in the work of ministering to suffering humanity, uplifting, educating them how to believe … in Jesus Christ our Saviour.'[53] She recognised that in some instances women could minister better than men[54] and that, therefore, they should be paid from the tithe funds reserved exclusively for the gospel ministry. They should be paid whether they asked for it or not.[55]

Ellen White was never formally ordained in the church, but she claimed that God himself ordained her to a special ministry.[56] As Roger W. Coon, an Associate Secretary of the Ellen G. White Estate, pointed out,

> She held the credentials of an ordained minister, first from the Michigan Conference and later from the General Conference (on one of the certificates [1885], the word 'ordained' is crossed out by the stroke of a pen; on some it is not – they were issued every year).[57]

Although she did not conduct marriages, the 'ordinance of the Lord's Supper' (Eucharist), or baptisms, she was paid the salary of an ordained minister. She never endorsed the ordination of women to the gospel ministry, but neither did she condemn it. The closest she came to approving the ordination of women was in 1895, when she wrote:

> *Women* who are willing to consecrate some of their time to the service of the Lord should be appointed to visit the sick, look after the young, and minister to the necessities of the poor. *They should be set apart to this work by prayer and laying on of hands.*[58] (emphases added)

This 'enigmatic exception', as Michael Pearson observed, 'seemed to pertain to the traditional Adventist role of deaconess'.[59] This concurs with the opinion of Ellen White's personal secretary, Clarence C. Crisler, who wrote in response to a query that this statement refers 'primarily to the ordination of God-fearing women as deaconesses in local churches.'[60]

Whether because the issue of women's ordination was not current in her time or to preserve the unity of the church, Ellen White, while highly recommending women's participation in the gospel ministry,[61] fell short of publicly supporting their ordination to that ministry. She called for the total utilisation of all the church's resources, including the talents, abilities and commitment of its women, for missionary endeavour of bringing the good news of Jesus to people around the world. She advocated placing women in all positions for which they were qualified and called by God. 'Her silence', Coon perceptively concluded, 'for she spoke neither in favour of ordination nor against – "proves" nothing conclusively beyond the fact that this subject was not one of her high-proprity burdens during her ministry (which ended in 1915).'[62]

The Renewed Concerns for the Role of Women in the 1970s: Symposium at Camp Mohaven

Just as there was a decline in women's participation in the leadership positions of the Seventh-day Adventist Church between 1915 and 1970,[63] so there was a decline also in theological discussion of the issue of women's role in the church. Owing to changing attitudes regarding women's role in the early 1970s, the General Conference commissioned some of the denominational leading scholars to write on different topics relating to the issue.

The first stage[64] of this scholarly endeavour was undertaken in 1973 when at Camp Mohaven, Ohio, more than 25 theologians and church leaders (men and women in almost equal numbers) met to discuss 26 papers[65] prepared for this first Council on the Role of Women.[66] The clear consensus was 'that women were discriminated against in denominational employment, and in church life in general, and that this contradicted the spirit of the gospel'.[67] Leona Running, Professor of Biblical Languages at Andrews University, argued that there were dangers in trying to apply biblical passages without giving due attention to their historical context.[68] Kit Watts, an editor at the Review and Herald, linked the issue of the role of women with such institutions as slavery and polygamy.[69] But one of the most important contribution was from a prominent theologian of the church, Raoul Dederen, who suggested that the role of women in the church cannot be linked to such theological concepts as the order of creation, the Fall, the ministry instituted by Christ or the sex of members of the godhead. He firmly believed that the issue of women's role in the church must be linked to the idea of the priesthood of all believers. In an open society such as ours, the church's responsibility is to employ every resource possible for the main task of Christianity, which is to spread the gospel to the world.[70]

Several years later, at the second stage of this scholarly undertaking, many more male theologians and scholars of the church were asked to be involved. Theologies of creation and redemption, so prominent in Ellen White's writings on equality, received a thorough exegesis for the first time. Gerhard Hasel, a leading Adventist scholar, contributed a study on woman as described in the first three chapters of Genesis.[71]

Gerhard Hasel – Theology of Creation

From Genesis 1 Hasel concluded that in God's purpose for humankind there exists full equality between sexes. He showed this by reference to several indicators from Genesis 1: (a) 'man' (adam), as a generic term for mankind, was created as 'male and female', (b) the creation of both was in the image of God, (c) they equally shared in the divine 'blessing', (d) they were mutually assigned to 'rule' over the animals, (e) they received the common power to 'subdue' the earth, and (f) they had a common vocation to be God's vice-regents on earth (Gen 1: 26–7). Hasel concludes, therefore, that

> in Gen 1 man (*adam*) is created last as male and female, and is thus truly the crown of creation. Both man and woman share their creation in 'the image of God' which lifts them above all other creatures and places them together in a special relationship to God. Both man and woman find their full meaning neither in male alone nor in female alone, but in their mutual relationship and communion. Both man and woman receive the divine blessing with the power to propagate and perpetuate the human species; both man and woman are given the task to 'subdue' the earth and 'rule' over the animal kingdom, indicating their common position as viceregents over God's creation. This heaping up of aspects in the creation, nature, and responsibilities of adam ('man') indicates that both male and female were created by God as equals. Neither man nor woman was superior or inferior to the other, neither was subordinated to the other. Man and woman were equals, each certainly with his own individuality.[72]

The more detailed account of creation in Genesis 2 does not stand in the tension or opposition to the picture derived from Genesis 1. Rather Genesis 2 presupposes and complements the compressed statements of Genesis 1. Hasel investigates two main terms: (a) *ezer* rendered as 'help meet' (KJV), 'helper' (RSV, NIV, NASB), 'partner' (NEB, NAB) and 'aid' (Speiser, Anchor Bible); and (b) *kenegdo* rendered as 'fit for him' (RSV) or 'suitable for him' (NAB,NASB). Hasel's conclusion is that since the noun *ezer* ('helper') is employed primarily to God (Ex 18: 4; Deut 33: 7; Pss 20: 3; 33: 20; 115: 9–11; Dan 11: 34, etc.), and sometimes to animals, the term itself does not specify positions within relationships. Therefore, the term 'helper' must be determined from the context of additional content, (i.e. *kenegdo*) literally meaning 'like his counterpart', 'corresponding to him' or 'alongside him'. So, concludes Hasel, 'as God is man's superior helper and animals are man's inferior helpers, so woman is man's equal helper, one that fits him'.[73]

The fact of Adam's creation prior to Eve's Hasel argues against – the so-called 'order (priority) of creation' argument: it does not imply any superiority on Adam's part. The creation of the first human being (male) is incomplete without the creation of the creature created last (female). Woman's creation is not an afterthought but a completion and culmination of the creation. The writer of Genesis used a *'ring composition'* 'where the first and last (second) correspond to each other in importance.[74]

In Genesis 3 we encounter the fall of man which disrupted all relationships. And even there 'the divine declaration that man shall "rule" (*masal*) over his wife (3: 16) indicates that she is not reduced to a slave or an animal to be "ruled" (*radah*) as animals are (Gen 1: 26, 28)'.[75] Also, Genesis 3 implies that this 'rulership' is restricted to the marriage relationship in order to maintain harmony in marriage during the era of sin. This type of rulership is described in the New Testament as the Father is the head of Christ in the relationship of the equality of a triune God (1 Cor 11: 3). The implications of these observations Hasel believes to be of immense importance for the modern understanding of the role of women in the church. Since the 'plan of salvation and the message of the gospel are concerned with the reproduction of the image of God in men under the guidance of the Spirit of truth', Hasel maintains that the responsibility of the church is 'to bring about the reproduction of the image of God in man, to restore harmony between God and man, and establish equality and unity in the human family where there is now inequality between man and women'.[76] This, for Hasel, means utilising all manpower and womanpower resources in the completition of the gospel commission.

Kenneth L. Vine and Jerry A. Gladson – Old Testament Views

Kenneth Vine and Jerry Gladson, at the time both prominent Adventist theologians, see the creation story as the primary source of God's ideal for the role of women. Everything else in the Old Testament indicates that 'man's adulteration and abuse of his powers debased womanhood'.[77] And, adds Vine, 'this abuse spreads far outside the marriage relationship to include all women, and to reduce their position in some societies to little more than goods and chattels-property owned by the man as he owned a house, land, animals, and slaves.'[78]

God's original plan of marriage as a monogamous unit developed into bigamy and then into polygamy. The Mosaic laws, which were given in this cultural setting in which women were already downtrodden, were aimed at improving conditions within that social and cultural setting.

And yet even within this restricted setting for women's activity and leadership, Gladson finds that women were publicly active, sometimes assuming very important leadership roles. One basic and fundamental role was the female prophet (Miriam, Ex 15: 20; Deborah, Judges 4: 4; Huldah, 2 Kings 22: 12–20; Isaiah's wife, Is 8: 3; and Noadiah, Neh 6: 10–14). Also there were some 'wise' women whose roles must have included advisory leadership (2 Sam 14: 2ff; 20: 16–22). Deborah occupied the dual role of prophetess and judge, implying even some kind of military authority (Judges 4: 4). Gladson concluded that although there is a lot of prejudice against women in the Old Testament and they are generally regarded as subordinate to men, there are also a number of positive aspects of womanhood that are vividly described through 'feminine imagery' of Isaiah 54: 5–6, Lamentations 1: 17, Proverbs 1: 20–1, 4: 5ff, 7: 4, 8: 1–3, 9: 1–6 and 14: 1. In passing he touches on the point that even God, although predominantly described in masculine terms, is occasionally characterised by feminine imagery. Such is the case in Isaiah 49: 14–16 and Deuteronomy 32: 18, for example. And lastly, Gladson sees in Joel 2: 28ff the 'advance word' of the Old Testament through which the Messiah will, as Jeremiah announced, bring a 'new freedom for all (from least to greatest) including women'.[79]

Walter F. Specht – Jesus and Women

The analysis of Jesus' attitude to women produced by Walter Specht, a prominent Adventist scholar, leads him to believe that Jesus championed women's rights. Jesus 'never looked down on women or spoke of them as inferior'.[80] Specht approvingly quotes Alicia C. Faxon saying that, 'In all four Gospels, Jesus is never reported as acting or speaking to women in a derogatory fashion. He always treated them as equals, individuals, and persons'.[81] Women had a prominent place in Jesus' teaching and in his ministry.

When challenged by the Pharisees about the concept of marriage, Jesus did not point to Moses and the provision in Deuteronomy which was a concession to man's 'hardness of heart'. Instead, Jesus indicated the original intention of the Maker testifying to the origin of the creation account. Specht observes that, 'in dealing with the Pharisees' question our Lord placed the wife on a status of equality with her husband. He did not recognize a double standard of sexual morality.'[82] Overall, Jesus' position on women might have been called 'revolutionary'.

Specht raises several new arguments in the quest for the equality between sexes. Specht depicts Jesus in the story of the adulterous woman (John 7: 53–8; 11). Jesus was provoked to give judgment about this woman, and hence be trapped into saying something that could be used against him. But after an initial silence and writing in the sand, Jesus asserted implicitly full equality between the woman caught in the act of adultery and the righteous Pharisees: 'If any one of you is without sin, let him be the first to throw a stone at her' (John 8: 7). This was a 'devastating rebuke to male arrogance'.[83] Implicitly, Jesus established equality status for all people regardless of their gender.

Specht then turns to another incident in Jesus' ministry which occurred in Bethany, 'the village of Martha and Mary' (John 11: 1). On one occasion when Jesus visited these two followers and friends, Mary took a seat at his feet and eagerly listened to his teachings. Just as Paul was educated 'at the feet of Gamaliel' in Jerusalem (Acts 22: 3), Mary took the same position at Jesus' feet. Although 'in Judaism, women, as a general rule, were not allowed the privilege of studying under a rabbi', observes Specht, 'our Lord did not hesitate to impart His teachings to her [Mary] and her sister [Martha]'.[84] Jesus was not bound by the Pharisaic notions of his day such as, for example, 'Better to burn the Torah than to teach it to women'.[58] Instead, he enjoyed discoursing with women who hungered for spiritual food (see, for example, the discourse with a Samaritan woman to whom he disclosed his identity as the Messiah). Martha and Mary proved that they knew Jesus' teaching about 'the resurrection at the last day' (John 11: 23–32). No greater affirmation of faith was made by any of Jesus' followers than when Martha responded: 'Yes, Lord; I believe that you are the Christ, the Son of God, who was to come into the world' (John 11: 27).

This acceptance of women as followers Specht sees as 'unprecedented in the first century'. On this point there is a striking difference between Jesus and other Jewish rabbis. As Jesus travelled throughout the land, he was accompanied by the twelve disciples and a band of Galilean women (Luke 8: 1–3). The women even provided financial support for Jesus' ministry (Luke 8: 3; Mark 15: 41), which was an absolute departure from rabbinical teaching. They were eyewitnesses to the death, burial and resurrection of Christ (1 Cor 15: 1–4) and were the first to receive the message of the resurrection (Luke 24: 8–9). Overall, concludes Specht, 'Jesus definitely championed women's right to honour and dignity'.[86]

Sakae Kubo – 1 Timothy 2: 11–15

1 Timothy 2 deals with prayer and worship. In order for Paul to write 'Let a woman learn in silence with all submissiveness', Sakae Kubo, a New Testament scholar whose influence extends beyond Adventist circles, believes that 'there was something in the Christian gospel that brought a sense of liberation to women'.[87] If they had not begun acting less passively than heretofore, Paul would not have needed to lay down some rules of conduct for them in public worship.

While Kubo observes that exegesis of 1 Timothy 2: 11–15 points towards a subordinate position of women and prohibits them from teaching, he believes that the passage needs hermeneutical explication because 'there are elements which stand in tension due to man's situation in sin'.[88] Kubo parallels the question of women's role with issues of polygamy and slavery which are socially accepted in the Scripture, although they stand against biblical principles laid down through the total thrust of the Scriptures.[89] He concludes that developments already existing in the church are against a literalistic application of 1 Timothy 2: 11–15. However, if this text is applied to the ordination of women, it does not deal with the issue at all.

Kubo develops one more theological point worth considering. The three general statements of Paul which directly speak 'of the breaking down of barriers in Christ (1 Cor 12: 12–13; Gal 3: 27–8; Col 3: 9–11) all appear in *baptismal context*'[90] (emphasis added). As Kubo argues:

> Baptism is specifically mentioned in the context of the first two; and in the last, reference is made to putting off the old ways and

> putting on the new self that is concretized in Christ. Baptism is thus looked at as *the great equalizer*. When one is baptized in Christ there is no longer male or female, slave or free, Jew or Gentile ... The very event of initiation into the Christian community destroys the barriers between groups out of which the old world had lived.[91] (emphasis added)

Baptism, which men and women undertake in the Christian context (unlike Jewish circumcision), is the great equaliser putting all people on the same level. Hence, Christianity unlike Judaism, is 'international, classless, and without sex bias in its basic insight'.[92]

Others from Biblical Research Institute of Seventh-day Adventists – BRIAD

Frank Holbrook, the director of BRIAD, agrees with Kubo that 1 Timothy 2: 11–15 is a general principle of Paul's time. However, he thinks that it is culturally conditioned and must be contrasted with the apostle's general treatment of the subject of equality: 'There is neither Jew nor Greek, there is neither slave nor free, there is neither male nor female; for you are all one in Christ Jesus' (Galatians 3: 28). Therefore, none stands above another. Nevertheless, as Holbrook rightly observes, 'it is evident from the records of the NT that the implications of such perspective could not always be realized in that age because of certain deep-seated social institutions and viewpoints held by the society at that time.'[93]

The slow process of social and religious equality started with Jewish–Greek relationships at the time of Paul; the process of slave-free relationships took much longer to resolve within the Christian community; and lastly, male–female relationships still have a long way to go before it is fully resolved.

Betty Stirling, although primarily dealing with the modern social conditions which desire the full participation of women in church activities, elevates the concept of the priesthood of all believers. In her view, this concept 'implies the equality of believers', including women.[94] While Raoul Dederen believes in the same concept, he does not equate it 'with any "clergy" or professional group'.[95] Rather, the concept of the priesthood of all believers is understood to mean all Christians. Hence, says Dederen, 'The Christian life, then, is by definition a priesthood, a ministry, performed in response to God's call addressed to all sinner'.[96] The question that remains, however, is how far the bounds of ordination can properly be extended. This question, in Dederen's conclusion, is followed by another: 'We should ask how far existing forms of the ordained ministry in the Seventh-day Adventist Church are adequate and in harmony with God's plan, and what new forms might be required'.[97]

Adventist Theology of Womanhood after 1973

Wadie Farag

Immediately after the commission of the General Conference to study the issue of women's participation in the work of the church, articles began to appear in denominational periodicals discussing the issue from different perspectives. Wadie Farag, a pastor of an Adventist College in Canada, introduced yet another theological concept in examining the relationship between men and women. Farag argues that the priority of man does not imply his superiority. He illustrates his point by reference to 1 Corinthians 11: 3, 'The head of every man is Christ; and the head of the woman is the man; and the head of man is God.' If Christ is divine and equal to God, how can God be the head of Christ? Farag solves the problem by asserting that, although God and Christ are both divine and equal, God has priority in the Godhead. So, in a kind of theology of parallelism, Farag assumes that 'man and woman may have different distinctive duties and one be the head of the other, and yet they are equal before God'.[98]

However, Farag fails to describe what this 'priority' comprises, or if it is distinct from superiority. Also, he does not explain in what sense God the Father is head to Jesus Christ. In other words, a number of questions arise which need answering before one can adopt the explanation of his model: Is that 'priority in the Godhead' constant or temporary; Does it change so that God the Son takes priority at some point in time or does it always stay the same? And lastly, Is the 'priority' of a hierarchical nature or does it merely describe purpose?

James Londis

In a commendable article 'God as Woman – Blasphemy or Blessing?',[99] James Londis, a leading thinker in Adventism, raises several issues regarding the role of women. He first discusses the concept of *Imago Dei*. To the questions, 'Is God male?' and 'Is "maleness" divine in a way "femaleness" is not?', his answer is 'No'.

When one says that God appears in bodily form it is quite different from when one claims that God is a body. God is described to us in terms we can comprehend, and they include both masculine and feminine imagery. 'God is pictured as carrying Israel in the womb, as birthing and suckling his people, as comforting them as a mother comforts her child, and as wanting to "gather them as a hen gathers her chicks"'.[100] God is neither male nor female, nor a combination of the two. In order to relate intimately to God as a person we imagine him in a bodily form. But Londis warns us not to 'suppose that God's bodily form in such appearances is identical to his substance'.[101] Since God is not male, but God's image reflects itself in both the male and female part of 'man', man and woman equally represent God. Hence the equality between man and woman.

Another point that Londis raises regards a woman deacon – Phoebe. He notes that the Greek term *diakonos* when applied to men is rendered 'deacon' in English, but when Phoebe is referred to as *diakonos*, the phrase is translated as 'servant' or 'helper' (Rom 16: 1). It is inconsistent with the original, where *diakonos* implies a leadership position within the church.

Londis argues that extra-canonical documents record intense competition between the apostle Peter and Mary over priority of witness to the resurrection of Jesus. This reflects the church's struggle over the leadership role of women as early as the second century. 'Otherwise', observes Londis, 'discussion over who was the first witness to the risen Christ would be pointless'.[102]

In Londis' view, the principle of the full humanity of men and women, which is the *sine qua non* of God's will, has been restricted to men. It is not known what security that full humanity will bring to women, but it surely will illuminate the meaning of such aspects of church's theology as anthropology and ecclesiology. 'Male and female together, in full humanity, provide the balance needed for theological insight'.[103]

Lastly, according to Londis, for a follower of Christ only his example would be appropriate – and Christ's example can be described through the theology of service. It is true, argues Londis, that in relationships power imbalances can be for socially sound purposes, e.g. raising children or instructing students. The aim of the superior is to raise the inferior to equality. That type of relationship, although imbalanced in terms of power, can be described as a *relationship of service*. Jesus is the prime example of such a relationship. Jesus came as a *servant* leader, as one who humbled and 'emptied' himself (Phil 2: 5–11). In God's kingdom, the path to power is through weakness, the path to glory is through humility, the path to life is through death.[104] And God is pleased when power is distributed rather than centralised and accumulated. To the world it is 'foolishness' that God becomes weak and vulnerable. This is the reason why the cross is such a powerful symbol. For centuries men had the power. The aim was for the superior to raise the inferior to equality. It was supposed to be a relationship of service although men were to use the tool of power to end the inequality. Londis believes in the words of his article title, that 'The Gospel Demands Equality *Now*'.

Richard Davidson and Skip MacCarty

Richard Davidson and Skip MacCarty attempt to give a summary of their theological insight through a question-and-answer type essay. In addition to the arguments discussed above, they point to several new insights relevant to the role of women. First, they argue that in Ephesians 5: 21–23, the home is not the model for the church, but the converse. It is the church and Christ's headship over it that is the model for the home. This means that 'we should not use the home model to structure the man–woman relationships in the church', because to do so would be an 'inappropriate reversal and backward application of the biblical model'.[105]

Secondly, they argue that Jesus did not choose any women to be his apostles for the same reason that he did not choose any God-fearing Gentile – due to the extreme prejudice of the people he came to call first. The immediate cultural and social context did not permit Jesus to choose a woman to be his disciple; this act would have jeopardised and undermined his ministry.

Lastly, Davidson and MacCarty see the 'husband-of-one-wife' requirement of 1 Timothy 3: 1–7 and Titus 1: 5–9 as ruling out polygamy and not as a prescribed commandment. They assert that the same phrase, 'husband of one wife' is used not only for elders but for deacons too (1 Tim 3: 11–12); yet in Romans 16: 1, Paul makes reference to 'our sister Phoebe, a deacon of the church'. 'How could there be a female deacon', ask Davidson and MacCarty, 'if the "husband-of-one-wife" qualification was to be interpreted in a prescriptive, literalistic manner?'[106]

Beatrice S. Neall

The most comprehensive theology of womanhood in the Seventh-day Adventist Church came from Beatrice Neall,[107] an associate

Professor of Theology at Union College. Looking at the theology of creation, she recognises that, 'As God is a fellowship of three beings who live in a love relationship, so man, in God's image, was created to be a fellowship of male and female and child living in a love relationship'.[108] Contrary to the opinion that 'the female adam was in the image of the male, and hence, inferior to him', Neall understands the text to indicate that man as the image of God is both male and female.[109] Therefore, one can see feminine imagery of God as well as masculine. In addition to the examples mentioned earlier, Neall lists God's name *El Shaddai*, which can mean 'God, my breast' – that is, God the source of my nourishment and comfort. She concludes, 'Since God describes himself by male and female attributes, it takes both male and female to image him'.[110]

Secondly, in looking at the creation story, Neall perceives that woman was created to be a suitable helper to man. She translates suitable literally – 'as if in front of him [the man]'; 'I will make a helper as if in front of him'. If an inferior position were implied, argues Neall, 'the writer would have used a preposition meaning after or behind'.[111] Both creatures were formed by God himself – the creation of woman from the rib of man implying that she was made to stand by his side as his equal. They were created of one flesh ('bone of my bones and flesh of my flesh') and then told to become one flesh (Gen 2: 23–24). 'The unity of substance was to be constantly nurtured by an even closer unity of relationship'.[112] The Fall introduced a hierarchy into the marriage relationship. However it soon spread to all other spheres of social life. The question is how to understand the pronouncements of Genesis 3. Is the curse of God a command for the human race or a description of the outcome of sin? What is the mission of the church: to perpetuate the results of sin or to redeem the race from the curse? Neall asks further:

> The sentence imposed by Genesis 3 is death. Is it permissible to try to extend or enhance life? The sentence of Genesis 3 is toil and sweat. Is it permissible to invent ways to lighten work and avoid sweat? The sentence of Genesis 3 is pain in childbirth. Is it permissible to find ways to reduce or eliminate such pain? The sentence of Genesis 3 is subjection of the wife to the husband. Is it permissible to find a better method of living in harmony?[113]

For Neall the answer is very clear: Jesus came to 'redeem us from the curse of the law by becoming a curse for us' (Gal 3: 13).

Thirdly, Jesus' attitude towards women both in his contact with them and in his preaching was remarkable. He compared God with a woman looking for a lost coin (Luke 15: 8–10), he compared the Kingdom of God to a woman making bread (Matt 13: 33); he spoke of ten virgins (Matt 25: 1–13) and of a persistent widow pleading for justice (Luke 18: 1–8); he praised a poor widow who put all her money into the offertory box (Mark 12: 41–4). He talked publicly to the Samaritan woman. He instructed women and defended Mary's right to learn. He had a group of female disciples from the beginning to the end of his ministry (Luke 8: 1–3). Women stayed by Jesus when the men forsook him and fled. They were present at the outpouring of the spirit at Pentecost (Acts 1: 13–14). Although the gospels 'give no technical term for ordination ... the empowering each time was the fullest evidence of ordination'.[114] In Peter's sermon at Pentecost, he emphasised the importance of the Spirit's descent upon the women by quoting Joel 2: 28–9. This text, observes Neall, 'long a favourite of Seventh-day Adventists in defending the call of Ellen White, asserts that the gift of the Spirit in the last days is universal (all flesh); there is no sex discrimination (sons and daughters), or age discrimination (young men and old men), or class discrimination (menservants or maidservants)'.[115]

Texts that deal with women in the New Testament Neall categorises into three groups: prescriptive, descriptive and corrective. The first category, *prescriptive texts*, includes the account of the Holy Spirit at Pentecost introducing new freedom and power for *all people*. This same new order Paul describes in Galatians 3: 28 – in Christian baptism all differentiation has died, spiritual as well as social. In the same letter Paul rebuked Peter for practising social discrimination against Gentiles (Gal 2: 11–12). In Jesus there is a mutual interdependence and mutual appreciation of the sexes.

The second category, *descriptive texts*, is found in the number of references to women in leadership positions in the first Christian church. These texts are subtle and without any need on the part of the author to justify them. For example, texts such as Acts 21: 8–9, Philippians 4: 2–3 and Romans 16: 1–2 can be included in this category.

The third group, *corrective texts*, can be illustrated by the two passages which apparently contradict the other passages mentioned before, namely I Corinthians 14: 33–35 and I Timothy 2: 11–15. While in the first instance Neall sees the local congregation of

Corinth being in chaos (I Cor 5: 1; 11: 21; 14: 23), apparently with the newly liberated women leading out and therefore being rebuked, in the second text she believes that Paul's concern lies with those women who, untaught in the law, were being not only 'led astray, but were promulgating "doctrines of demons", "silly myths", and "old wives' tales" (1 Tim 4: 1.7)'.[116] Hence, Neall concludes on this point, 'To women who aspired to teach, but were themselves deceived by false teachers, Paul spoke of Eve's vulnerability to deception. His use of Genesis was illustrative rather than normative for all time'.[117] Neall believes that the texts in question are 'case laws', laws which 'do not have the enduring force of fundamental law, and may with time be changed or dropped'.[118] She illustrates this with Jesus' application of one such 'case law':

> Jesus distinguished between the two kinds of law in case of the woman taken in adultery (John 8: 1–11). He upheld the Ten Commandments law against adultery by telling the woman, 'Go, and sin no more'. But he bypassed the case law that said, 'If a man is found lying with the wife of another man, both of them shall die' (Deuteronomy 22:22). He did not regard that law as binding in his day.[119]

Paul's statements prohibiting women from speaking in churches, in a similar way, are case laws for that particular time in that particular situation. They are not universal laws, not even in every church of Paul's time.

Lastly, Neall discusses the concepts of subordination and submission. Jesus is the model for women in his equal/subordinate role to the Father (1 Cor 11: 3). Jesus' dependence on the Father was evidence of his deity (John 7: 18). Although Jesus derived his power from God (John 5: 19) and was subordinate to him (John 14: 28), he nevertheless was equal with God (John 5: 18; Phil 2: 6). Neall points out that the Father and Son can and do exchange roles at times. The Father 'has given all judgment to the Son' (John 5: 22), and during Christ's earthly ministry the Father 'gave all things into his hand' (John 3: 35; 13: 3). Neall's right conclusion is that:

> The heavenly model illustrates that man/woman relationship should be characterized by harmony, consultation, and working together, with no independent decision-making. There can even

be exchange of roles, with one or the other leading out in different areas.[120]

Through the example of Christ's relationship with the Father we can freely say that the ideal for husband and wife is to be in a relationship of mutual submission which Paul declared in Ephesians 5: 21: 'Submit to one another out of reverence for Christ'. Only mutual submission would be in the spirit of servanthood that Jesus introduced.

Others

Among those who opposed the ordination of women to the full church ministry two European theologians are worth mentioning, Samuel Bacchiocchi and Bryan Ball. Although neither Bacchiocchi nor Ball opposed the idea of women ministering and serving in the church, they both fall short of endorsing women's ordination. Ball suggested that a great caution should be exercised before the church approves the ordination of women to full gospel ministry. Not only should this be the case because of cultural differences that the international Adventist church must take into account, but also on theological grounds, the church must resolve all objections which arguably stem out of the New Testament.[121]

Bacchiocchi argued more forcefully that ordination of women to gospel ministry should never be allowed in the Seventh-day Adventist church. According to him, woman was created second in the order of creation and, therefore, has a submissive role. Neither in the Old nor in the New Testament were women assuming the role of a priest. Just as Christ is the head of the church, the man must assume the role of the head of the family, according to Bacchiocchi, the priestly role.[122]

When Ball's and especially Bacchiocchi's views were published in 1986, the editors of *Spectrum* were overwhelmed by replies which argued for the ordination of women to the gospel ministry. It is doubtful whether this is a sign that the majority of Adventists believe that women should be ordained because *Spectrum* is a left-of-centre journal read mainly by Western Adventist intellectuals.

The theological discussion of the role and status of women in the church continues until the present day. It will do so until the ordination of women to the full gospel ministry is accepted and approved by the church. Many theologians of the church have realised that 'it is only tradition and custom, not our doctrines or deliberate reflections that have kept us from ordaining women to the ministry'.[123] Beside the tradition and custom and the preserving of the unity of the world-wide church, the greatest reason for theological disagreement on the issue is due to different application of principles of interpretation of the Scriptures.

PRINCIPLES OF INTERPRETATION IN RELATION TO THE ROLE OF WOMEN

Many of the modern Adventist scholars would fully agree with Kubo that 'the most important task in studying the Bible and ordination of women is that of arriving at a principle for interpreting Scripture'.[124] There are two basic models of interpretation that Kubo depicts: a literalistic view of Scripture which those who oppose the ordination of women often assume, and more flexible interpretation, whereby the New Testament elements point beyond the period which they enunciate. Kubo prefers the latter when he approvingly quotes Krister Stendahl: 'It is – as always in truly Christian theology – to discern where the accent should lie now, the accent in the eschatological drama which we call the history of the church and the world'.[125] By this principle of interpretation which looks for the modern application of the biblical principles Kubo sees no biblical barrier to ordination. He believes that with the role of women it is just as it was with the issue of slavery, 'those who argued for emancipation were more truly biblical than those who used "irrefutable biblical argument" for their view'.[126]

Kubo argues elsewhere that a theologian must determine which text deals with a specific case and which is applicable as a general principle.[127] 'The first is to understand the biblical teachings aright and the second is to read discerningly the historical situation and context in which one lives'.[128] He favours the second model on the basis of which he concludes that 'in addition to commitment to a call, ability is the only criterion by which selection to this [ministerial] office is determined'.[129]

Jerry Gladson is another author who talks about appropriate exegesis and hermeneutics of the Bible. He suggests that before the proper meaning of a given text is determined, one must take into account the historical, grammatical, syntactical, literary and sociological context. And yet, contrary to many contemporary theologians who use the historico-critical approach, 'the divinity of Scripture will also have to be maintained as an integral part of the whole'.[130] Gladson concludes that 'God spoke to people where they were and He attempted to raise them from that level to His ideal'.[131] Just as it was with slavery issue which was defended by an incorrect hermeneutic in the past century, and the polygamy issue still unresolved in some churches today, the issue of the biblical role of women may be resolved by applying this type of hermeneutics today: the result would be 'the full utilization of feminine talent in the community of God'.[132]

Frank Holbrook develops the concept of cultural conditioning a step further. He argues that there are two distinct reasons why, in the Old Testament, women were so treated. The first he labels 'the deep-seated social customs of the surrounding cultures'. There is, throughout the Old Testament, an accommodation to custom with respect to different social institutions including the role of women. Secondly, Holbrook finds a certain accommodation due to 'the hardness' of the human heart. It is *progressive revelation* that a modern theologian must consider in order to arrive at God's ideal. Holbrook does not indicate whether this incorporates 'natural revelation' or not. But, for Holbrook, this progressive revelation discloses 'more clearly perspectives of the divine heart' and the conscience of mankind becomes more enlightened.[133]

In a highly focused study on the principles of interpretaion, Beatrice Neall raises six major points: (1) a theologian must determine the original intent of the writer, i.e. exegesis (2) a theologian must apply the text to our own time, i.e. hermeneutics. A task for hermeneutics is found in determining, for example, whether Paul's statement, 'I permit no woman to teach' is a universal command, or counsel for a specific situation. (3) Neall establishes several principles to guide us in the whole exercise of hermeneutics. One of them is that 'the pre-Fall state is the ideal to set before men and women today'.[134] Many practices which are quite common in Scripture do not represent God's ideal for humanity. Such are, for example, polygamy, slavery, meat-eating and use of alcoholic beverages. The Adventist mission to call the world 'back to Eden' is fundamentally right. (4) Jesus Christ is the supreme revelation of God to human kind. He is also the supreme example of how human beings should relate to one another. Therefore, the example of Jesus must be carefully considered in the study of the role and status of women. (5) an interpreter needs to be very careful with the argument from silence.

In a case when the Bible is not explicit on a subject, as is the case in the study of the role of women, one must look at the 'trajectory' of Scripture. Says Neall,

> if one can see the direction a missile is pointed and calculate its velocity, one can predict where it will land. For example, on the issue of slavery, the Bible assumes its existence and gives no command to abolish it (Paul even tells slaves to obey their masters); but the biblical principles of brotherhood, the dignity of humanity, freedom to choose, and the need to develop one's gifts, all lead in the direction of abolition. Concerning both slavery and the role of women, it is necessary to determine the trajectory of Scripture.[135]

And finally, (6) the question for an interpreter of Scripture should be, 'What is God actually doing?' It is a similar argument to Holbrook's 'progressive revelation' concept, because it allows the work of the Holy Spirit to influence and lead Christians in modern times as he was able to do in ancient times. Neall illustrates this with Peter's example. Peter believed, based on the biblical evidence, that Jews should not associate with Gentiles (Lev 20: 26 and Neh 9: 2). The Holy Spirit was an instrument in changing his theological misconceptions by acting contrary to Peter's expectations (Acts 10: 28.44–5). God was moving, and Peter had to learn to move with him. 'How is God moving today? Does he use women to teach, to lead, to exercise authority? ... God's actions should be a check on our interpretation of Scripture'.[136] In other words, progressive revelation is leading us to the point when we shall have to accept the inevitable: the full ministry of women based on the full equality regardless of race, nationality, economic status or gender.

Several others attempts[137] have been made in the discussion about principles of biblical interpretation in the year following the general Conference Session in Utrecht in 1995. All these attempts, important as they are, expose the cracks in Adventist hermeneutics which need to be addressed more comprehensively if the church intends to maintain unity among its scholars and theologians.

Although the Seventh-day Adventist Church has not recognised that 'moving of God' world-wide and applied it to its policy of ordination of women to the gospel ministry, the outcome of this 'moving' seems inevitable. It is difficult to deny the direction of the general biblical principles which are derived in doctrines of creation, redemption, Christ's emancipation of women, the first Christian church's use of women, and the guidance of the Holy Spirit in modern times. The question that remains is *not whether* but rather *when* the fully equal ministry will be granted to women.

Part III
Social Theology in Seventh-day Adventist Scholarship

6

Reasons for Social Concern in Modern Adventism

INTRODUCTION

The reality of a double shift of approach in matters of social concern became obvious from the study of such human rights issues as racism and gender inequality. This can be seen from original, if peripheral, involvement with issues of social justice and human rights among the pioneers of the church, through indifference to social matters in the mid-history of the Seventh-day Adventist church, to the situation now where social justice and equality have become prominent towards the end of the twentieth century. The reasons for this change are not so obvious. Therefore we shall now attempt to explore why there has been renewed social interest among the church's scholars. Chapter 6 examines this through the study of important themes of Adventism, while the focus of Chapter 7 is more on the historical development (and liberation) of contemporary Adventist theology, especially from World War II to the present day.

There would seem to be at least seven major factors for this progression in social awareness within modern Adventism, although it was not entirely lacking among the first Adventists. In these early days of the movement social concern appears to have been obscured and marginalised by the proclamation of the gospel, the task which for Adventist pioneers was the principal reason for the movement's existence (Rev 14: 6–12).

The same objective of 'winning of men's souls' was rivalled by social improvements as late as the mid-1960s. In an editorial in the *Review and Herald*, Francis Nichol, the prominent editor of the *Seventh-day Adventist Bible Commentary*, wrote:

> the business of the church should be the saving of men's souls, that we should leave to others the task of improving society. …

> This is not the way to bear testimony to what we believe to be the right program for the church. We think these social reformers are mistaken as to what should be the great objective of the church. We are confident that it is the winning of men's souls.[1]

However, this was becoming an increasingly weaker voice among Adventist scholars.

Numerous articles addressing different social injustices have appeared in Adventist publications since the early 1960s. Increasing interest became apparent in areas of racial, tribal and sexual unity, world poverty, peace achievements, refugee protection, human rights matters and political influences on social justice. As George Colvin observed, 'the disengagement from society that [Adventist] tradition has produced may be eroding.'[2] The most important move in this direction on the administrative level of the church were probably four statements issued prior to the 1985 General Conference Session by the then president of the General Conference of Seventh-day Adventists, Neal Wilson. These statements, although criticised by some for their autocratic methodology,[3] dealt with such issues as drug abuse, the family, racism and peace. The obvious question that comes to mind is why did such change come about? This chapter attempts to answer this question in the light of what prominent Adventist thinkers have suggested.

HOLISTIC THEOLOGY

Holism – in Adventist circles often referred to as 'wholism' – was considered by some Adventist scholars in the 1980s to be the 'church's most single important contribution to theology'.[4] Its leading exponent, the bioethicist from Loma Linda University, Jack Provonsha, explains his view:

> Man is unity, a marvellously interpenetrating, interacting unity of one dimension with another. … This is why the health of the body is also a moral issue. What happens to a man's body is important to his entire personality and character, and thus may have eternal implications.[5]

'A Christian ethic', Provonsha argues, 'becomes an ethic of health'.[6] In Adventist circles the notion that the human body is the temple of the Holy Spirit and that we should 'honour God with our body' (1 Cor 6: 19, 20) is often used to support the idea of the church's health message. Consequently, as Bull and Lockhart observe, 'physical and spiritual well-being become difficult to separate'.[7] It follows that religious commitment, as seen by Adventists, can and should bring immediate material benefits. So from the future emphasis of the eschaton the focus has been reversed to the present life of a believer. Hence Adventist writer Don Hawley concludes that 'laying aside all discussion of future life, *it would pay any man or woman to live the Christ life just for the mental and moral rewards it affords here in this present world*'[8] (emphasis in original).

'Individual' and 'individuality' are important concepts in Adventist theology and because, as one editor of *Review and Herald* pointed out, 'the Adventist world view is keenly aware of *the dignity of personhood*',[9] modern Adventist scholars have made a link between holism and the social influence of Adventists on wider society. Thus Roy Branson suggested that 'a unique contribution [to society at large] is the Adventist experience; not the way to achieve salvation, but an overflowing of the gospel in a distinctive way of life.'[10] He continued:

> Because Adventists worship a God who will resurrect us *individual* and *whole* we appreciate the body and commit ourselves to preserving its health. The future is as real as the skin we touch. In the Adventist experience the Christian hope is made flesh. ... [Because of Adventist influence] the entire United States developed an appetite for wholesome grains made into wheat and cornflakes, and defied years of habit to adopt lighter, more nutritious breakfasts. Millions nearly addicted themselves to the protein-rich peanut butter developed in Battle Creek.[11] (emphasis added)

Branson then went further by establishing the point that, because Adventists believe that the gospel of Jesus 'affects all life' (holism), they established institutions to demonstrate the power of the gospel. Hence, Adventists have set up the largest Protestant educational system in the world and the largest Protestant healthcare system in America. Also, as Branson pointed out,

> Adventists send more physicians from the United States to other countries than do the next thirteen most active Protestant denominations and Catholic orders combined. ... Food is also the focus

of the $15 million annual budget of Adventist World Service (SAWS). Agricultural demonstration projects in Chad, Haiti, and Zimbabwe show government ministries how crops can be grown on previously barren lands.[12]

Holistic theology made a significant contribution to elevating the idea of personhood and, therefore, significantly influenced Adventist scholarship to focus on the well-being of people and to concentrate on eliminating anything that would prevent the full development of physical, emotional, economic, mental and spiritual abundance that people can have here and now (John 10: 10).

CONTINUITY OF THE EARLY ADVENTIST INTERESTS

In an editorial in the *Adventist Review*, the editor observed that Adventism in its early history was very sensitive to 'equality and to infringement of freedom'. 'Our pioneers', the author continued, 'unabashedly opposed slavery and gave aid to equality and to the 'underground railroad'. Later, led by Ellen White, they crusaded against the slavery induced by alcohol.[13] This renewed interest in social order to which Adventist pioneers devoted their time and effort has become a focus of study for a number of Adventist historians in the late twentieth century.[14]

If the social awareness of the present generation of Adventist thinkers can be linked to the involvement of church's pioneers in the social problems of their time, the present social consciousness would gain more credibility because of its consistency and continuity.

While W. G. Johnson proposed in broad terms that 'like Ellen White and the pioneers opposing the social evils of slavery and alcohol, we must "call sin by its right name", protesting the exploitation and dehumanization of our fellows',[15] Branson dealt more specifically with what our own contribution to the social debate should be. He suggested that Adventists should do something about the powerful US tobacco industry which year after year ensures that the federal tax revenue subsidises the cultivation of tobacco, while the same time the federal government has cut by two-thirds the funds for established programmes (Adventist 5-day Stop Smoking Clinic included) informing the public about the direct link between smoking and 300,000 deaths each year on the soil of the North America. In his view, Adventism as a movement should give itself 'utterly for the fragile, the weak among God's creatures, even if it meant challenging principalities and powers.' If the pioneers of Adventism were ready to fight slavery and the alcohol industry, their heirs, being consistent with their past, should help 'break the power of forces systematically contributing to a third of a million fatalities' in America that are directly linked with smoking.[16] Yet the greatest obstacle to that fight was a constant reminder for more than a century that the second coming of Christ will take place in the very near future.[17]

THE 'DELAYED' ADVENT

Fritz Guy, a theologian and Professor at the Seventh-day Adventist Theological Seminary, observed in a well-argued article on the 'Adventist Theology Today' that this notion of the 'imminent' Advent raises several important questions: 'Does the fact that Christ has not yet returned call for a re-examination of Adventist eschatology? Can the church believe and proclaim an "imminent" Second Advent for an indefinite length of time? If so, what is the meaning of the idea of "imminence"? However, if not, is there any way to continue an authentic (and not merely nostalgic or cultural) Adventist theology?'[18]

As another church historian put it, 'Seventh-day Adventists became aware that there might be a "delay" before the second coming' defining this 'delay' in terms of human attitudes and expectations and not as the fulfillment of God's promises.[19] Some Adventists found it difficult to deal with the fact that Christ has not yet returned, others suggested solutions which are directed towards social involvement. Of the latter group three scholars deserve special attention.

James Walters, an ethicist from Loma Linda University, calls the ethic oriented towards the Second Coming an 'ends-oriented ethic'. He criticised this type of ethic because it characteristically produces what he called 'ethical egoism' or 'corporate egoism'. In his opinion this is an inadequate ethic because 'achieving even laudable ends does not justify compromising our duty to respect human beings and their autonomy'.[20] Walters suggests that, 'Even when the end sought is as commendable as the Second Coming, if a person has himself exclusively in mind as the beneficiary, he is an ethical egoist.'[21]

Walters' proposal is to turn from the 'end-oriented ethic' to the 'ethic of duty', which is based on the doctrines of creation and kingdom of God. The problem is that he omits to suggest what to do, in this case, with the doctrine of the second coming and how to reconcile the two types of ethic deeply rooted in the church's theology and history.[22] Nevertheless, even Walters recognises the fact that 'because Adventists keenly anticipate a soon-coming, perfect world, they are typically not so concerned with how persons ought to relate to one another here and now, but with how to reach future goals or ends.'[23] Although Walter's proposal for the 'ethics of duty' is a valid one, it lacks full elaboration of how to avoid the consequences of an ethic that is so deeply based in the most fundamental of Adventist doctrines.

Michael Pearson, Head of the Department of Theology, and a lecturer in Christian Philosophy and Ethics at Newbold College, Bracknell, describes the particular dilemma of dual aspects of the second coming as *an ambiguity*. Pearson believes that, like other evangelical Christian groups, Adventists experience the 'tension produced by the dual imperatives, "Prepare to meet thy God", and "Occupy till I come" (Amos 4: 12 and Luke 19: 13).'[24] He recognises that,

> There is something odd, at first sight anyway, about an organization which, on the one hand, proclaims that Christ's return is imminent, and, on the other, regularly engages in the construction of institutions costing untold millions of dollars. One can understand Gaustad's observation that, while Adventists were 'expecting a kingdom of God from heavens, they worked diligently for one on the earth'.[25]

Then Pearson offers an analysis of what is happening in contemporary Adventism and how the perceived 'delay' of Christ's coming is reflected in the life of the church in a very pragmatic way. He suggests that,

> The longer the delay in the fulfilment of the advent hope, the greater is the emphasis on occupation rather than preparation. The longer the occupation, the greater is the tendency towards concerns of this world and diversification of interests. The increasing demand among rising generations of Adventists that their church address itself to issues of a socio-political and ethical nature is part of a pursuit of relevance in face of an advent which appears reluctant to materialize.[26]

Pearson, therefore, states the inevitable development within the Adventist theology towards more socially oriented concerns which are direct result of the delay of *parousia*. What he does not explain is where this trend ultimately leads to and what to do with the still strong and influential theology of the second coming. This is a contribution which James Londis, the director of The Washington Institute for Contemporary Issues, makes.

Londis, like Walters and Pearson, recognises that there has been a long delay in the second coming, which has brought a theological crisis among Adventists. In his opinion the delay has caused some Adventists embarrassment and a sense of abandonment at best, at worst it was 'a force pushing many Adventists into disbelief'.[27] Many Adventists, believing in the 'imminent' Second Coming during their lifetime, thought that they would not age but be translated without seeing death. 'Now when they are ageing and dying', Londis continues, 'the God of their childhood is dying, and they are left wondering whether any God exists.'[28] Out of this bitterness and despair Londis suggests there is only one way to go.

He looks at Matthew 24 and 25 and identifies the present Adventism with the first Christian community. Matthew, sensing the anguish over the delay in his own community, tells about Jesus answering the disciples' question about the 'time' of his coming with several parables. Londis believes that the parable of the sheep and the goats is a direct answer to the disciples' question, 'When are you returning?' And it seems to Londis that this is the solution to our pain over the delay. Jesus tells us that the best way to maintain a living experience of his presence during the delay is by immersing ourselves into the offering of the world; or, in Mauriac's phrase, 'assume the anguish of another'.[29]

Londis' suggestion, therefore, is that as we wait for the Messiah to come again, we have a definite task to fulfill which will give us a sense of purpose and belonging. The task is to get socially involved, not only theoretically, but also in everyday Christian experience. Londis suggests that social concern for justice and human desire for fulfilment beyond death are both built into our nature. 'As they bend down into human misery their eyes are lifted up to divine glory,' Londis concludes, 'they sense that even as human beings by nature hope for fulfillment beyond death, we also by nature want justice to be done, righteousness to triumph, and mercy to prevail'[30] – two ideas perfectly legitimately side by side, even supporting each other.

PRAGMATISM

There is no doubt that ethical reflection in Adventism was, like many issues of a predominantly American church, in a greater measure influenced by pragmatic philosophy.[31] Many times the church found it necessary to address particular ethical issues because its members found themselves in moral difficulty. It is doubtful, as Pearson suggested, whether pragmatism is 'one of the greatest gifts bequeathed to the Adventist church by its American origins'[32] not least because 'the major disservice of such an approach has been that the church has failed to demand of its scholars and leaders, until very recently, a careful investigation of ethical concerns'.[33] The result of this type of approach is inconsistency in Adventist moral action and scarce ethical *a priori* reflection.

George Colvin suggests that Adventists head to address the 'hot topics' of the times. Yet Adventism 'must develop the ability to do so based on a well-considered, well-founded, and consistent set of principles founded on the Bible, on rational thought, on empirical research, and on political analysis'.[34] Colvin notes that Adventism has never developed 'the kind of thoughtful foundation in such areas that is absolutely necessary to ensure consistent, intelligent, and informed positions in social, economic, and political concerns.' Furthermore, he believes that this is not even possible employing the pragmatic approach which Adventists usually employ (i.e. waiting until the church is pressed by circumstances which embrace and involve its members). Before the church 'is led (as it inevitably will be) much further into such [ethical] matters', Colvin proposes,

> Adventism needs to do its homework. If it does not, its actions and statements will be incoherent, irrelevant, and frivolously modish at best; at worst, they will be dangerous or actively harmful to the Church, its members, and the general society. Even less than in earlier ages, the world is unforgiving of the ignorant.[35]

By means of systematic rational ethical reflection, Adventist scholars can avoid many pitfalls of inconsistency which are at times intensified by the fact that Adventism is an international denomination.

DOCTRINAL PURITY VERSUS DOCTRINE OF LOVE

As we have noticed earlier, James Walters labelled some of Adventist ethics as 'ethical egoism' and 'corporate ethical egoism'. He illustrated his point by using the notion of human rights:

> the Adventist interest in religious liberty originally came from concern about protecting our own religious interests, not from universal concern that human beings, by virtue of being human, have the inalienable right to autonomy of religious practice.[36]

Recognising the fact that as a group, Seventh-day Adventists were sometimes ethically selfish, protecting only their own interests, Johnsson pleaded with the Adventist public in *Adventist Review*. 'We must not keep to ourselves, becoming vocal only when our self-interest is threatened'.[37] Branson called Adventism's preoccupation with itself 'the besetting sin'.[38] Whatever it is called, it became obvious that too often what mattered most to Adventists was of some self-interest. This was mostly evident in Adventist 'passion for doctrinal purity'. As Kent Seltman put it figuratively: 'We are guilty of overtly minute examination of structural pillars, but never stepping back to view the temple built on the foundation of Christian love. Consequently, in recent times, some of us seem aligned with the tradition of militant Christianity, where being right is more important than being kind.'[39] Seltman further asserted that, 'Christ did not die on the cross for doctrinal purity but for human beings. ... The mark of the Christian is not possessing doctrinal purity but a willingness to die for a friend.'[40]

The pride of many Adventists was in purity of doctrine and in understanding God's revelation better than anybody else. Seltman challenged this idea with the concept of brotherly love which should be the main motivating factor in deciding who is the true Christian. And the motivating factors such as love, care, and 'Christian brotherhood' would have much greater impact and effect in our social relations to the world.

REMNANT EXCLUSIVENESS RE-EXAMINED

The once almost totally exclusive 'remnant theology' of early Adventism, in which the Seventh-day Adventist church viewed itself as the only right and acceptable church, with all other churches belonging to 'Babylon', has been changed to much milder options. For some contemporary Adventists the term 'remnant' does not mean anything at all; for others, especially in recent years, re-examination of the concept of 'remnant' is a central task; and for yet another group of Adventists, the idea of the remnant is nothing more than a 'distinctive colour in the Christian rainbow'.[41] But whatever the meaning of biblical remnant is[42] (and there is little doubt that Adventist theology needs to elaborate more on the concept), Adventist attitudes towards other Christians and churches have changed considerably. This can best be illustrated by an editorial from the *Adventist Review* dealing with the distinctive Adventist world-view:

> We are not the only people through whom God is working out His will, for instance. We are not to be exclusive, ignoring or patronising other Christians. We are not necessarily better people than others; only God knows the heart.[43]

The process of denominationalisation started with a desire to be recognised as a church. Inevitably this led to a complex of characteristics which, as Bryan Wilson observed, included 'increased tolerance of other movements, attenuation of distinctive commitment, diminished emphasis on boundaries and boundary-maintaining devices'.[44] Such a process is likely to lead to greater relativity of peculiar beliefs, and open up a whole area of concern which is common to other groups whose approval Adventists were seeking. This process has inevitably led Adventist scholars to the point where they are reappraising the church's teachings, history, presuppositions and self-interpretation.[45] In return, Adventist scholarship has accepted a whole new field of concern (inclusive of social concern) and is able to address the wider community of believers. Some specific Adventist concerns and theological insights might, in such a way, contribute to wider general Christian thought.

RADICAL DISCIPLESHIP

By re-examining Adventist roots and discovering that 'the pivotal 16th century antecedents of Adventism are the Reformation radicals, most notably the Anabaptists',[46] Adventist scholars proposed a programme of renewal for the church, a much more audacious and socially oriented programme. Anabaptists (and Mennonites as their heirs) understood the doctrine of discipleship as the essence of the gospel. By discipleship they meant responding to the personal call to follow Jesus in a new and radical way. This type of discipleship brought to the believer a 'new life', the life of commitment. As Charles Scriven asserted:

> Anabaptists believed that true Christian witness, true Christian evangelism, confronts not only individuals but also nations and institutions. Witness must deal with public life and its goal must be the transformation of all society. The church is an exemplary community precisely in order to heal the nations, to be God's agent in bringing injustice and war to an end.[47]

Hence Scriven concluded with the application and a call to the Adventist community: 'The radical Protestant element in our past teaches us this about Adventist identity: that through the witness and example of *radical discipleship* we are to transform human consciousness and thus transform society.'[48]

This line of thought, without any doubt, is reflected in a number of contemporary Adventist theological proposals which resemble the idea of 'radical discipleship'. Branson detected two groups of scholars presently representing Adventist theology: (a) those who speak from within Adventism to other Adventists in order to preserve the purity of the denomination, and (b) those who adopt terminology from outside Adventism to make Adventism more Christian. 'But what is desperately needed',[49] he continued, 'are people who speak distinctively and movingly from within Adventism to the larger community; voices who, from the core of Adventist particularity, express a universal message for our time; people who allow the power of the gospel to challenge those who oppress the vulnerable.'[50]

This proposal almost coincides with George Colvin's in which Adventist scholarship is challenged to look outside and instead of sorting out internal problems and doctrinal differences offer something to the wider community in order to contribute to the improvement of modern society which Adventists are part of:

> If done well, this approach could place Adventism high in the ranks of organizations contributing to the improvement of

> modern society; and the contributions Adventism could make in this way are far more important and much cheaper that those it can make by providing facilities for high-technology medicine, now the only field in which Adventist institutions have a world-wide reputation.[51]

Colvin called these matters the 'matters of the spirit'. These also include the contribution Seventh-day Adventists could make in the area of social ethics. It remains to be seen whether Adventism will take that route or not.

7

Adventism's 'New Theology'

INTRODUCTION AND DEFINITIONS

Examination of several aspects of Adventist theology has revealed that contemporary theologians, faced with theological and pragmatic dilemmas, have striven to find the reasons for the church's existence. The longer they perceived the delay of the *parousia*, the more prominent the Master's command, 'Occupy till I come', became. In this chapter the reasons for renewed social interest among the church's leaders and theologians will be traced, by focusing on the historical development of general contemporary Adventist theology in the second half of the twentieth century.

'New theology', it will be argued, of a much broader definition than is intended by the derogatory use of the phrase in some Adventist circles, can be identified as the basis for current interests in socio-political and socioethical thought among Adventists. How 'new theology' developed and the primary reasons for the liberation of Adventist theology are the main focus of this chapter.

The somewhat arbitrary term 'new theology' was made prominent within Adventism in the 1980s applying to – for those who coined the term – negative aspects of the direction Adventist theology was taking. The term has never been clearly defined and has been used almost exclusively by the 'traditionalists' within the church. 'New theology' embraced that part of Adventist theological thought which sought to bring Adventism closer to Evangelicalism, and hence desired to make it more Christian and less sectarian and cult-like.[1] Contrary to its intended derogatory use, the term can also apply to progressiveness of thought and development in Adventism. In this way it is in line with the pioneers' idea of the 'present truth' – that truth that is 'peculiarly appropriate' in the present conditions in which the church lives and works.

Early pioneers used the term 'present truth' in a very liberal and diverse way. Joseph Bates applied it to the 'shut door' theory, James White defined it as 'present duty' and Ellen White said that 'the truth for this time embraces the whole gospel'.[2] *Present Truth* was also the name of the first Adventist publication issued from 1849.[3]

There are several factors which directly influenced theological 'liberation' within Adventism and it is useful to mention them before we outline the diversity of Adventist theology and the main proponents of the two major fractions.

EARLY FACTORS CONTRIBUTING TO THE 'LIBERATION' OF ADVENTIST THEOLOGY

Emphasis on Education after the World War II

In the aftermath of the international upheaval following World War II, Seventh-day Adventists were scattered around the globe without coherent organisation and with loose ties. In order to restore communication with the church in Europe and other parts of the world, the American leadership of the General Conference – the highest body within the Adventist organisational structure – encouraged youth congresses, educational conferences and other types of meeting, which took place in the late 1940s and early 1950s.

Education of the new leadership force was also high on the agenda as the recruiting of leaders was essential if the church was to continue to grow. Since education was an important part of Adventist philosophy[4] from the beginning of the organisation of the church, and owing to the fact that Adventists established their school system in its early history,[5] it was understandable that the leadership of the church wanted to reestablish strong educational institutions for its members after the war. The priorities of quality education, and therefore the inevitable changes and adaptations in the curriculum in the advanced Adventist schools, were recommended in the hope that Adventist schools in Europe and Australia would be recognised and eventually accredited by their government's accrediting bodies.[6] Also, students in Adventist secondary schools were encouraged to sit national examinations at the end of their secondary education. All this meant that attendance was increased at Adventist schools, the recognition and support of the church's educational system was improved, and the educational attainments of both members and workers of the church rose considerably.

Publication of the SDA Bible Commentary

With the establishment of the Seventh-day Adventist Theological Seminary in 1937 and because of the demand for qualified teachers and lecturers, there was an increased number of professional Adventist theologians, scientists and biblical archaeologists. In the 1950s there was more pressure on the Adventist community to clarify its theological positions on various doctrinal issues as encyclopaedia editors and writers on contemporary religious history and thought requested information about Adventism. At the same time Adventist theologians from different scholarship backgrounds contributed to the important *Seventh-day Adventist Bible Commentary (SDA BC)*,[7] a monumental eleven-volume work started in 1952 and finished in 1957, and sponsored by the Review and Herald, an official Adventist publishing house.

Publishing of *Questions on Doctrine*

However, the single most important contribution to the contemporary theological debate among Adventists was a book *Seventh-day Adventists Answer Questions on Doctrine*,[8] which was prepared by a representative group of Seventh-day Adventist leaders, teachers and editors and approved by more than 250 representative Adventist leaders throughout the world. *Questions on Doctrine* was published in 1957, having been finally authorised by the General Conference officers. In its introduction the editorial committee stated that 'this book came into being to meet a definite need', namely to 'set forth our basic beliefs in terminology currently used in theological circles' where the questions arose about whether Seventh-day Adventism is an Evangelical Christian denomination or a sect which does not belong to the Protestant Christian heritage.[9] The book is a direct result of a series of dialogues between on one side two non-Adventists, Donald Grey Barnhouse, a Presbyterian minister from Philadelphia and editor of the influential Evangelical journal *Eternity*, and Walter R. Martin, the director of cult apologetics for Zondervan Publishing Company, and on the other several prominent Adventist theologians of the

1950s, notably LeRoy E. Froom, Walter E. Read, R. Allan Anderson and T. Edgar Unruh.

Adventist-Evangelical Dialogue

It all started after Unruh, a Seventh-day Adventist minister and an administrator, commended the Presbyterian Barnhouse for his radio presentation of the doctrine of righteousness by faith as found in the book of Romans. After initial surprise on the part of Barnhouse and after several letters exchanged communication stopped between the two. However, Barnhouse passed Unruh's name to Walter R. Martin who was at the time commissioned to write a book against Adventism's 'doctrinal errors'. Martin, as an honest researcher and a good scholar, asked for representative books on Adventist theology and an opportunity to interview administrators and scholars of the church. This developed throughout the following two years into a series of conferences.

In the course of communication with Adventists, Martin's attitude and understanding of the church changed considerably. Two of the conferences took place in Dr Barnhouse's home. Dr Barnhouse and his son Donald Grey Barnhouse, Jr, a theological adviser on the staff of Billy Graham's evangelistic crusades, were active participants. They too had misconceptions regarding Adventist teachings on the doctrine of Christ, atonement and the relationship between justification and sanctification. They admitted their conceptions were mistaken and decided to publish their findings in the magazine *Eternity*, although they knew that their subscribers would be displeased. After Martin and Barnhouse Senior published a series of articles in which they stated that they found Adventism within the parameters of Biblical orthodoxy more than one sixth of the subscribers of *Eternity* cancelled their subscriptions in protest.[10]

As Keld Reynolds, a former teacher and administrator at Loma Linda University and the associate secretary in the Education Department of the General Conference, observed in an admirable work *The Church Under Stress, 1931–1960*:

> These 1955–56 dialogues were of considerable historical importance, because they forced the Adventists to sort out their beliefs: a first basic category that they shared with conservative Christians of all ages, a second category in which Adventists

> stand with some Christian bodies but not with others, and a third category representing Seventh-day Adventists alone and justifying their separate denominational existence.[11]

Furthermore, as Walter Martin's understanding of the Adventist theology increased, he asked for refinement of idiosyncratic Adventist language and clarification of Adventist theological concepts. As a result the group of Adventist scholars and administrators prepared written answers which were published in *Questions on Doctrine* with the approval of the General Conference and over 250 representatives of the church. Three years later, in 1960, Martin's book *The Truth About Seventh-day Adventists*[12] appeared, reporting accurately and honestly what he had learnt about Adventism and citing Adventist proofs exhaustively.

Despite the suggestion of Richard Schwarz, an historian at Andrews University, that *Questions on Doctrine* 'had a unifying and stabilising influence in the Adventist clergy and seminarians throughout the world,'[13] not everyone within the church was happy with it. A small fraction of these was led by the most vocal critic, M. L. Andreasen, a long-standing educator and lecturer in the Adventist Seminary.

Andreasen claimed that *Questions on Doctrine* was a threat to traditional Adventist understanding of doctrines such as the divine human nature of Christ, the role of the Christ as priest, the doctrine of perfection and the incompleteness of the atonement on the cross. He also accused the church leaders of having revised the writings of Ellen White in order to harmonise them with their newly adopted views. These claims were immediately refuted by the leaders of the church, and the denomination as a whole has made a significant step into 'Christological advancement'.[14] However, Andreasen's claims would be taken up again in the 1970s with renewed vigour and not without serious consequences.

'SOTERIOLOGICAL ADVANCEMENT' OF THE 1960s

If, as Geoffrey Paxton suggested, the 1950s were characterised by 'Christological advancement' in Adventism, the 1960s can be adequately described as the decade of 'soteriological advances' within the Adventist theology. (Paxton was an Australian Anglican clergyman who lost his chair as a president of a theological seminary in

Australia because of his interest in Adventism and his controversial book *The Shaking of Adventism*.) What was implied by the changes of emphasis in *Questions on Doctrine*, especially in regard to the nature of Christ and the completeness of salvation on the cross, was inevitably to be spelled out in the area of such prime doctrines of the reformation as justification by faith alone and salvation in and through Christ alone. This task was accomplished by a new generation of competent biblical scholars and theologians such as Edward Heppenstall, Desmond Ford and Hans LaRondelle.

Heppenstall was the first to write directly against 'perfectionism'. Contrary to the widespread belief of Adventists before the 1950s, Heppenstall wrote in 1963 in an article entitled 'Is Perfection Possible?' that

> It is fatal to believe that if only we could become totally surrendered to Christ, the sinful nature would be eradicated. ... The basic doctrine of the Christian faith is salvation by grace alone. ... Salvation by grace alone means that absolute perfection and sinlessness cannot be realised here and now.[15]

The process which was started with *Questions on Doctrine* denying Christ's sinful human nature was logically carried to the conclusion that human beings cannot become sinless before the second coming of Christ. By the end of the decade it was obvious that the two streams of thought had emerged in the theological circles of the church. Opposing Edward Heppenstall, the then Dean of the Theology Department at the Andrews University, and his followers of whom Australian theologian Desmond Ford was the most outspoken, were Robert Brimsmead of Australia, Herbert Douglass and Kenneth Wood, associate editor and editor of the Review and Herald respectively.

THE SHAKING OF ADVENTISM – A POLARISATION BETWEEN THE 'NEW' AND 'OLD' THEOLOGY

The debate between the two schools of thought was carried into the 1970s and then intensified after publication of Paxton's *The Shaking of Adventism*. The newly formed scholarly journal *Spectrum* provided the venue for both sides to express themselves and to expound their viewpoints. Reviewing Paxton's book the representatives of the 'new theology' (Paxton's term),[16] Fritz Guy, Desmond Ford and Hans LaRondalle appeared alongside Herbert Douglass, the representative of the 'traditional theology'.[17]

The 1970s became a decade of 'polarisation and crisis' as the 'new theology' gained more credibility among the laity and as it was opposed more intensely and forcefully by the keepers of the traditional Adventist teachings. It eventually led to two most explicit proponents of the 'new theology', Brimsmead[18] and later Ford, leaving the denominational work. As one observer pointed out, 'the Ford case revealed, [that] there existed an even stronger commitment to hold to tradition' than was thought in the previous two decades.[19]

John Clifford and Russell Standish published a book *Conflicting Concepts of Righteousness by Faith in the Seventh-day Adventist Church: Australasian Division*[20] in 1976 in which they argued forcefully against 'the Ford–Brimsmead mateship' and counteracted their theology of justification by faith and Christ's sinlessness with theologies of perfection, the sinful human nature of Christ and the denial of original sin. Ever since that publication, Russell Standish, an Australian surgeon, and his twin brother Colin Standish, a Lecturer in Psychology and the then Academic Dean and President of two Adventist colleges, have published books attacking the 'new theology' of which they believed Ford was 'the best known proponent'.[21] We shall now examine the theologies of Ford and the Standish brothers as they most explicitly represent what is now termed the 'new theology' and what we would call the 'old theology' in order to distinguish it from the traditional Adventist theology established by the Adventist pioneers in the nineteenth century.

DESMOND FORD AND THE 'NEW THEOLOGY'

As a student of Edward Heppenstall, Desmond Ford accepted the Adventist faith believing deeply and consistently in salvation by faith in Jesus Christ and the impossibility of perfection. He believed in original sin which penetrates and affects every human being (Rom 3: 10–23) and the impossibility of a sinless life on earth. He wrote strongly against 'perfectionism' in many articles of the official Adventist press. 'The consecreated believer', asserted Ford,

> has sin in him but no sin on him, just as Christ had sin on Him but no sin in Him ... every converted soul still has his old nature

> to fight. ... Our old nature will be finally destroyed at glorification when our Lord returns. Then we will have sin neither in us nor on us.[22]

Ford's views on the nature of man and the nature of Christ were in sharp contrast. Although Jesus took human nature upon himself, it was perfect humanity as God intended by the creation (as Adam's humanity was before the Fall). It was by no means the sinful humanity which human beings had received ever since Adam's fall. For this Ford used the Adam–Christ theology of Romans 7. Although Jesus is our 'Example', his primary purpose in coming to the earth is to be our 'Substitute'. In Ford's Christology the substitution is primary and the example of Christ is secondary.

Ford's gospel-centredness was welcomed by many scholars and leaders of the church. His positive and charismatic personality gained him many sympathisers and followers within the Adventist community. However, when Ford voiced concern about the very sensitive subjects of the doctrine of sanctuary and the pre-Advent investigative judgment, the leaders of the church felt uneasy. They were compelled to address openly the issues which were lying on the shelves of Adventism throughout its history.[23] Six months' leave, resources and an appointed guidance committee were given to Ford to prepare a study on the issues which he had raised. Ten months after his initial speech at the Pacific Union College on 27 October 1979, which caught the attention of the leaders of the church, a conference of 115 scholars, administrators, editors and leaders of the church was called at Glacier View Ranch.[24] The outcome of the meeting which took place 10–15 August 1980 was, to say the least, surprising to most who attended: Desmond Ford was called to resign his teaching position and he was stripped of his ministerial credentials.

Ford had prepared a position paper for the Glacier View conference, which was sent to all the participants several months earlier. The lengthy document was entitled 'Daniel 8: 14, The Day of Atonement, and The Investigative Judgment'.[25] In it Ford spelled out what he regarded, and the majority of Adventist scholars accepted,[26] as the analysis of the exegetical problems of the books of Daniel and Hebrews within Adventism. Furthermore, he went as far as saying that the former Adventist positions on the major doctrines (in traditional Adventism called the 'pillars' of the faith) were unbiblical and wrong. He dealt primarily with the eschatology of the church and with the role of Ellen G. White. Touching a very sore point in Adventism, Ford was either to push the church into a new era, or initiate a retreat to the pre-1950s position.

Ford offered solutions to the church's eschatological dilemmas through the so-called 'apotelesmatic (repeated fulfilment) principle'. By the apotelesmatic principle Ford meant that biblical prophecies have more than a single fulfilment, dual or more. He equated this principle with what Strand called 'the philosophy of history' approach and suggested that 'the apotelesmatic principle is the very key we need to authenticate our denominational appropriation' from such eschatological passages as Daniel 8: 14,[27] and that, in his opinion which he elaborately illustrated, Seventh-day Adventists have 'always acknowledged the apotelesmatic principle'.[28] But Ford's proposition was not accepted.

Ford also proposed a 'homiletic place' for Ellen White instead of a prophetic one ('pastoral' rather than 'canonical'). Officially this proposal was not accepted either. However, his influence has been felt among Adventists ever since. The questions Ford raised have not been fully and comprehensively resolved, even though there is a strong desire to answer them and a group of scholars from Andrews University and from the Biblical Research Committee have made an enormous effort to address them. Hence, the division which was created in the aftermath of the Glacier View conference, and which resulted in many ministers leaving the ministry and in some cases deserting the church, has not fully disappeared.[29]

The greatest threat to Adventism in Ford's theology was a threat to its uniqueness. If all doctrines which Ford challenged were changed, the leaders of the church felt that it would leave the Adventist church without a purpose and basis. They feared that the church would become just another Protestant denomination instead of being the special church raised by God for a special task in the last days of world history. As Ford rightly observed, the threat to the sanctuary doctrine was indeed the threat to the Remnant theology which played such an outstanding role in traditional Adventism. However, Ford also observed that some leading men of the church are

> playing 'Let's Pretend' with reference ... to the Remnant theology cherished by the traditional believers. The vast majority of our scholars believe that the church is composed of all who trust in the merits of Christ, whatever their denominational sign. They

> know that Christ is no polygamist and has but one bride – the church invisible. No denomination should ever be set forth as *the* church. The faithful in each denomination belong to the larger worldwide flock.[30]

If this was to be the direction of Adventist self-understanding, as indicated by the most recent scholarship[31] (but not without objections),[32] then it is a definitive movement from the traditional and indefensible position that only Adventist people belong to the remnant church. This claim to exclusiveness and the task of the remnant to proclaim the third angel's message of Revelation 14 have been the *raison d'être* of the Seventh-day Adventist Church, some believe. How it would cope with the 'new' view of being a part of the larger body of believers and at the same time retain its distinctiveness is to be seen in the future of the Adventist community.

RUSSELL AND COLIN STANDISH AND THE 'OLD THEOLOGY'

One of the ways to deal with the issues that Ford raised was to withdraw into the conservatism of what we have called, for lack of better terminology, the 'old theology'. The strongest proponents of this line were Russell and Colin Standish. Ironically, neither of them was a biblical scholar or theologian but credentialed ministers who were 'deeply concerned in the issues presently affecting the church, and have carefully studied our landmark beliefs'.[33]

The Standish brothers rose directly in defence of what they believed were the traditional teachings of the Seventh-day Adventist Church. In practical terms, they opposed Ford's theology. They labelled his teachings the 'new theology' which, in their opinion, has been used by Satan in an endeavour to derail God's remnant church. The 'new theology' was always present in Adventism, the brothers suggested. From as early as 1844 there were Adventists who could be categorised as proponents of 'new theology'. Such are, the Standishes proposed, Dudley M. Canright who wrote against the sanctuary message; Albian F. Ballenger, a 'heretic' who believed in a gospel built upon justification alone; Louis R. Conradi who was 'a constant critic of the Spirit of Prophecy';[34] William W. Fletcher; and more lately Desmond Ford. This appears to be self-contradictory when the Standishes match the Adventist 'new theology' with theologies of men from the mid-nineteenth century up to the present day. It is either new theology, or it is not new.

What was difficult for the Standish brothers to accept was the fact that 'in many [of] our colleges, theologians, trained in the universities of apostate Christianity, were already teaching these errors as if they were God's truth.'[35] By 'these errors' they meant salvation by faith in Jesus Christ, the son of God, the complete atonement on the cross, and anything else that would contradict the remnant exclusivist theology.

They, and other authors of the same persuasion, disagreed on every point of the developed Adventist theology which started its 'liberation' in the 1950s.[36] The emphasis on the human sinful nature of Jesus ('just as we are'), the denial of the consequences that original sin had on all born after Adam, the nature of sin which was understood not as a state in which we are born, but only 'wilful or negligent violation of God's law',[37] the possible and, indeed, absolutely essential perfection (defined as behavioural sinlessness) before the coming of Christ, the prophetic role of Ellen White, and acceptance of the investigative judgment which begun in 1844 were of the greatest concern to the 'old theology'. The desire of the proponents of this view was to return to the pre-1950 theology. However, this was far from possible.

Although Colin and Russell Standish attracted a fraction of newly converted believers as well as a group of existing conservative Adventists, and despite the fact that they had some support from a small group of the right-wing denominational leaders, the group was, after a substantial time had elapsed, labelled as an 'offshoot' dissident group[38] and, especially in the most recent years, marginalised as the divisive and destructive 'extreme conservative wing of Adventism'.[39] However, independent organisations such as Hope International with its powerful mouthpiece *Our Firm Foundation* and Colin Standish's Hartland Institute still attract a fraction of very conservative Adventists and are gaining more supporters in America, Australia and England. The so-called 'Independent Ministries' of Hope International and the Hartland Institute are presently the greatest force of division within the Seventh-day Adventist church. Ironically, the Standishes maintain that 'Truth has never divided the church.'[40] They felt called like the prophet Isaiah to 'cry aloud, spare not' (Is 58: 1). And in their appeal to the ministers and leaders of the Adventist church they concluded that,

> the Seventh-day Adventist Church today is a divided house. No longer can it be seen as one unified body established upon the pure Truth of God. We must recognize that we are in the civil war. We know that civil wars are bloody wars and that the damage in the terrible battle that is being raged in the Seventh-day Adventist Church will be tragically high. But there can be no Switzerland in this war. We either stand in the army of Jesus Christ or we stand in the army of Satan. If we are not for Christ, we are against Him. If we do not stand for His Truth, we stand for error.[41]

Although we can only guess at the reason for military terminology, it does go consistently with the Standishes' views of God. However, the most important is yet another of many inconsistencies in which they encircle themselves. They are not 'for Christ' as most Christians throughout the history of Christianity found him in the Scriptures.[42] Their emphasis is only on the Christ 'like us' (his sinful human nature), and not on the incarnate God (his divine nature). To take their argument to its logical conclusion, if they are not for Christ, they do not stand for his truth. However, they are utterly convinced of the opposite and the church has just started to react in a slow process.

CONCLUSION

A recent article in *Christianity Today* suggested that there are three groups of Adventists co-existing. Its author, Kenneth R. Sample, correspondence editor of the late Dr Martin's Christian Research Institute, proposed the following three tendencies: (1) Evangelical Adventism, (2) Traditional Adventism, and (3) Liberal Adventism. The question, 'Which is the true Adventism?' stands. In a commendable article Woodrow Whidden, Associate Professor of Religion at Andrews University, proposed a new and refreshing approach to Adventism by suggesting a more meaningful and descriptive terminology of 'essential Adventism', 'processive Adventism' and 'non-essential Adventism'.[43] It remains to be seen whether this will be the direction of the future debate.

The 1980s brought a real crisis to the church, which was forced to examine whether it is 'more sure of its denominational distinctiveness than it is of the gospel'.[44] The outcome of this examination is not yet clear, although the light at the end of the tunnel, for their more optimistic observers is brighter in the early 1990s. The inevitable point is that there is no turning back. The younger generation of Adventist scholars is unable to accept the same level of exclusiveness implied in the pre-1950s remnant concept. Nevertheless, they are ready to search for a meaningful identity for the church and the reason for its existence within the parenthesis of, for example, such essential doctrines as the second coming of Christ, the value of moral law in a permissive society, the rest and universal blessing of the Sabbath and the holistic approach to human nature.

Contrary to the 'old theology' which allows no room for improvement, change and diversity, the modern generation of scholars desire a greater variety of Adventist thought. In a recent article about the Adventist church, Alvin L. Kwiram correctly recognised that

> Adventism needs more, not less, pluralism and ferment. We need more vigorous and informed contributions from conservatives. Conservatives are our 'institutional engineers', they tend to provide a context for continuity and stability. But we also need the liberal, 'artistic' elements to bring to Adventism an even greater sensitivity to human needs to issues of justice and mercy. We need an inclusive church that relishes a pluralism of viewpoints.[45]

Kwiram suggests that Adventists do not need to reject the past nor ignore it. But neither should they live in the past, as some would desire. Instead, they should dare to 'build on the past, not live in it'. Or as another contemporary author put it, 'faithfulness to God demands dynamic, changing involvement with God's sovereign role in history, a sensitiveness to our place and condition in the last quarter of the twentieth century, an openness to the ongoing revelation of God in our experience, in nature, in His Word'.[46] How far this changing involvement in God's history will be allowed in Adventism is obscure. The process of change has started. The denomination's great emphasis on education, as the historian Gary Land has rightly observed, 'had inadvertently produced intellectuals who, on the basis of new experiences and new information were in various ways reformulating Adventism'.[47] The questions which must be left open are how much reformulating the church will allow, and will there ever be a reconciliation between the directly opposing views on major Christian doctrines of salvation and Christ? It is yet to be seen how this reformulating of Adventism will affect members' involvement in society, especially on the socio-political questions of human rights.

An analogy comparing the SDA church with a new model of a car, proposed by one Adventist, is useful in this context. It has been suggested that a new body has been fitted to an old chassis without much having been done to redesign the engineering of the vehicle. The question is whether the car will function efficiently under modern road conditions. Some believe that the future of the car is in the export market, others think that it will become a collector's item.[48] If the church desires to stay effective on the road and does not want to become a collector's item, or even worse that it gathers rust and dirt and eventually falls apart, it must find contemporary relevance. And the only way to get its engineering adjusted to the use of unleaded petrol and other modern essentials to be constantly fit for the road, is to address issues of life and death, and therefore issues of social ethics.

By balancing the doctrine of the second coming with the notion 'Occupy till I come' (Luke 19: 13), clarifying the doctrine of creation with all its implications of equality, the value of human life and granted freedom, upholding the law as a standard of moral conduct which does not allow violation of other persons' freedom, looking at man as a whole being with implications for the importance of caring for his physical as well as spiritual aspects of life and uplifting the notion of redemption and liberation in Jesus Christ accomplished on the cross for all who accept it, the Seventh-day Adventist church has much to offer to the community in which it lives and operates. The 'new theology' with its yet unprobed aspects is the direction to pursue. Because of the trend of the 'new theology', Adventism restarted its pioneers' interest in social change, it developed the basis on which it could build the theology of human rights and it is finding the present truth for the 1990s. However, it needs to continue to be new, progressive, inventive, creative and existential to be meaningful to every generation. It needs to build on the old and every time surpass it. It needs to be truthful to its past, and yet look to the future. It needs to be practical and efficient as well as theoretical and well thought out.

Part IV

Theology and Ethics of Human Rights: The Seventh-day Adventist Perspective

8

Philosophical Basis for Human Rights

WIDER PERSPECTIVE OF HUMAN RIGHTS

Having examined several areas of social concern within the Seventh-day Adventist church, a need for a systematic and coherent theology of human rights emerges. The Adventist church, like most other Christian bodies, has never attempted to produce a comprehensive theological basis for human rights. There were sporadic attempts within Christendom to justify the notion of human rights on the basis of the doctrines of creation and incarnation and on the basis of so-called natural law. Most of these were of an apologetic character. Lately, in Reformed circles, Jürgen Moltmann has engaged in theologising about human rights via theologies of hope and the future aspect of the Kingdom of God. A more comprehensive theology of human rights, taking into consideration all these ideas, and also more peculiar Adventist theological contributions, has not yet been attempted. This is the purpose of the last part of this volume.

It would be foolish to claim that only Christian theology deals with human rights. To disclaim the relationship between Judeo-Christian thought and human rights, on the other hand, would be even more incorrect. The question which must be asked is: What is the relationship between Christian theology and human rights? Are human rights at the end of the day, as one theologian put it, theological or ideological considerations?[1]

ORIGINS OF HUMAN RIGHTS

A number of thinkers disagree on the point of origins of the concept of human rights, mostly (but not entirely) depending, it would seem, on their scholastic background. Many non-Christian thinkers argue, from a political or philosophical standpoint, that human rights originate in and were developed from *Magna Carta*, from the Enlightenment, John Locke's philosophy, in the humanism and secularism of the eighteenth and nineteenth centuries, from the French Revolution, and after World War II from the establishment of the United Nations.[2] Some theologians and ethicists accept this explanation.[3] Some dismiss any relationship between the Christian message and human rights. Carlos Nino, for example, wrote that 'human rights are instruments created by human beings [and are] among the greatest inventions of our civilization'.[4] Others have argued that, although 'there is much in Christian and Muslim tradition that could be used to support a human rights policy, the contemporary concept of human rights does not occur'.[5]

Some scholars, on the other hand, while not disputing the fact that Christians can make no claim to an exclusive concern for human rights, argue that the notion of human rights is grounded in Judeo-Christian tradition.[6] This is especially so 'in the value of the created order',[7] according to Richard Harries, Bishop of Oxford, as he expressed it in his lecture to the British Institute of Human Rights at King's College, London. He argued against the idea that 'the concept of human rights is usually … a secular notion'[8] by showing that the American Declaration of Independence in 1776, which influenced the French declaration in 1789, had been based on a Christian belief in the Creator. The American Declaration stated that 'all men are *created* equal, [and] are endowed *by their creator*, with certain inalienable rights.'[9] In the same way, the French made their declaration 'in the presence and under the auspices of *the Supreme Being*' (emphasis added).[10] It is therefore doubtful whether the notion of human rights in its modern form can be divorced from the Christian tradition.

However, one could easily understand the concern which some raise against the Christian 'privatisation' of human rights in the view of Christian history. And yet, despite the fact that 'people of various cultures now are laying claims to this idea',[11] the notion of human rights 'being revealed by a long historical process [should not] embarrass theologians'.[12] What Harries sees as 'the doctrinal truths of the Bible … spelt out as the result of a process of development'[13] and consequently ethical truths therefore taking time to be seen in their fullness, Adventists have come to term the 'present truth'.[14] It is a belief in the progressive revelation by which different biblical emphases are seen as essential at different times of human history.[15]

While it may be true that human rights are a 'philosophical idea whose related concepts may be rooted in diverse traditions',[16] the modern tone to the human rights debate is inevitably a result of what Jürgen Moltmann calls, 'the process of Christianization of societies and states'.[17] However, no matter how much influence the Christian perspective of human dignity has had on the notion of human rights, in practical terms this should not be taken 'as implying an "ecclesiastical go-it-alone", or a "Christian solo-run" on the highly charged field of human rights'.[18] What it should imply is that Christians can freely engage in the debate which they believe has certain roots in their tradition and theology. Also they could contribute to the debate by inserting their specific theological considerations, which could, in turn, enhance the whole doctrine of human rights in the modern world.

EXTENT AND NATURE OF HUMAN RIGHTS

If there is a disagreement about the origins of human rights, there is even more disagreement in qualifying and defining what human rights actually are. In *A New Dictionary of Christian Ethics* David Little defines human rights as 'a set of justifiable or legitimate claims',[19] while Douglas MacLean calls them 'the most basic and universal moral demands which any individual can make'.[20] He goes on to say that human rights are 'a complex of liberties, claims, powers, and immunities. What unifies them is a core of ethical "advantages" to the individual. These advantages are the "freedom and control" [and] "ethical autonomy" of the rights-holder.'[21]

Wellman, on the other hand, defines them too narrowly when he asserts that human rights can be seen as 'an ethical right of the individual as human being vis-à-vis the state'.[22] Indeed, the debate about individual rights versus social rights is still very much present in the contemporary literature.[23] An individual could have an ethical right vis-à-vis other individuals or some other institution beside the state. Some groups (minorities, the poor, blacks, women, to name but few) could have their rights denied within the context of Wellman's definition.

One view suggests that human rights cannot be a gift, tolerance, or privilege to be conferred.[24] David Lyons, in the Introduction to the remarkable collection of papers on *Rights*, also accepts that

> rights go beyond mere favours and privileges. One cannot claim a right to other's kindness, to their unselfish sacrifice, or to their compassionate benevolence. There are two sides to this important truism. Rights do not secure all that is valuable in human relations. ... But rights concern what we can rightfully claim.[25]

Looking from the perspective of the other, though, it is 'natural to associate rights with others' obligations because of the connection of rights with what is mandatory rather than optional on the part of others'.[26] In other words, human rights are not only 'claims' or 'universal demands' but also become 'others' obligations' when being observed from the perspective of the person against whom rights are being claimed. However, Joel Feinberg argues that 'claim' is the best description of what human rights are all about. In order to understand, and especially observe what rights are, it is essential to observe 'claims'. After all there is a verb 'to claim', but no verb 'to rights'. He concludes that one 'could learn more about rights through claims than through the abstract definition of rights, [even] if one were possible'.[27]

Among human rights theorists the discussion about duties, benefits, obligations, goals, liberties and rights and their correlation is still very lively. Ronald Dworkin, in the course of a discussion on John Rawls' theory of justice, suggests an initial classification of political theories into three groups: goal-based, right-based and duty-based theories.[28] Dworkin then argues that,

> any particular theory will give ultimate pride of place to just one of these concepts; it will take some overriding goal, or some set of fundamental rights, or some set of transcendent duties, as fundamental, and show other goals, rights, and duties as subordinate and derivative.[29]

Dworkin opted out of right-based political morality, while John Mackie took it a step further by applying it to moral theories in general, arguing that morality is right-based.[30] Goals, or about what is good as an end, duties, or about what is obligatory, and rights, or about what ought or ought not to be done or what people are entitled to have or receive or do (hence liberty) are closely interwoven. As Jeremy Waldron postulated, 'If P's having a right is *defined* in terms of Q's having a duty, how can some theories be right-based while others are duty-based?'[31] And he concluded,

'Now, of course, most people feel both sorts of concern'.[32] However it was Joseph Raz, Fellow and Tutor in Jurisprudence at Balliol College, Oxford, who balanced all these three out. Although based on purely humanistic presuppositions, and therefore a limited viewpoint, his conclusion asserted that morality is neither exclusively right-based, nor duty or goal-based. Instead, Raz supported 'a pluralistic understanding of the foundation of morality'.[33]

Jo Renee Formicola in *The Catholic Church and Human Rights* classified essential inherent rights into three groups: personal security, civil/political rights and economic/welfare rights.[34] This or a similar classification is fairly widespread among modern philosophers, politicians and theologians. However, a holistic approach to them must be maintained. In Moltmann's words, 'all human rights, be they social, economic, religious, or political are *interrelated*. They must be taken as a *whole*. The churches should give them equal importance and seek the application of all of them.'[35] While Adventists have always applied a 'wholistic' approach to its theology and ethics,[36] they have failed to take this same wholistic consideration in viewing human rights. The importance of the balance among social, economic, religious and political human rights is something that Adventists, as well as the wider Christian community, must come to terms with.

While O'Mahony rightly observed that 'human rights are prior to legal definitions, to legislation or any form of social organisation' and that they are 'what people are entitled to – not what society or state is willing to give',[37] this still does not give us the full definition of *human rights*.

BASIS OF HUMAN RIGHTS

Thus far, the definition of 'rights' has been examined. The word 'human' must now be considered. The view to be taken of man and his nature will also determine rights which could be given him; in other words, by definition human rights depend on a definition of 'human'.[38] While it is generally acceptable that human rights rest on human dignity, not everybody agrees what 'human dignity' is and where it is rooted. For this, Christians have to examine the doctrine of man in order to define what 'human' is. Human dignity derived in such a way could be the root of human rights. To consider man's nature within the biblical context is the task of theological anthropology. O'Mahony has rightly observed that, 'to speak of a person's liberty, life and security as his or her right is in fact a curious legalistic formation. What we really want to protect is not the person's rights but the person himself'.[39] O'Mahony, therefore, although indirectly and unintentionally, defines 'human' in terms of personhood.[40] And personhood, from a Christian perspective, is without doubt derived from the dignity of human beings being created in the image of their creator.[41]

Another question worth pursuing is whether human rights can be said to be 'absolute' rights. In other words, are human rights claims 'unexceptionable' as well as 'inalienable'? To this question Gregory Vlastos, with a careful clarification, answers 'No', while Alan Gewirth say 'Yes'. Vlastos argues that Locke has been misunderstood to say that natural rights are absolute. Vlastos proposes, in his opinion together with Locke, that 'natural rights are subject to justified exceptions', i.e. the claims of any human right can be overruled in special circumstances.[42]

Gewirth also recognises that many claims are not absolute. He illustrates this with the most plausible right: the right to life. He reasons:

> This right entails at least the negative duty to refrain from killing any human being. But it is contended that this duty may be overridden, that a person may be justifiably killed if this is the only way to prevent him from killing some other, innocent person. … It is also maintained that even an innocent person may justifiably be killed if failure to do so will lead to deaths of other such persons. Thus an innocent person's right to life is held to be overridden when a fat man stuck in the mouth of a cave prevents the exit of speleologists who will otherwise drown, or when a child or some other guiltless person is strapped onto the front of an aggressor's tank, or when an explorer's choice to kill one among a group of harmless natives about to be executed is the necessary and sufficient condition of the others' being spared, or when the driver of a runaway trolley can avoid killing five persons on one track only by killing one person on another track.[43]

However, argues Gewirth, some human rights can be perceived as absolute. 'A right is absolute', says Gewirth, 'when it cannot be overridden in any circumstances, so that it can never be justifiably infringed and it must be fulfilled without any exceptions'.[44]

The criteria of justification of an absolute right must be based on a certain supreme principle of morality. While Gewirth terms it *the Principle of Generic Consistency*, he recognises that others might easily identify it with the Golden Rule, the law of love, the categorical imperatives and/or the principle of utility. After establishing the basis for absolute rights, Gewirth explores a few examples: namely, the principle of respect for the rights of all persons to the necessary conditions of human action, and hence respect for the persons. He concludes, 'The principle hence prohibits using any person merely as a means to the well-being of other persons',[45] what others have labelled 'the equal right of all people to be free'.[46]

Legitimate objections have been raised, from a different perspective, to whether we could talk about any rights at all from a Christian standpoint. The argument that is put forward is that the Bible does not speak about our rights and privileges, but rather about duties and responsibilities.[47] However, even if we accept that the Bible is primarily concerned with duties and responsibilities of individuals and groups both in relation to God and also in relation to their fellow human beings, it would still mean that our responsibilities were other people's rights: two sides of the same coin. Further, one could say that Christian ethics of human rights is not primarily concerned about 'my rights', but instead its concern is to protect 'your' rights or the rights of the 'other'. In this way Christian ethics and a theology of human rights bring the most radical contribution to the general discussion about human rights.

Contrary to Karl Marx's assessment that 'nothing in these so-called human rights goes beyond egoistic man', and that 'behind the noble ideal of human rights lay, in short, one single interest: that of the possessor',[48] the Christian idea of human rights should be based on selflessness and sacrifice for the rights of other.[49] As Roy Jenkins illustratively put it: 'Bread for myself is a material matter; bread for my neighbour is a spiritual matter.'[50]

Lochman acknowledges that Christians must be prepared for self-criticism as they consider their history and the present situation. How often, asks Lochman, have the churches begun to engage actively and resourcefully on behalf of human rights when their own interests were not involved? However, the interest in human rights must go 'beyond egoistic man', if it is to have any weight. This going beyond, understood from the perspective of a Christian, 'becomes the criterion, and marks our passage from ideological to the theological struggle for human rights'.[51] And Lochman concludes that 'the particular task of the Church on this field is to be outgoing towards other ... and to be counsel for defence of our fellow-men's rights'.[52] In other words, as propounded by a group of Lutheran Christians, 'Christian responsibility must take special care to ensure that human rights are defined and applied as the rights of the other person, whom God has also created, liberated and called to serve him'.[53]

An additional perspective is raised by Jürgen Moltmann when he asserts that

> declarations of human rights ... are effective only insofar as there are men who are prepared to take upon themselves the right and duties of men and stand up for the oppressed for the sake of humanity. The rights of freedom are effective only insofar as there are free men who intercede for the liberation of the enslaved men.[54]

Therefore, it is not sufficient for Christians to think about the rights of others; only when it is done in a selfless way can the struggle for human rights be effective. Only through this selfless renunciation, argues Moltmann, can believers find themselves and their true being.[55]

Furthermore, the self-renunciation of the Christian for the cause of the rights of others is not limited to legal rights, but also, 'beyond the call of duty', to moral, even though sometimes not yet legally recognised rights. After recognising the naturalness of associating 'rights with other's obligations because of the connection of rights with what is mandatory rather than optional on the part of other', David Lyons argues that

> not all requirements correspond to rights. It is often said, for example, that one should be charitable and generous – that one has a duty to behave in that way. This appears to make good sense, even though no other person could have a right to one's charity or generosity (for if the other had a right, then what would be required of one would not be classifiable as charity or generosity).[56]

In other words, while human rights differ from acts of charity and benevolence, Christian responsibility should go beyond the call of duty as far as legal rights are concerned, and include also natural (moral) rights[57] such as, for example, the equal right to be free. Consequently, this kind of liberty would imply non-exploitation of the peoples of the Southern hemisphere to the point of starvation while the West swims in luxuries and products of cheap labour and unequal distribution of resources. Such understanding of human rights does not only include the principle of equal distribution, but also benevolence in order to balance the world's resources with the world's consumption.

The last example vividly illustrates the important point in the debate about human rights: a relationship between individual rights and social rights. Elaine Pagels suggests that individual human rights derive from participation in society.[58] It is true, as one philosopher put it,[59] that it was the liberal tradition that stressed the liberty of the individual against society. And one need not lose this emphasis as one appraises the concept of human rights. However, the problem arises when the issue of justice for groups, minorities, or as in our example above, whole countries have their rights denied, and their social and economic freedom refused.[60]

Moltmann recognises that 'one has had to learn not to conceive of human rights as "individual freedom" rights anymore'.[61] The similar thought can be found in the summary of the fourth plenary meeting of the World Council of Churches in Uppsala in 1968 which reads:

> in the modern worldwide community the rights of the individual are unavoidably tied to the fight for a better living standards for the socially disadvantaged of many nations. Human rights cannot be secured in a world of gross inequality and social conflicts.[62]

O'Mahony sums it up well when he declares that 'personal freedom and social justice belong together'.[63]

Dealing with human rights one must bear in mind that life comprises more than human rights. There can be no responsible morality if we do not look at the realities of life from a wider perspective than just focusing on human rights.[64] Martti Lindqvist's proposal, for example, can serve in projecting a part of the wider perspective:

1. The concept of right has to do with three levels of the human community: (a) individuals, (b) social systems and institutions, (c) the law of the nations.

2. Justice is not a property of individuals and their actions, but a predicate of social systems and institutions.
3. The concept of right cannot be understood correctly if reference is being made only to the things human beings are entitled to. Speaking about rights means speaking about duties and obligations.[65]

This threefold statement would sum up the discussion if it was not lacking one thing which a Christian perspective adds. As Lochman puts it, 'In a theological sense, human rights are in no way to be defined or constituted either as predicates of nature or some timeless "essential humanity", or as the result of some historical materialistic process of self-deliverance'. There is, Lochman continues, some kind of 'the inner potential of faith in God as personal motivation in the quest for human rights'.[66] This theological basis of human rights needs considerable examination if a greater insight into the Christian ethics of human rights is to be achieved.

9

A Common Theological Basis for Human Rights

Seventh-day Adventists have contributed to Christian theology by a number of theological observations which had been either neglected or forgotten during the history of the Christian church. Some of these theological considerations, as will be argued in the next two chapters, have been helpful in the development of social concern. Others have had the opposite effect. Hence, through Adventist history, different theological emphases have led to inconsistency in the realisation of social ethics and, in particular, of the ethics of human rights. The aim of this chapter is, therefore, threefold. First, to pursue areas of theology through which Adventists could learn to be more consistent in their application of social ethics. Secondly, to investigate a common theological basis for human rights that Adventists share with other Christians, in order that a greater degree of understanding and cooperation can be initiated between Seventh-day Adventists and the wider community. Finally, to explore several theological aspects through which Adventism could contribute to the development of theology and ethics of human rights.

In the context of ethics of human rights Adventists could learn considerably from some of the aspects of Christian theology, which, while present in Adventist beliefs, are not as strongly emphasised from a socio-ethical perspective as they should be. These doctrines will be our focal point here.

CREATION

Creation *ex nihilo* is one of the fundamental beliefs of the Seventh-day Adventist church.[1] Moreover, the Genesis account is accepted literally by the majority of Seventh-day Adventists, as the 'authentic account of [God's] creative activity'.[2] The official Adventist explanation of the fundamental beliefs of the church goes as far as iterating that 'the days of the Bible's Creation account signify literal 24-hour periods'.[3] Beside Genesis 1 and 2, numerous other texts of the Old and New Testament are cited. It ends with the very significant text for Adventists, which they believe describes the people living at the end-time and proclaiming the three angels' messages of Revelation 14, calling everyone to 'worship him who made the heavens, the earth, the sea and the springs of water' (Rev 14: 7).

Creation *ex nihilo* of the Genesis account, however, although viewed by Seventh-day Adventists in a literal way, has rarely been interpreted in the context of human rights or social ethics.[4] In most instances, the creation story has been linked to Sabbath observance and with an attempt to prove the validity of the seventh day rest. Also the doctrine of creation gave strong support to the Adventist understanding of family life. However, the creation story is also the primary basis for human rights. The theology of creation is, as Richard Harries pointed out, 'the foundation for a consciously Christian approach to human rights.' He continued:

> God makes man in his own image and respects the worth and dignity of what he has created. ... Such is the value of human persons in the eye of their maker that he himself becomes a human person.[5]

Richard Rice, a contemporary Adventist theologian, in his elaborate book *The Reign of God*, rightly suggests that 'the doctrine of creation ... circumscribes or defines our lives, setting boundaries on our activities and aspirations.'[6] Implicitly, Rice concluded, the doctrine of creation warns us against violating any of the basic conditions of our existence. And the basic condition of our existence is the brotherhood of all humanity, which assumes equality of races, sexes, nationalities and economic positions.[7]

Image of God

By being created in the image of God, the first human beings were different from the rest of the creation. Adam and Eve were creatures, but at the same time they became persons bearing the likeness and image of God (Gen 1: 26–8).[8] And personhood implies both moral 'uprightness' (Eccl 7: 29) and a function which one theologian describes as man's 'creative mastery of existence'.[9]

Mankind's divine image and dominion over the lower creation is mentioned in one breath. But there is no mention of dominion of one human being over the other.[10] The image of God implanted to both created human beings implied their equality, companionship and compatibility (Gen 2: 18–24). Rice observes that

> God never intended human beings to exercise dominion over other human beings. The idea of the image of God confers a dignity on every individual. Since all bear the image of God, one human being should never be the property of another. Neither race, nor sex, nor age elevates one person or group to a position of sovereignty. The concept of the image of God rules out all forms of slavery – economic, political and sexual.[11]

Since we are created in the image of God, we share God's dignity. Human beings are invested with responsibility as stewards of creation.[12] This implies, as Roy Jenkins remarked: 'Harm another being – or allow him to be harmed – and we damage the God whose image he bears.'[13]

Moltmann rightly observed that Adam was not the first Jew, but the first man. Consequently, 'if God the Creator fashioned man in his image on earth, then the inner dignity, freedom and responsibility of man extends impartially beyond every human community and state organization.'[14] This gives a responsibility to all human beings to be their 'brother's keepers', because the universal fatherhood of God established through creation implies the universal brotherhood of men and women in every place and at all times of human history. And it is human dignity which springs from the image of God in man that leads us to human rights.

Human Dignity

Moltmann, in his treatise *On Human Dignity*, argues that 'the dignity of the human being is not itself a human right but a source and ground for all human rights, and all human rights promote respect for the singular worth of human beings.'[15] Moltmann further described the distinction between human rights and human dignity in more detail:

> Human rights are plural, but human dignity exists only in singular. Therefore, the dignity of human beings takes precedence

> over the many rights and duties which are bound up with being human. The dignity of humanity is the one indivisible, inalienable, and shared quality of the human being. The different human rights portray a wholeness because the human being in his or her dignity is a totality. The completeness of the catalogs and lists of human rights is not identical with this totality. The light of totality falls much more from the human being's dignity onto every fragment of his or her human rights.[16]

In other words, human dignity comes first and human rights come second as an application of human dignity.

Many non-Christian thinkers agree that human dignity is the prime basis of human rights.[17] However, as Ronald Dworkin points out, the idea of human dignity is usually associated with Immanuel Kant.[18] The challenge to this notion that comes from Richard Harries is most appropriate. Harries rightly argues:

> One wonders why Kant is singled out rather than the framers of the legal codes of the Old Testament, or Jesus, or Aquinas, to suggest just a few of the thousands of pre-Kantian alternatives. For the worth and dignity of the human person is basic to the Judeo-Christian-Islamic tradition.[19]

The dignity of humanity comes directly from the creator and from the 'image of God' given to the first created pair.[20] In such a way the Judeo-Christian-Islamic concept of creation and the image of God contribute to the understanding of the dignity of humanity which must be the cornerstone of any human rights debate.

Nature of Man

If it is true that the moral basis of human rights follows from what a person's nature is and how people perceive each other,[21] then we need to look at the biblical understanding of the nature of man. Although man[22] after the Fall experienced separation from God and had fallen from the humanity originally intended, he still continued to carry the image of God with him into the sinful world. Although 'the image of God in them [human beings] was marred and they became subject to death. ... God in Christ reconciled the world to Himself and by His Spirit restores in penitent mortals the image of their Maker.'[23] So Christians are called to the restored image of God which reflects the dignity of mankind, a basis of human rights.

Rice argues that sin has a social dimension and involves our relationship with other human beings. 'Rejecting the sovereignty of God', he rightly suggests, 'inevitably leads us to ignore the rights of other people'.[24] And the only adequate prescription Rice can think of is to keep to the law: 'love your God and love your neighbour'. The two commandments are inseparable – 'we cannot observe one without observing the other, and failing to keep one inevitably leads us to violate the other.'[25]

While original sin has affected individual lives as well as social structures (violation of human rights could be cited as one of the proofs of this fact), it is believed that through Jesus Christ a new humanity (new creation) is available to all (Gal 6: 15). Jesus has restored the image of God which Christians have the privilege and duty to develop in their lives. And this is why Christians ought to be the first to condemn human rights abuses, injustice and inequality between people world-wide.

Moltmann develops the idea of this new humanity a step further:

> If God acts as the liberator of man in an inhuman history, then the goal of Israel as well as of Christianity is the new, just humanity of God. The historical monotheism of the Old Testament leads logically to the notion of one humanity. Before God, all individual destinies and national histories merge into a single and common world history. The late Israelite expectation of the coming kingdom of the Son of man ... and the Christian proclamation of Jesus as the Son of man and the new man display a theological and future-oriented concept of humanity.[26]

Through Jesus' restoration of the image of God and dignity of humanity, the Christian view of man is again, as far as social ethics is concerned, positive, futuristic and constructive. Bearing in mind that the effects of the Fall are still with us (Rom 7: 14–25), we trust in Jesus' mission of restoration of which Christians should be the first to benefit, and then help others benefit too.[27]

Conclusion

Seventh-day Adventists, as believers in the creation account of the first three chapters of Genesis, have a great opportunity to explore in depth the applications of the doctrine of creation in the context of social ethics. While maintaining their strong belief in the God of creation and the mankind being created in the image of God, Adventists should study more the creation's implications in regard to the issues of human rights. The meaning of creation rather than its actuality – what creation should mean to human relationships rather than whether it happened in six literal days – should be the Adventist concern at the end of the twentieth century.

KINGDOM OF GOD

Christian Theology of the Kingdom

Study of the life of Jesus reached its highest peak in the nineteenth century. Towards the end of the century increasing doubt began to be felt as to the possibility of writing a *scientific life* of Jesus. Instead interest turned towards the *teachings* of Jesus. And Jesus' teaching about the Kingdom of God occupied the central position. Albrecht Ritschl (1822–89) brought the concept of the Kingdom of God into sharp focus.[28] He became the great 'theologian of the Kingdom of God' and had a large following.

Jesus of Nazareth was a prophet who preached the coming of the fulfilled 'Dominion of God', according to Ritschl.[29] When Jesus preached the nearness of the Kingdom this did not mean that the Kingdom of God is a future reality, but that it has become effective with his first coming. Jesus' inmost intention was to 'educate a select group of people for entry into the Kingdom of God'.[30] Consequently, Ritschl gives a definition of the Kingdom of God in purely ethical form:

> The Kingdom of God consists of those who believe in Christ, inasmuch as they treat one another with love without regard to differences of sex, rank or race, thereby bringing about a fellowship of moral attitude and moral properties extending through the whole range of human life in every possible variation.[31]

Hence, Ritschl regards the Kingdom as something the Christian possesses and, essentially, an ideal belonging to an ethically-determined society. There is little doubt that the Ritschlian idea of the Kingdom of God bears the stamp of 'Kant's this-worldly interpretation of the Kingdom of God'.[32]

In the view of Ritschl, Kant and the ideological founder of the Social Gospel movement in America, Walter Rauschenbusch, the Kingdom was construed to mean the exercise of the moral life in society. It was thought to be both immanent in individual religious experience – as perceived by Adolf Harnack – and also to be realised gradually in an ideal society on earth.

The 'Social Gospellers' emphasised such things as the fatherhood of God and the brotherhood of men. The Kingdom of God was presented as the lost social ideal of Christianity within which all committed Christians must organise themselves according to the principles of love and solidarity. Therefore, it was the task of believers to work out the coming of this Kingdom, of which 'the ennoblement of culture and of society is regarded as an element'.[33]

The Ritschlian interpretation of the Kingdom of God, with both Harnack's and Rauschenbusch's elaborations, lost sight of the eschatological nature of the Kingdom of God as proclaimed by Jesus. However, when this essential concept of the Kingdom had been rediscovered by Ritschl's own son-in-law, Johannes Weiss, Ritschlianism declined very rapidly.

As Richard Hyde Hiers and David Larrimore Holland noted in the elaborate introduction to Weiss's *Jesus' Proclamation of the Kingdom of God*,

> This most important contribution remains his recognition of the eschatological beliefs of Jesus and the early church and especially his willingness, against the stream of the contemporary theology, to try to discover what Jesus really understood the Kingdom of God to mean.[34]

In Weiss's own words,

> The Kingdom of God as Jesus thought of it is never something subjective, inward, or spiritual, but is always the objective messianic Kingdom, which usually is pictured as a territory into which one enters, or as a land in which one has a share, or as a treasure which comes down from heaven.[35]

For Weiss, the Kingdom of God was not primarily an ethical relationship of love between God and man but, first, a religious and therefore an eschatological event.[36] He then specified this eschatology as the apocalyptic eschatology, or the one looking into the future realisation of its fulfilment. Weiss also wrote that 'the actualization of the Kingdom of God is not a matter for human initiative, but entirely a matter of God's initiative.'[37] He viewed the Kingdom of God entirely as a future reference. However, the Kingdom was not to develop gradually as the Social Gospel hoped. Weiss emphasised that 'either the Kingdom is here or it is not yet here!'[38] And lastly, Weiss believed that the only appropriate attitude Christians should adopt towards the Kingdom is one of passivity. Christians can pray that the Kingdom might come, they can long for it, but they can do nothing to bring it into existence. Contrary to the then contemporary theological belief that the Kingdom of God is an assignment, Weiss believed that the Kingdom is a gift, and therefore solely the prerogative of God.

Although Weiss shifted the emphasis of the theology of the Kingdom from purely this-worldly and moralistic to eschatological and theological grounds, he had difficulty in reconciling some sayings of Jesus which appear to be outside the apocalyptic-eschatological frame. While Rolf Schafer accuses Weiss's apocalyptic eschatology as a standard of authenticity amounting to a *petitio principii*, Hiers and Holland are more sympathetic to Weiss by describing his interpretation as an 'exaggerated exegetical emphasis'. Whatever one terms it, Weiss had either to 'correct' such texts to fit his view, or eliminate them for one reason or another.[39] However, this does not take away from Weiss's greatest contribution of bringing the eschatology of Jesus into a prominent and undeniable position within New Testament scholarship.[40] Since his time, as Lundstrom concluded in his thesis, 'very few scholars have denied the eschatological nature of the Kingdom of God'.[41]

Ever since the contributions of Ritschl and Weiss to the discussion about the timing of the Kingdom of God little new has been added. Rudolf Bultmann proposed to express the essential meaning of Jesus' eschatology in purely existential categories. To him the eschatological interpretation must concentrate upon the present subjective moment of existential decision-making. Hence the demythologising of the New Testament which could be also described as de-eschatologizing. On the other hand, in Karl Barth's interpretation of the New Testament eschatology, the emphasis is on the past objective events of Jesus' incarnation. The incarnation of Jesus is the beginning of eschatology. However, as Hiers and Holland observed, 'each interprets eschatology primarily in terms of his respective theological interest; neither takes chronological futurity seriously'.[42]

In *Christ and Time*, Oscar Cullmann gives a new and interesting approach to the debate. For him Christ stands in the middle between the beginning and the end of time and history. Cullmann believes that the end is yet to come as the 'final completion' of the plan of salvation. But for him the question of 'when' does not make any difference, because 'the "end" as the meaning of redemptive history ... is Jesus Christ, who has already appeared.'[43] In the latter respect one can see Cullmann's thought moving closer to C. H. Dodd's idea of 'realised eschatology.'

C. H. Dodd wrote in *Parables of the Kingdom* that the Kingdom of God 'is not merely imminent; it is here'.[44] He maintains throughout his work that Jesus believed that the Kingdom of God was entirely present; there would be no future coming of the Kingdom, nor the Messiah, nor Judgment. Dodd defined the Kingdom of God as

> the ministry of Jesus as 'realized eschatology', that is to say, as the impact upon this world of the 'powers of the world to come' in a series of events, unprecedented and unrepeatable now in actual process.[45]

It is unfortunate that Dodd's insight of realised eschatology was not balanced with the future aspects of the Kingdom which Weiss proved to be unavoidable in any New Testament study of the Kingdom of God. The two concepts wedded together would give more accurate picture of the New Testament evidence both of Jesus' and the early church's understanding. Perhaps Jürgen Moltmann has come close to this realisation in his study of the significance of the eschatological future and the realisation of this hope in everyday life of the Christian on the basis of the past action of Jesus.[46] Moltmann understood that

> the future is anticipated in hope, it is in the process of coming. ... The Christians must understand themselves as co-workers of the promised kingdom of God and its universal peace and its righteousness. For they live not for a future which has not began yet but which has already arrived in Christ and which – coming from him – will change the world. Only this eschatological horizon of the hope for the one future of the world from the one God is wide enough to confront faith with the present needs and necessities and to introduce it into life.[47]

Moltmann asserts that this hope for the future realisation of the Kingdom motivates and drives Christians to work for social change and the realisation of human rights in the present, present and future being linked in the 'human striving' on the account of the redemption in Jesus. 'The Kingdom of God', argues Moltmann,

> can only then be understood as the real future of the world if it becomes present in history as redemption and as goal of the human striving, as absolution in forgiveness of sins and as goal of new obedience. The surplus value of the future above and beyond the attained and the attainable shows itself not only in permanent surplus of incentive, but always as redemption from the compulsions of the instincts, only in this doubleness of anticipation and already arrived grace (*Zuvorkommenheit*) of redemption and mobilization, does the future work into the misery of the present in a humanizing way. It is exactly this double impression of the future upon history which we discover in the resurrection of the crucified one and in the cross of the risen Christ.[48]

The Kingdom of God,[49] edited by Bruce Chilton and published in 1984, is one of the latest attempts of the New Testament scholarship of the 1970s and 1980s to revive the debate about the Kingdom of God. These latest attempts have not been able to resolve the old tension between the this-worldly and eschatological aspects of the Kingdom. However, in some of the contributions this was not the primary task. Instead, they tried to find the reasons for one or the other concept (Michael Lattke, Norman Perrin and Bruce Chilton), or deal with the relationship between eschatological and ethical components of Jesus' preaching of the Kingdom (Hans Bald). As Chilton concluded in the introduction to the book, only 'time will tell whether a fresh consensus will emerge'[50] in the debate that was started by Jesus and the New Testament writers and later in the Enlightenment period by Ritschl.

Seventh-day Adventists and the Kingdom

Ellen G. White and the Kingdom

The founders of the Seventh-day Adventist church and its pioneers of the second half of the nineteenth century did not say much about the Kingdom of God as a present reality. When the phrase was used in Adventist circles between the middle and the end of the nineteenth century, it usually meant the second coming of the Lord. Ellen White wrote in 1888 that 'the events which were generally expected to take place before the coming of Christ, such as the universal reign of peace and the setting up of the kingdom of God upon the earth, were to be subsequent to the second advent.'[51] White stated very specifically that 'not until the personal advent of Christ can His people receive the kingdom'.[52] And then, after quoting 1 Corinthians 15: 50, she continued,

> Man in his present state is mortal, corruptible; but the kingdom of God will be incorruptible, enduring for ever. Therefore man in his present state cannot enter the kingdom of God. But when Jesus comes, He confers immortality upon His people; and then He calls them to inherit the kingdom of which they have hitherto been only heirs.[53]

Opportunely, this eschatological-apocalyptic emphasis of the Kingdom of God preceded Weiss's 'discovery', which stirred theological circles at the very end of the nineteenth century.[54]

Beside many references to the future aspect of the Kingdom in White's writings,[55] there are several other aspects of the Kingdom of God which she touches upon: the Kingdom of righteousness,[56] conditions of entrance into the Kingdom,[57] appearance of the spiritual and the not worldly Kingdom,[58] and the Kingdom in the context of biblical prophecy.[59] But probably the most distinct contribution of Ellen White to Adventist theology of the Kingdom is her division of the Kingdom of Grace and the Kingdom of Glory.

In *The Great Controversy*, White wrote that the Kingdom of God has two distinct aspects with respect to both time and purpose. 'As used in the Bible,' wrote White, 'the expression "kingdom of God" is employed to designate both the kingdom of grace and the kingdom of glory.' White continued after quoting Hebrews 4: 16,

> The throne of grace represents the kingdom of grace; for the existence of a throne implies the existence of a kingdom. In many of His parables, Christ uses the expression, 'the kingdom of heaven', to designate the work of divine grace upon the hearts of men.
>
> So the throne of glory represents the kingdom of glory; and this kingdom is referred to in the Saviour's words, 'When the Son of man shall come in His glory, and all the angles with Him, then shall He sit upon the throne of His glory: and before Him shall be gathered all nations.' [Matt 25: 31.32] This kingdom is yet future. It is not to be set up until the second advent of Christ.[60]

Although the kingdom of glory points to the future apocalyptic and literal Kingdom established on earth after Jesus' 'work as a mediator shall be ended',[61] the kingdom of grace was 'instituted immediately after the fall of man, when a plan was devised for the redemption of the guilty race'.[62] However, the kingdom of grace was not actually established until the death of Jesus. 'The kingdom of grace, which had before existed by the promise of God, was then [at the death of Jesus] established.'[63] Despite the fact that throughout early Adventist history the concept of the Kingdom of God had a very strong bias towards the future establishment of the Kingdom at the second coming of Christ, Ellen White indicated in her writings an understanding of the Kingdom in such a way that it incorporated both the future and the present aspects of the kingdom of grace and the kingdom of glory. Only very recently have several contemporary Adventist scholars taken this dualistic concept of the Kingdom of God and elaborated upon it with special references to social ethics.

Modern Adventists and the Kingdom

The most distinct point in the modernisation of Adventist theology can be marked by the appearance of the book *Seventh-day Adventists Answer Questions on Doctrine*, the work of a representative group of Seventh-day Adventist leaders, Bible teachers and editors intended, as the subtitle suggests, to be 'an explanation of certain major aspects of Seventh-day Adventist belief'.[64] The concept of the Kingdom of God reappeared in a fresh form in the book after a period of half a century in which other theological interests and pragmatic needs had preoccupied Adventist thinking. However, the discussion about the Kingdom only appeared in the general discussion on Adventist hermeneutics and, more specifically, within the framework of the eschatological prophecies and the millennium.

Questions on Doctrine briefly reviews three different approaches to prophetic interpretation: postmillennialists, amillennialists and premillennialists. The postmillennialist, it is claimed, 'interprets the "kingdom prophecies" as wholly symbolic descriptions of a future golden age of the church, a millennium of worldwide righteousness, to be brought about by a larger measure of the present means of grace, not by direct intervention of God.'[65] This would prepare the world for the second coming of Christ at the end of the millennium.

'The amillennialist', according to *Questions on Doctrine*, 'denies any millennial kingdom; rather, he equates it, like Augustine, with the triumph of Christianity in the present era.'[66] The premillennialist expects the present reign of evil to grow worse until the personal coming of Christ ends this age in a supernatural way and the millennial kingdom begins. After the millennium, the final earthly Kingdom of God is established as an eternal state in the new heavens and new earth.

Although SDAs can easily be described as premillennialists, *Questions on Doctrine* reiterated that,

> Unlike most premillennialists today, Seventh-day Adventists hold that the kingdom promises are fulfilled in the experience of the church – today the 'kingdom of grace' in the hearts of Christians, and eventually the 'kingdom of glory' in the eternal state.[67]

And therefore, it concluded, Adventists 'differ from other Christian groups in our views on the kingdom prophecies'.[68] It is very significant that White's idea of the Kingdom of Grace and the Kingdom of Glory is elaborated. Two aspects of the Kingdom, now and not yet, going hand in hand together as two phases of the same kingdom.

Adventists' view of the Kingdom prophecies is then explained in detail. God made promises to Abraham (Gen 12: 1–3; 13: 14–17) and later to Israel at Sinai (Ex 19: 5, 6). These promises were conditional, significantly marked by an *if* (Lev 18: 26–8; Deut 7: 9–12).

These, and other promises,[69] were ratified by the covenant between God and his people. The earthly kingdom of Israel, and its remnant – the kingdom of Judah – fell into apostasy and were taken into captivity. The royal line of David lost the throne until the Messiah should come, 'whose right is to reign'. At this hour of Israel's history, God sent messages through Jeremiah and Ezekiel about a 'new covenant'; an 'everlasting covenant'. God would restore them as God's holy nation, as a living demonstration of his love and care (Jer 31: 27–34; 32: 36–41; Eze 37: 19–28). *Questions on Doctrine* calls these promises 'the New Testament gospel in the heart of the Old Testament'.[70]

> The 'restoration' or 'kingdom' prophecies ... speak of long life and Edenic conditions of the earth, of Israel's righteousness and world leadership. ... The house of David was to be restored, and finally the Messiah was to come ... and was to rule the kingdom in righteousness and finally bring in eternal peace. However, the golden age was not to be altogether one of peace; apparently the jealousy of enemies was to bring war, which would end in final

> victory for God's people (Ezek 38: 39) before the second coming of Christ, and the transition to the eternal state.[71]

The books of Ezra, Nehemiah, Haggai, Zechariah and Malachi show how the Israelites fell short of the restoration envisaged under the new covenant. And then came the Messiah who began to preach, 'The time is fulfilled, and the kingdom of God is at hand' (Mark 1: 15). While Jews were preoccupied with earthly matters and material aspects of the kingdom, they had forgotten the spiritual. And the Carpenter of Nazareth offered 'the blessings of the new covenant, of the renewed heart, of the Spirit within'.[72]

Because of the conditional nature of the kingdom prophecies to the nation of Israel, and the failure of Israelites to keep their part of the covenant, Jesus pronounced that 'the kingdom of God will be taken away from you and given to a people who will produce its fruit' (Matt 21: 43). Many were to come from the west and the east to the kingdom of heaven (Matt 8: 11, 12), some among the Gentiles proving themselves worthy of being called 'Abraham's children' more truly than the Jews because they 'would do the works of Abraham' (John 9: 39). Hence, 'the children of the flesh' were replaced by 'the children of the promise' (Rom 9: 6, 8) – the spiritual seed of Abraham.

There is a continuation of the kingdom promises from the Old Testament to the New Testament. Christians – both Jew and Gentile – have become the children of Abraham when they accepted Christ in faith (Gal 3: 7.8.16.29). Both classes of Abraham's seed, claims *Questions on Doctrine*, 'are to receive the Abrahamic promises. Paul does not say that the *earthly-kingdom promises* to Israel belong to the Jew and *heavenly-kingdom promises* to the Christians, but rather he speaks of the inheritance of the *world* by *all* the seed (Rom 4: 13, 16)'.[73] Therefore, Christians are heirs of the new-covenant prophecies and the new-covenant kingdom (1 Pet 2: 9; Rom 2: 28, 29).

The Christian church is now the vehicle for bringing God's blessing to the world. Its head is Christ, who now rules in the hearts of his people. One day, he will rule in person in his eternal kingdom. As *Questions on Doctrine* put it:

> It is 'the kingdom of God … within you' (Luke 17: 21), which 'cometh not with observation [margin, "outward show"] (verse 20), but grows like a mustard seed' (Matt. 13: 31, 32). Such is the spiritual kingdom to which we must now belong if we are to

enjoy the blessings of the future kingdom of glory. Thus the kingdom prophecies will finally be fulfilled, not in the presence of sin and repentance, birth and death, war and plague, but in the new earth.[74]

Questions on Doctrine does not see a paradox, or even tension, between the two aspects of the kingdom. It makes an additional contribution in proposing a concept of continuity of the covenant, promise and prophecy of the kingdom from the Old to the New Testament. It therefore talks not only of the present and future aspects of the kingdom, but also of the link between these two and the past aspects described and promised in the Old Testament. *Questions on Doctrine* sums it up in this way:

> The new covenant, first offered by the prophets of old in connection with the kingdom promises, was mediated by Christ (Heb 9: 15), ratified by His blood (Heb 13: 20), typified in the Lord's Supper (Luke 22: 16), and reiterated in the Epistles. Thus it became a reality in the church, and the new-covenant kingdom exists now in its first phase, which is commonly called the 'kingdom of grace', until at the second advent it will become the visible 'kingdom of glory', which will continue on after the millennium as the eternal kingdom established on the new earth.[75]

Therefore, *Questions on Doctrine* suggests, what was the phase of promise of the kingdom in the Old Testament became the first phase of the Kingdom of God in the life, death and resurrection of Jesus and will be the second phase of the same Kingdom at the time of second advent when the eternal Kingdom of God will be established on the new earth.

Only in the second half of the 1980s did a number of Adventist scholars attempt to revise the concept of the Kingdom of God and link it to social involvement. In 1985 Richard Rice, Professor of Theology at La Sierra University, California, embraced the concept of the Kingdom within his title *The Reign of God*.[76] A year later Roy Branson[77] and in 1987 John Brunt[78] examined the concept of the present and future Kingdom of God and what relationship it has to Adventist social ethics.

Rice's idea of the Kingdom of God is not so much 'the territory over which God rules, as to his ruling activity'.[79] After contrasting C. H. Dodd's views of the Kingdom as purely present reality with

Norman Perrin's views of the Kingdom being brought in the future by the dramatic divine activity, Rice opts for George Eldon Ladd's understanding of the Kingdom as a 'twofold interpretation of the expression'.[80] Rice quotes Ladd interpreting the Aramaic word *malkuth* ['kingdom'] to be 'either a monarch's kingship, his reign, or it can be the reality over which he reigns. It is our thesis [originally Ladd's but also Rice's] that both meanings are to be recognized in the teachings of Jesus, and that the primary meaning is the abstract or dynamic one, for it is God's kingly act establishing his rule in the world which brings into being the realm in which his rule is enjoyed.'[81] Hence the title of Rice's book – *The Reign of God.*

The Kingdom of God was the theme of Jesus' ministry and, according to Rice, the central topic of his preaching. His miracles and illustrations of the nature of life in the kingdom served as the signs that the Kingdom of God was near. But Jesus' emphasis 'on the priority of the spiritual dimension of the kingdom of God to its material and political dimensions'[82] led to widespread disillusionment among the people who hoped for the Messiah. However, Rice wrote, 'As the Sermon on the Mount illustrates, the kingdom of God is fundamentally a matter of values and attitudes, rather than power and position. Until certain spiritual conditions were fulfilled, the kingdom of God would not be visually manifested.'[83] The most important condition Rice asserted was that people's 'relation to the kingdom depended entirely on their personal response to [Jesus]. Only if people accepted him as the source of spiritual life could they enter the kingdom of God.'[84]

Another condition for the Kingdom lies, according to Rice, in 'extending God's sovereignty in the world'[85] by loving others. Practically, this means 'working to bring about a state of affairs that resembles the way things are in the kingdom of God. This involves striving to relieve human suffering wherever we find it. It means opposing oppression and working for freedom and justice in human affairs.'[86] Social change is part of the good news of salvation; it is not in competition with it. However, Rice does not suggest that by social involvement Christians could bring about the Kingdom of God on earth.[87] This, Rice suggests, is not a contradiction but ambiguity.

> The position of Christians in the world, then, is ambiguous. They are in the world, but not of the world (cf. Jer 17: 15–16). They commit their lives to loving others because this is what it means

> to follow Christ, and because they believe this is worthwhile in the scale of ultimate values, but they do not expect it to make sense in our present situation. [In a similar way] the reign of God is present reality, but it will not be fully realized until the future. As a result, we cannot identify the kingdom of God with any achievable state of affairs in the present, but we cannot relegate it entirely to the future, either.[88]

Although the Kingdom is yet to 'fully arrive', Rice concludes that 'we can never abandon the attempt to live as citizens of the kingdom here and now'.[89]

Roy Branson takes the idea of the Kingdom of God in relation to Adventism a step further. He links Seventh-day Adventist eschatology to 2 Peter:

> Seventh-day Adventists are anxious for the soon return of their Lord, and would be grateful if He appeared at any moment. But also like Peter, Adventists have an eschatology that allows them to sustain a lively hope and active life for as long as proves necessary.[90]

He then notes several areas in which Adventists had sustained that hope in active life: exhibiting the meaning of Christ's victory through 'individual members' lives and the character of the institution [the church] has ventured to establish'.[91] In particular Branson is thinking about hospitals and medical institutions, welfare departments, missions, schools and numerous educational institutions which Adventists have established throughout the world. But also he writes about direct social involvement of the early generation of Adventists who were fighting 'vigorously those defiant powers violating God's creation and creatures'. Branson continues,

> The church challenged the institution of slavery, calling not only slavery an evil, but also the religious and political institutions that supported it. Adventists opposed parties that did not assist the black man after emancipation. They opposed ineffective medical institutions, and battled liquor interests.[92]

However, Branson warns of the danger Adventists could and unfortunately on occasions have faced. He suggests that confident Christians during the early twentieth century made a mistake in thinking they would, with God's help, transform society into a loving, peaceful and just world. They thought that the social gospel could usher in the Kingdom of God. Adventists substituted the social gospel with the ecclesiological gospel thinking that 'if the Seventh-day Adventist church only works hard enough, the kingdom will come'.[93]

Branson does not see the problem with the social gospel in so far as Christians are concerned about the conditions of their fellow men. He perceives the problem in the fact that they 'confused Christianity with being able to create a perfect human society.' In the same way, Branson observes,

> The problem with the ecclesiological gospel is not that the church thinks that it should witness to what Christ has done or that the church believes that God works evermore fully in the lives of members – it is that the church thinks that its good works achieve the salvation of the world.[94]

Therefore, the exclusiveness of the church in both salvation history and social work can be damaging as well as anti-Christian. The only way to make any sense of a group which expects the Kingdom of God from heaven and, at the same time, works diligently to represent the Kingdom of God on earth must be to appreciate and understand the eschatology of Seventh-day Adventists. Branson describes Adventists as people who 'celebrate God's action past, present and future; that they have a thoroughly biblical eschatology that justifies their intense and sustained effort here and now to demonstrate the character of the Kingdom of God.[95] So he, in a similar fashion to *Questions on Doctrine* 30 years previously, links God's past, present and future action into a united whole from which springs a dynamic Christian faith, active in the present world (first phase) and yet expecting the future phase of the Kingdom of Glory after the return of Christ.

John Brunt has approached the whole discussion of the Kingdom of God from a dual perspective as the title of his book *Now and Not Yet* suggests. Brunt's main thesis is that the New Testament eschatology is concerned with both present and future aspects. Following Dodd's 'realized eschatology' to some extent, Brunt suggests that eschatology was realised in Christ's life, death and especially in his resurrection. Unlike Dodd, however, Brunt does not see the realised eschatology completed in the first century. He also speaks of the significance of the future aspect of eschatology. In fact, he links the two by saying that 'what Christ has already done provides the assurance that His promise about the future is reliable'.[96] In other words, the *already* of the New Testament eschatology provides the 'down payment' for the *not yet*.

The characteristics and values of 'God's government' (Brunt's expression for the kingdom of God) are realised grace through Jesus' sacrifice, which must be understood and accepted by recipients of the Kingdom (cf. Matt 20), exercised *humility* of the true citizens of God's kingdom (cf. Matt 5), and accepted *service* as exemplified in the life of Jesus (Mark 10: 42–45). Brunt argues that such a survey

> of some of the values of God's government reveals the difference between His government and the governments that we know in this world ... in the long run, it is love, not force; service, not status; humility, not hubris; that will have the last word. God's government offers an alternative counterculture to this world, and in the end all will see that what it values is the same as that which endures for eternity.[97]

After examining Jesus', Paul's and John's concepts of the Kingdom, Brunt concludes that the New Testament eschatology as a whole manifests the dual character by including both the 'already' and the 'not yet' perspective.[98] From this New Testament perspective he determines that the church's attention has a dual focus too: 'a vision of the future and a present work to be done'.[99]

For Brunt, however, the concept of the two ages is not only chronological but also moral. As he argues, 'the two ages are shaped by different values. The pattern, or shape, of this present world is characterised by evil. Jesus Christ reveals a different pattern, which will characterise the world to come.'[100] However, the world to come, argues Brunt, is not just something in the future. We can in the present begin a way of life that fits its pattern or shape. Paul, in Romans 12: 2, is cited in support of his argument: 'Do not conform any longer to the pattern of this world, but be transformed by the renewing of your mind.' Christians are called 'to let the future begin now. The not yet has everything to do with the now.'[101]

After analysing the dualistic concept of the kingdom of God, Brunt asks how this type of the eschatological 'already/not yet' model affects our socio-ethical responsibility in the world. He argues that this 'already' of eschatology should not minimise or detract from the 'not yet'. Instead, the 'already' should serve as the motivating factor in working towards the 'not yet' aspect of the Kingdom both in the general character of the moral life and in giving the specific shape to the moral life.[102]

Brunt realises that 'eschatology can [and often has] become an excuse to shun ethical responsibility'. However, he argues, 'when properly understood, eschatology – in fact the eschatology of the book of revelation and Advent eschatology today – should have precisely the opposite effect. Eschatology and ethics should go hand in hand.'[103]

The 'eschatological motivation' as a response both to what God has done and what he has promised to do for us is listed in three separate categories. First, a person whose life is motivated by appreciation for God's generosity can 'never be unconcerned about the needs and sufferings of other people merely because it will all be taken care of when Jesus comes'.[104] Secondly, the general cosmological concept of 'already/not yet' has direct implications for the individual life also. 'Just as the kingdom has already come to this world, yet awaits its final manifestation, so the individual life has already been transformed by God's grace, even though final perfection comes only in future.[105] Anyone who is in Christ becomes a brand new person, the old has gone and the new has come already in the present life (cf. 2 Cor 5: 17 and Phil 1: 6). And thirdly, the Christian ethic must never be legalistic. Christians do not obey rules in order to go to heaven. They respond to the eschatological 'already' of a generous God by living in ways that show appreciation and desire to please him. Brunt points out that 'We do not obey in order to receive a reward. Rather, the law reveals the principles that will motivate those who want to please God and who desire to begin living now according to the principles of the kingdom to which He calls us.'[106] Christians are motivated out of love rather than by fear of punishment (1 John 4: 18–19).

When Brunt takes his dualistic model from the theoretical into the practical sphere of everyday living, he concludes that although Jesus was crucified as a revolutionary, Jesus' disciples did not fight because he had proclaimed that his kingdom was not of this world (John 18: 36). 'Jesus destroys all illusions that the kingdom can be fully manifest in the political structures of this world. The kingdom cannot come by fighting or overturning one political structure in favour of another.'[107] Yet, Jesus did not accept the political structures of his day without criticism and he was a threat to them. Hence,

> the realization of the 'not yet' aspect of eschatology has significance for political ethics. If the kingdom is beyond history and will be fully realized by God's action, then it is inconsistent for Christ's followers to try to bring it now by fighting and violent revolution. Such means are not in keeping with the principles of the kingdom.[108]

In the same way, Christians are advised not to engage in violent revolt but to resist the power of the political tyrant by non-violent means and by championing the cause of the oppressed. Pacifist resistance is, for Brunt, the imperative for every Christian. 'Those very principles of the kingdom that keep us from violent revolution also impel us to be concerned not only for ourselves but for all the oppressed'.[109]

The last point raised by Brunt deals with the commitment to the principles of the Kingdom of God. The fact that the future Kingdom has already broken into the present in the person of Jesus Christ activates Christians to commit themselves to the principles of that Kingdom. And commitment must make a difference now, for we cannot possibly be committed to the principles of God's Kingdom without showing now that we accept and live by them. Since Christ makes his Kingdom a place where tears are wiped away, suffering and death are ended, and poverty, disease and hunger are abolished, argues Brunt, 'commitment to Christ's kingdom implies commitment to the destruction of pain, suffering, hunger, poverty, and even death'.[110] Of course, all these cannot be abolished before the return of Christ. Nevertheless, the Kingdom can be anticipated and people can be committed to its principles in this world.

Those Christians who really understand and accept the 'already/not yet' concept of the Kingdom cannot but bring a taste of the Kingdom to the world. Brunt concludes that

> there can be no sharp dichotomy between the future vision and present action. Hoping for the kingdom can never make Christians indifferent toward their neighbour. Hoping for the kingdom means caring about the neighbours now, because that's what the kingdom is all about. ... Hoping for the kingdom is caring for and living for what the kingdom stand for.[111]

It was Jesus who linked our entrance into the future Kingdom with our concerns for our neighbour in the present anticipation and implementation of the Kingdom principles. In the last parable of the Olivet discourse in Matthew 25: 31–46. Jesus pointed to the final judgment and to the values, concerns and actions that will characterise those who have set their minds on the Kingdom. 'Our fitness for the future kingdom is necessarily related to our present attitude toward principles of the kingdom.'[112] Brunt is convinced that 'Christians with a vivid vision of the future promise can still act responsibly in the present, contributing to the betterment of this world while hoping for the next'.[113]

Conclusion

In the middle of the nineteenth century, the Kingdom of God was perceived by most Christian scholars as the present Kingdom, which Christians should work towards and make real on earth. Contrary to that opinion, the early Seventh-day Adventists meant by the Kingdom of God the eschatologic-apocalyptic Kingdom established by God at the end of the millennium. With Ellen White, this emphasis within Adventism shifted. White proposed the concepts of the 'kingdom of grace' and the 'kingdom of glory', which gave foundation for other Adventist thinkers to develop the idea further. Initially in the 1950s with the movement of 'Adventists-towards-evangelicalism', and especially in the 1980s with the new breed of Adventist theologians and ethicists, Seventh-day Adventists experienced a new emphasis on a number of issues and doctrines, including the Kingdom of God. This time, the dual nature of the Kingdom, expressed as two phases or stages, not only affected the theological discussion of the timing of the Kingdom, but also opened up a discussion about the moral and ethical effects of the Kingdom of God. For the first time the doctrine of the Kingdom of God resulted in considerations of a socio-ethical nature. The conclusion was that 'eschatology and ethics must go hand in hand'.[114]

The ethical reasoning that springs from the concept of the Kingdom of God must be taken very seriously. There is no doubt that Jesus, both in the Synoptic gospels and in the Gospel of John, reiterated the dual concept of the Kingdom.[115] While Jesus proclaimed that his Kingdom would come with power and glory after he had gone to the Father to prepare the place for his followers in the eternal Kingdom, and while he taught disciples to pray for this future Kingdom to come and instructed them to wait for him, Jesus also encouraged them to proclaim that this same Kingdom is at hand in their time, that it is within them, and that they need to make a personal commitment in order to enter it.[116] Jesus' proclamation of the Kingdom included serious ethical implications: preaching the good news to the poor, proclaiming freedom for prisoners, healing the sick, releasing the oppressed and proclaiming God's favour (Luke 4: 18–19).

Jesus' ethical implications of the Kingdom are expressed in the most explicit way in the Sermon on the Mount. There, the inhabitants of the Kingdom are the poor, those who mourn, the meek, the hungry and thirsty for righteousness, the merciful, the pure in heart, the persecuted and the peacemakers. These are the true salt and light of the world (Matt 5: 1–16). In order to take the part in the Kingdom, it is not sufficient for Christians simply to talk; they must do 'the will of my Father who is in heaven' (Matt 7: 21). And, in such a way, God's will was fully manifested in Jesus' life – the unselfish life for others in every moment of his earthly existence as he 'made himself nothing, taking the very nature of a servant' (Phil 2: 7).

Employing this kind of humility of Jesus, looking after the 'least of these brothers of mine', helping our 'neighbour' in need as the Samaritan had done, is the true Christian response to the message of the Kingdom. Entering into the sphere of the Kingdom of grace here and now is not only a possibility for a Christian, it is a requirement. For, as Brunt pointed out, 'how can we possibly be committed to the principles of God's kingdom without showing now that we accept and live by them?'[117]

However, commitment to the principles of God's Kingdom here and now does not take away from the anticipation of the final fulfilment of the promises of the second phase of the same Kingdom when Jesus comes. Commonly described, the Kingdom of glory is a biblical concept of the eschatological Kingdom established by God in his own time, which nobody knows. Jesus' command, 'Occupy till I come' has ethical implications for human rights in the world we live in. The command gives Christians direction as well as a sense of belonging to the Kingdom which was promised in the Old Testament period, expected by God's people of all ages, verified by the Jesus' sacrifice and the resurrection, and proclaimed and acted out by many faithful believers throughout the centuries. For contemporary Christians the 'eschatological vision of our future hope actually contributes to the content or shape of our daily lives. It helps us see how we should live responsibly here and now'.[118] How we treat others in this world will not bring about the Kingdom of God, but it should prove that this Kingdom is in our hearts, that we are the new creatures who entered the sphere of the Kingdom of grace and that we anticipate the fulfilment of promises of the Kingdom of glory in the near future.

10

Adventist Basis for Human Rights

In the course of the history of Christianity, Adventists believe, certain biblical teachings have become distorted or lost. Some of these were brought into sharp focus by Seventh-day Adventists. A few of these theological emphases became helpful in developing social ethics. Others, however, appeared to be contrary to social involvement. The previous chapter dealt with issues which are common to Adventist as well as non-Adventist Christians. Now we turn to theological insights which, in part, form Adventist identity and which contribute to a Christian theory of human rights, namely emphasis on the moral law, the concept and meaning of the Sabbath, the role of prophets and prophetic communities, and finally, the implications of the belief in the second coming of Christ.

COMMANDMENTS-KEEPING PEOPLE

The Decalogue

The moral law, as an expression of the character of God and as God's desire for human fulfilment, was always high on the agenda of Adventist theology.[1] Adventists regard the Decalogue as a great moral guideline binding upon all people who desire to live in perfect harmony with God and with other human beings in every age. It is not, and has never been, the means of salvation (Rom 4: 1–3; Heb 11). However, the fruit of salvation is obedience to these precepts that God himself gave to humanity (Ex 31: 18).

Jesus and the Moral Law

For a complete understanding of what God means by his moral law, a Christian must turn to the God Incarnate. Jesus, in his most remarkable sermon about the law (some call the Sermon on the Mount the second Sinai),[2] claimed that he did not come to abolish the law but to fulfil it (Matt 5: 17). He continued:

> anyone who breaks one of the least of these commandments and teaches others to do the same will be called least in the kingdom of heaven, but whoever practices and teaches these commands will be called great in the kingdom of heaven.[3]

When challenged to give an account of what he thought was the most important commandment, Jesus did not allow himself to be drawn into making the mistake of selecting one and overemphasising it. Rather, he summed up the law and the prophets in a remarkably concise but powerful phrase borrowed from Deuteronomy: '"Love the Lord your God with all your heart and with all your soul and with all your mind". This is the first and the greatest commandment. And the second is like it: "Love your neighbour as yourself"'.[4] Asked on another occasion the question 'Who is my neighbour?', Jesus answered eloquently in a parable that our neighbour is everyone who is in need, regardless of race, nationality or caste (Luke 10: 29–37).

The Universality of the Moral Law

The universality of the Old Testament account of the moral law (Ex 20: 1–17 and Deut 5: 1–22) and Jesus' elaboration of it (Matt 5–7) require from people respect for and protection of human rights. If God is interested in relationships between human beings, and he demonstrated the desire to regulate these relationships with the last six commandments of the Decalogue and with the numerous sayings of Jesus, his children should uplift these regulations and apply them to every situation in life.

Applications for the 'Commandments-keeping People'

The commandments-keeping people, as Seventh-day Adventists desire to be known, should be the first to foster good relations with their neighbours. Whenever there is a violation of the love-principle in the world they ought to be among the first to condemn it and to seek ways to eliminate injustice, inequality, bad relationships and violation of human rights in general in order to be true to their calling as the people of the law.

SABBATH[5]

Its Importance

One of the very important commandments describing the Judeo-Christian God as the Creator of the Universe in a special way,[6] Adventists believe, has been sadly neglected by Christians. The fourth commandment calls people to 'remember the Sabbath day by keeping it holy' (Ex 20: 8). Seventh-day Adventists have thought this feature of their belief so important and distinguishable that they included it in their name. They are the Sabbath people.

However, most of the Adventist studies about the Sabbath have attempted to prove that the seventh day is the Sabbath and that the fourth commandment, as part of the moral law, is relevant to all people at all times.[7] The meaning of the Sabbath and the relationship between the doctrine of Sabbath and social conscience had emerged only recently in Adventist writings.[8]

Its Meaning

Sakae Kubo was among the first to point to the meaning of the Sabbath observance and its 'relationship to our practical Christian life'.[9] He raised several points worth noting. Using Philo's expression that the Sabbath is 'the birthday of the world' and consequently a 'festival, not of a single city or country, but of the universe',[10] Kubo points to the universality of the Sabbath. And the universal Sabbath makes no distinction among people. Instead it makes all people equal before God.

God's presence is not limited to any special place or country, building or people. God selected nothing within space to be his medium through which he could be in contact with his created beings.[11] Indeed, if he had appointed a place or a building to be his holy special place, this would have favoured only people living nearby. Instead, God chose a segment of time to come closer to people. Time is universal, and therefore no person stands in a place of advantage. 'With time all are equal. The Sabbath becomes a worldwide blessing'.[12] And if people worldwide are equal because of their identical access to the Sabbath rest, God points towards the ideal social structure in which all human beings share the same status regardless of their origin, economic status or gender. The Sabbath, in such a way, presumes human rights, and promotes them on a regular weekly basis in a very powerful and meaningful way.

Its Social Application in the Context of Human Rights

But the Sabbath doctrine does not involve only the Sabbath day; it concerns the other six days of the week as well. The atmosphere and the principles of the Sabbath will not only 'extend beyond the worship service to the dinner table and the living room'[13] on the seventh day, but they would also become a part of the Sabbath attitude which ought to be practised throughout the week. In the words of Jack Provonsha,

> True Sabbath keeping touches the whole of life. The Sabbath sanctifies the week. One cannot be dishonest on Monday and truly keep the Sabbath, because the Sabbath keeping is essentially a posture toward God that is not a one-day-in-seven kind of activity.[14]

The concern for other people, which the Christian should have on the Sabbath, must be extended to a way of life which the Christian should exercise daily. The Sabbatical concern, which extends from the weekly Sabbaths to Sabbatical years also, was to teach the Jews about the needs of the less fortunate, the poor, the widows and the orphans (Ex 35: 12–33). In the similar way, Christians should develop a greater 'Sabbatical' conscience for the poor, the unfortunate, the unemployed, and the powerless whose basic human rights are denied.

Jesus and the Sabbath

Jesus is again the supreme example of the way God desired to have fellowship with man and how he intended the Sabbath to bring meaning to the worshipping community. As 'the Lord of the Sabbath' (Mark 2: 28), Jesus took pains to clarify the true meaning of the Sabbath. At the time of Jesus, the Sabbath had become a legalistic exercise of self-righteousness on behalf of different groups of believers who wanted to prove their perfection. Jesus, however, pointed out to the almost forgotten humanitarian function of the fourth commandment. As Bacchiocchi rightly notes,

> To counteract prevailing legal interpretations which restricted humanitarian service on the Sabbath to emergency situations only, Jesus intentionally ministered on this day to persons who were *not critically* but *chronically* ill.[15]

In such a way Jesus pressed the Sabbath into salvation history, making it a day intended for the benefit of humankind (Mark 2: 27).

Equality and the Sabbath

The Sabbath points to equality among all human beings. It is a memorial to God the Creator. Remembering weekly that God is our Creator, and that all human beings are only creatures among whom the differences are really non-essential, should encourage Sabbath observers to accept and respect others regardless of their occupation, ethnic or economic background or educational level. Rice observed that on the Sabbath day,

> differences of occupation and education lose their significance. We realize that what we have in common before the Lord is more important than the various structures that distinguish us during the week, so we can associate with each other as equals and enjoy each other's company as brothers and sisters in Christ.[16]

Rice extends his idea a step further when he asserts that the basic concept of the Sabbath must bring forth the idea of freedom. After all, claims Rice, 'the Sabbath is a day of freedom', and as such,

> the freedom from labor means freedom from bondage to other people. According to the fourth commandment, servants are not to work on the Sabbath. Since no one is subordinate to another on Sabbath, each person stands before God in his individual identity and dignity.[17]

So the Sabbath becomes the true means of liberation for humanity. It celebrates God's merciful act of liberation and deliverance from the bondage of Egypt (Deut 5: 15), but it also points to the ultimate liberation from sin and all its consequences which Jesus proclaimed and exercised both on the Sabbath and at all other times (Luke 4: 18; 13: 16).

Liberation and the Sabbath

As Charles Bradford remarks in his treatise on 'The Sabbath and Liberation', the Sabbath lay at the very heart of the first great freedom movement. Moses delivered God's message to Pharaoh: 'The Lord, the God of the Hebrews, has sent me to say to you: Let my people go, so that they may worship me' (Ex 7: 16). This was a direct appeal to Pharaoh to allow the enslaved people to observe the Sabbath rest. Later, God re-established the Sabbath as a sign of their liberation (Deut 5: 15). However, Bradford continues, this arrangement was to be permanent because 'Sabbath rest and Sabbath observance have something to do with human dignity and freedom. Yahweh never intended for one human being to tyrannize another, or for one nation to subjugate another nation.'[18]

Bradford calls Isaiah's description of the Sabbatical attitude in Isaiah 56: 1–7, 'Yahweh's manifesto', or God's sign of freedom, independence and liberation.[19] And 'Yahweh's manifesto' is relevant and applicable to the whole human family, especially to the outcasts – the poor, the powerless, foreigners (e.g. refugees) and eunuchs (politically and economically impotent). Bradford adds: 'The Sabbath is a sign in perpetuity and a constant reminder of the relationships that exist between human beings and their God and between human beings and their fellow humans – their brothers and sisters.'[20]

Bradford, as a black Seventh-day Adventist, identifies with the theme of liberation taken up by African-American and Third World theologians. He understands that 'they are closer to those parts of the world where the misery index is highest' and reminds us 'that God is on the side of the poor' and, as a result, they 'send out a ringing call for justice and equality'.[21] But Bradford cannot accommodate the idea of calling exclusively for secular, political solutions to human problems. In this respect Bradford sees liberation theology as not sufficiently radical – radical, in Bradford's definition meaning 'getting at the root of a matter'. He remarks:

> Political solutions are not the final end. They cannot possibly get to the root of the human dilemma – sin, rebellion against God. Political revolutions only throw out one group of robbers to be succeeded by another gang.[22]

However, there is an authentic theology of liberation which Jesus came to preach. It was Jesus who promised freedom to the nations – total freedom. His inaugural message is both radical and revolutionary. And Jesus' message 'makes the Sabbath the sign of liberation and independence'.[23] To support this point Bradford quotes, for example, from the book of Ezekiah:

> Therefore I led them out of Egypt and brought them into the desert. I gave them my decrees and made known to them my laws, for the man who obeys them will live by them. Also I gave them my Sabbaths as a sign between us, so they would know that I the Lord made them holy. ... Keep my Sabbaths holy, that they may be a sign between us. Then you will know I am the Lord your God.[24]

Ultimately, Bradford concludes, God is for freedom, liberty, dignity and for the empowerment of all people. Hence, now is the time for all people to make God's sign of liberation their banner.[25]

Kubo similarly believes that the theme of freedom not only reminds us of our deliverance and liberation, but it 'commands us to extend the blessing to those under oppression or servitude'.[26] It is not enough to enjoy one's own benefits of redemption. One must also work with God in bringing liberty 'to the captives, and recovering the sight of the blind, to set at liberty those who are oppressed, to proclaim the acceptable year of the Lord' (Luke 4: 18). Kubo rightly judges that 'Sabbath observance has integral social and humanitarian aspects that we dare not forget. The Sabbath as sign of redemption points in two directions – to our own redemption and to that of the oppressed. We must bring rest to those who live in servitude.[27]

Ironically, Seventh-day Adventists have repeatedly failed to recognise that Sabbath observance should initiate liberation beyond their own community. Even within the church, as was noticed earlier,[28] the principle of equality was not always practised rigorously. But, as Kubo concludes, if Adventists 'fail to practise true fellowship and genuine equality, they betray a lack of understanding of the Sabbath as a sign of fellowship and equality'.[29]

Human Rights and the Sabbatical Year

The extensions of the Sabbath idea found in the sabbatical year and the year of jubilee emphasises almost exclusively humanitarian aspects. From a week of days to a week of years God's desire for the poor and the oppressed to be liberated is the prime concern of the true Sabbath principle (Ex 23: 11 and Lev 25: 10). The idea of the land resting (lying 'unploughed and unused') on the seventh year focuses on the concern for the poor, the slave, the underdog, as well as the rights which go beyond mere human rights.[30] If one truly observes the Sabbath, one cannot remain satisfied only with one's own redemption, restoration and liberation. One must show concern for one's neighbour not only spiritually but also physically – and the Sabbath provides adequate opportunity for this.

Conclusion

The Sabbath, described in Hebrews 4: 3–10 as 'entering God's rest', is not imposed on human beings by their creator. It is a voluntary time which people have freedom to receive or reject. The fourth commandment begins with 'remember', suggesting that the Sabbath is God's gift to people and not something he wants to impose on them or demand from them. The basic principle of human rights is, therefore, uplifted and encouraged through the commandment about the Sabbath.

As a day of freedom, the Sabbath has important social implications. As Rice rightly concludes,

> It attaches such value to human beings that no person can ever be merely the property of another. A real appreciation for the Sabbath would therefore make slavery impossible. The Sabbath speaks against every practice that deprives human beings of their sense of worth and dignity. Oppressive economic and social structures, which make it impossible for people to provide for themselves, contradict the message of the Sabbath. Those who appreciate the meaning of the Sabbath will seek to eliminate such things.[31]

Seventh-day Adventists, believing themselves to be the true Sabbath-keepers, should be among the first to advance the ideas of justice, equality and freedom among all people within as well as outside of their community. If they fail to do that, the letter of the law might be observed but the spirit of the Sabbath-commandment would be totally lost.

THE ROLE OF THE PROPHETS AND PROPHETIC COMMUNITIES

Adventist understanding of the role of prophets and prophecies is primarily of a futuristic and apocalyptic nature. However, predicting the future and eschatological emphasis is only a secondary role of the prophets of ancient Judaism. Their primary role is socio-ethical. Since the Seventh-day Adventist church believes itself to constitute the prophetic minority at the end of world's history,[32] their role should be comparable to the role of the prophets in Jewish society. Hence the importance of examining that role, which by most Adventists is assumed to be almost exclusively eschatologically futuristic.

The Hebrew term *Nabi* is first used in connection with Abraham.[33] However it becomes a popular term with the 'historic' Moses.[34] Moses, as provider of the moral law, becomes a standard of comparison for all other prophets.[35] The Old Testament prophets had several important roles: they were political and religious leaders who proclaimed the law, guarded the spiritual life of the nation, mediated between the people and their God and predicted future judgment. They were interested in international affairs and the future in the same breath as they counselled and influenced social structures of their own generation in their own locality. They could therefore be described as *theological reformers*.

Four Elements of Prophetic Teaching[36]

Four essential elements emerge from prophetic teachings. First, the warnings which prophets bring are always a matter of life and death. Every warning, if not taken seriously, is followed by long-lasting consequences. The prophets called Israel to reject evil and death and choose God, moral behaviour and, consequently, life.[37]

The second element in prophetic teaching deals with God's care for those who are without proper protection within the existing social structures (i.e. slaves, widows, orphans, debtors, the homeless, strangers, etc.). The law requires[38] that there should be no unjust differences between people. But in real life this becomes perverted. Therefore, God promises to be a support and help to those who do not have anybody: he hears their cries, sees their suffering and brings help when his human agents fail to do so. The prophets talk about alienation of those who grab land and 'add house to house and join field to field' until they are alone in the land. This process of materialism,[39] mirrored in our own time and expressed in the accumulation of material goods beyond the point of realistic needs, ends in isolation and in the loss of any meaningful human existence and relationship among people.

Thirdly, God seeks obedience and justice rather than a formal worship or sacrifice. The sacrificial system and religious festivals were important; but ethical behaviour springing from right motives was even more important ('doing the truth' instead of only 'having the truth'). And the basic motive was love which responds to God's love, his choice and his call.[40] Therefore, the motive for ethical behaviour is a response to God's love which he expressed in the covenant relationship with human beings.[41]

The fourth aspect of the prophetic role is eschatological-apocalyptic. In this element of prophetic teaching the prophet goes outside his immediate domain and speaks about the global picture of human history. At its centre, prophetic eschatology is an affirmation that God will succeed in his desire for his creation, that he shall win the battle between good and evil and inevitably bring salvation to his people.

Adventists have usually emphasised the fourth aspect of the prophetic role. In its self-understanding as a 'prophetic movement', Seventh-day Adventism was usually thought of as 'a movement preoccupied with making predictions' as well as 'a movement with a special interest in studying and interpreting predictive prophecy'.[42] But, as Provonsha recently pointed out, Adventism as a prophetic movement should be defined more in terms of function and role, i.e. a people with a mission to the world.[43] However, Adventists should also consider other aspects of prophetic ministry, if they desire to be faithful to their prophetic calling. One of these aspects, and perhaps the first, is the social role of prophets.

Examples of the Primary (Social) Role of Prophets in Jewish Society

The prophets of the Old Testament did not invent new social, economic or moral responsibilities. They believed and affirmed that the ideal for Jewish society as a whole, and its people as individuals, was set in the legislation of the covenant between God and Israel. Justice, as a basis of the law and the pillar of society, was regarded by the prophets as binding for all ages. The guidance that the prophets gave to Israel regarding social, ethical and economic relationships were clearly based on the Mosaic Law as expressed in the

Ten Commandments. Of other prophets dealing with social ethics,[44] Amos, Hosea and Isaiah are typical examples of this.[45]

The Role of the New Testaments Prophets

The role of the prophets in the New Testament was not very different from that in the Old Testament. John the Baptist, whom Jesus called the greatest prophet of all times (Matt 11: 9–11), invited the people of Israel to repent and to produce good fruit (Matt 3: 2–10). After querying whether Jesus was the Messiah, he received a message from Jesus which he could understand, appreciate and identify with. Jesus said: 'Go back and report to John what you hear and see: The blind receive sight, the lame walk, those who have leprosy are cured, the deaf hear, the dead are raised, and the good news is preached to the poor.'[46] This was a powerful testimony to the prophet's concerns. There is little doubt that only a true prophet would recognise the Messiah in such a description. That is why Jesus used this approach in explaining his mission to the imprisoned prophet.

John the Revelator was concerned about social as well as eschatological matters. Writing both about and to the minority of Christians in a society which did not favour them a great deal,[47] the writer of the book of Revelation was concerned for their safety, their well-being and their rights, which were being violated through persecution.[48]

Jesus of Nazareth was greatly concerned with the social and economic justice of his time. He came to proclaim freedom to the captives, to release the oppressed and to proclaim the acceptable year of the Lord.[49] However, Jesus did not only preach about issues of social concern, he also practised his social beliefs.[50] He proved through his ministry that virtually nobody was outside of his interest. And he demanded nothing less from his followers. Even in the most famous of his eschatological discourses, when his closest followers asked him when he would establish his *parousia*, Jesus not only answered in terms of the outside events but also in terms of what his followers must do (Matt 24: 1–25: 46). Parallel to proclaiming the gospel, the task of the church was to feed the hungry, give drink to the thirsty, be hospitable to the stranger, clothe the poor, visit the prisoner and look after the sick. The social concern thus expressed was to be one of the primary tasks of the community awaiting the final realisation of the Kingdom of Jesus.

Applications to a Modern Prophetic Community

In short, there are several different roles that the prophets in Jewish society were called upon to fulfil. Most of the time Adventists concentrate on the prophets' eschatological role. However, in reality, this part of prophetic ministry was secondary to their role of calling the people back to the God-given socio-economic and ethical principles enshrined in the Ten Commandments and Jesus' elaboration (Matt 5: 17–48) and summary (Luke 10: 27) of them. As a 'prophetic movement', which Seventh-day Adventists believe themselves to be, the church should balance the proclamations about future events and eschatological predictions with calling people back to God-given principles of socio-economic justice, Christian ethics and human rights based on the moral law of the Old Testament and the explanation of it by the greatest of all Jewish prophets, and founder of the Christian church – Jesus Christ. As O'Mahony rightly observed: 'In biblical times justice needed a prophet. Today, as ever, prophets are needed. From its very beginnings, the Christian community had a prophetic role.'[51] Seventh-day Adventists, as well as all other Christians, are called to fulfil this role in the modern world.

SECOND COMING OF CHRIST

Relevance of Belief in the Second Coming

Until recently only religious people talked about the 'end of the world'. More recently it has become a concern of many thinking people. Today, more than ever, one can see the living relevance of Christian eschatology, and especially its crown, the second coming of Christ. Christian eschatology speaks directly to the present, as one observes such phenomena of the modern world as the possibility of nuclear annihilation, the real possibility of environmental disaster, overpopulation and prospects of starving to death or poisoning ourselves by pollution. As one Adventist commented, 'The doctrine of last things doesn't deal with the far-off future. It speaks to the present. It is as timely as the morning paper and the hourly newscast.'[52]

Although in the traditional arrangement of Christian theology the doctrine of the second coming comes at the end, it is not a footnote or an afterthought. Instead, the second coming becomes the climax to which all the rest leads, or as Rice framed it, 'the ringing conclusion of all that Christians have to say'.[53] Many biblical scholars hold that eschatology not only applies to part of what Christians believe, but to all of it. John T. Robinson, a well-known British theologian, is an example: '– all statements about the End … are fundamentally affirmations about God, [and] every statement about God is *ipso facto* an assertion about the end, a truth about eschatology.'[54] Rice's conclusion is that the second coming is a part of the process of human history. Actually it becomes the climax of this process. In his words, 'Christian faith interprets human history as a whole, not just its final segment. It views all of history in the light of God's saving activity, and it sees the end of history as the climax of the process.'[55]

Possible Negative Effects of Belief in the Second Coming

Overexcitement

Seventh-day Adventists, alongside some other Christians, believe in the Second Advent. The effects of this belief are important within our study of social ethics. As Samuel Bacchiocchi pointed out, in living the Advent hope two dangers exist: overexcitement and indifference. 'There have been Christians in every age who became so excited at the thought of Christ's imminent Coming that they gave up all efforts to work for their personal future or for that of the society in which they lived.'[56] Bacchiocchi illustrates this with a simile of the sinking ship:

> [Some Christians today] view the present world as a sinking ship and so they see no value in setting the course, polishing the brass or mending the sails. Rather than working on the ship, they spend their time on lifeboats, warning from a distance the passengers on the ship of its impending doom. They regard any attempt to improve social conditions as futile and unnecessary, since Christ at His Coming will destroy the present sinful world-order.[57]

Sakae Kubo, when expressing the charge which is made against a believer in the Second Coming, put it in similar terms:

> the person who really believes in the second coming of Christ and the end of our world is not alert to and cannot have any concern about improving human social conditions. He is so otherworldly that he loses all sense of involvement in our world.

> Wrapped up only in his own individual salvation, he feels nothing for his neighbour and his plight.[58]

This charge of isolationism and non-involvement was exposed head on by a non-Adventist theologian, Max Warren, when he said that

> The real reason for the failure of Second Adventism to win support lies in the fact that it affronts the moral conscience of the Church by its virtual abandonment of responsibility for the things of this world in deference to its preoccupation with the imminent return of the Lord and the end of history. Human life, in so far as it is involved in the life of Society, is held to lie so completely in 'the evil one' that the only safe action is for the Christian to wash his hands of it. On this view the salvation is salvation of the soul alone. No serious attempt is made to consider the soul's environment.[59]

Indifference

Another danger to which Christians who wait for Christ's imminent return are exposed to is indifference. In Bacchiocchi's opinion the vast majority of Christians have become neglectful, even indifferent towards Christ's Coming. They have made the present world the ultimate reality to live and work for. 'For these', Bacchiocchi continued, 'the present world is not a *waiting room* to the world to come, but a *living room* in which to live as comfortably and as relaxed as possible.'[60]

Kubo used the idea of the 'problem of delay', a prominent theme in modern Adventism, to explain how the prolonged delay between the proclamation of the 'soon' Second Coming and *parousia* can affect the Advent believers. On one side crying 'wolf' too many times, argued Kubo, 'can lead to a complete lack of response'. The opposite pole of this reasoning, however, 'concludes that if one does not expect an impending return, he can relax and live a careless Christian life'.[61] He resolves:

> The latter kind of reasoning controlled the servant who said to himself, 'My master is delayed in coming' and began 'to beat the menservants and the maidservants, and to eat and drink and get drunk' (Luke 12: 45); and this relaxing is a real danger to those taught that only a sense of Christ's immediate return can instill the urgency necessary for a fervent Christian life.[62]

It is therefore not the timing or the sequence of the Second Coming that should motive the Christian to moral behaviour but, instead, the certainty of his coming.[63]

It is interesting to note that motivation for ethical behaviour, in the context of the servant of Luke 12, was the coming of the Lord. So, contrary to the opinion that the Second Coming is a brake in Christian social involvement, it is rightly portrayed in Luke 12 as the motivating factor. Nevertheless, it is obvious from Christ's parable and Kubo's comments on it, that the imminence of the Second Coming should not be the only motivating factor in Christian ethics.

Bacchiocchi rightly called for balance between the two extremes of practical living of the Advent Hope. To be an 'adventist', a Christian who lives in the expectancy of Christ's Coming, concluded Bacchiocchi,

> means to avoid both the *overexcitement* which writes off the present world as doomed, and the *indifference* which makes the present world the ultimate reality for which to live and work. It means 'to live sober, upright and godly lives' (Titus 2:12), maintaining the delicate balance between being concretely involved in the salvation of this world, and not becoming so entangled in its affairs as to lose sight of the world to come.[64]

Positive Effects of the Certainty of the Coming

The need to explore the meaning of the doctrine of the Second Coming, especially in relationship to the Adventist social ethic, was met most eloquently by Sakae Kubo. He raised a number of aspects of the doctrine of the Second Coming which one should do well to look at. The question for Kubo is not 'if' but 'when' will Jesus Christ come? Jesus' return is guaranteed by his death, resurrection and ascension. Since these are accomplished facts, his coming is an absolute certainty.[65] Kubo used Berkouwer's sentence, 'The believer is called to an attitude that does not reckon but constantly reckons with the coming of the Lord.'[66]

Mistakenly, Adventists' emphasis on reckoning the possible time of Christ's coming (captured in a prominent phrase 'in our lifetime') led generation after generation of believers into disappointment at not yet seeing their Lord. However, the most important factor of the Second Coming need not be the imminence of Christ's return but its reality in our own experience. After all, Kubo suggested, 'the instant of [a person's] death is in effect for him the moment of Christ's coming. Thus in a real sense, Christ returns for everyone in his lifetime. The urgency of Christian living must centre around that point. The actual time of Christ's coming is not significant – only the fact of it.'[67]

The effect which this kind of understanding of the Second Coming would have on a believer is inescapable. Even if the Lord returns in 'our' time, as generations of Adventists believed, this may be seven or seventy years – there is no room for complacency. The imminence of Christ's second advent is in such a case a reality in every period of the church's history, from the time of the apostles to the present.

If Christians connect the actual Second Coming with 'the necessity to give more generously and to live more fervently', in other words to be concerned for their fellow human beings because of the nearness of Jesus' Advent, they will create the impression that only if they feel its approach, need they show concern to live urgently. And this was a trap that the servant in Luke 12 fell into. By implication it would mean that if Jesus' coming is not soon,

> we are justified in living less fervently, less urgently, perhaps even carelessly. In fact, that was the attitude of the servant who, because he felt that his master was delaying, began to beat his workers, to eat and drink and get drunk. But whether Christ's coming is a thousand years from now should not make one iota of difference in the way we live. That He will come should provide sufficient motive for a dedicated Christian life.[68]

The Future Determines the Present

While Rice argued[69] that the hope in the Second Coming sees the future in direct relation to the present to the point of the future actually impinging on the present, threatening to break in at any time, Kubo went beyond this understanding in suggesting that the future actually determines the present and the past.[70] He argued that 'before the incarnation of Christ, one's past determined the future and present'.[71] In Adam all die[72] was the judgment on all apart from Christ. 'All have sinned and fall short of the glory of God',[73] the apostle Paul wrote to the Romans. And since sin was our past and is our present in salvation history, it determined our future – death.[74] However, the Christ event reversed the whole process.

The future does not only *impinge* on the present, or *threaten to break in*, but, Kubo argued, it *enters* the present and *affects* it. 'Eternal life, the Holy Spirit, and justification we experience now, yet they are of the age to come. The ultimate certainty of the future blessing effected through the coming of the second Adam makes it possible to bring the future into the present.'[75]

The future, for some Christians, indeed becomes the 'opium of the masses'. They falsely think of the *parousia* as a compensation for their various lacks in the present life. Hope, in such reasoning, becomes only a wish projection of the deprived. The Second Coming, and what it will bring, becomes mere wishful thinking, a hope which is but a compensation for what people do not or cannot have here and now. Kubo's thesis, however, is that the *parousia* is not 'the promise of what we need or would like, but a fulfilment of what we even now experience.'[76] Kubo reasoned:

> And those who look to Christian hope as a compensation have a fragile hope because it depends on human circumstances. ... We grow beyond such hope when we become better educated and better employed. Our earthly mansions can take the place of the heavenly, our Cadillacs for the heavenly chariots, our stylish wardrobes for the white robe of righteousness, our table delicacies for the tree of life. Because so many Christians view hope in such manner, their hope diminishes as their bank account increases.[77]

On the other hand, Christians should not long for the *parousia* to the extent of ignoring the present. The *parousia* must not be a compensation, but a consummation. In the words of J. Fison, 'Present presence and future *parousia* do not disappear or coalesce in a timeless eternity. They are two inseparable but irreducible elements in that single reality of love, of which the more you have in the present the more you know awaits you in the future.'[78]

Fison pointed out that 'Without faith in the real presence, belief in the real *parousia* ... is phantasy: without faith in the real *parousia*, belief in the real presence is idolatry.'[79] Fison's influence on Kubo is apparent. The present hope, although not identical with the future realisation, is nevertheless closely related. The *parousia*, as Kubo understood, is the fulfilment of the present experience. Kubo quoted Brunner: 'The hope which springs from faith is so much a part of the life of faith that one must say: the future, for which it hopes, is the present in which the believer lives.'[80] And the consequences of such a view for social ethics are obvious. If the believer lives out now the hope of the future, such hope will inevitably penetrate the sphere of human rights. In other words, the justice and equality that the believer expects God to establish at the time of Christ's coming must be the same justice and equality which encompass the present life of the believer.

The Paradox of the Eschatological Motif

C. S. Lewis has been credited with the thought that 'only since Christians have largely ceased to think of the other world have they become so ineffective in this. The rule seems to be that if you aim at heaven, you get earth "thrown in". Aim at earth and you will get neither.'[81] Paradoxically, it is suggested, only a person who lives with a vision of the second coming can truly feel the concern for the present world. On the other hand, a person whose vision is limited to the present world cannot logically worry about love, right, justice and truth – about others.[82] Kubo, in support of this view, quotes Robert McAfee Brown:

> Among the New Testament Christians, the fact of the matter is that eschatology did not lead to irresponsibility or neglect of this world. On the contrary, *their concern with the 'age to come' made them live more responsibly in the present age*. This is the fact which can be documented.[83]

It is true that the first Christian church did not attempt to change the social order from the outside by revolution. Rather it worked from within by conversion. But the changes of its influence were nevertheless far-reaching. Paul, for example, by spreading the good news about the God made without hands touched the vested interests of the Artemis cult in Ephesus, by freeing the slave girl with the spirit of divination, challenged her and other owners of such girls, and by treating Onesimus in a new way dealt a mortal blow to those businesses which depended on people's ignorance (cf. Acts 19: 23–41; Phil 1: 8–16). And finally, the yeast of the early Christian era worked its way to the point, even if only unintentionally, to the establishment of a Christian state.

Kubo summed up the point about the paradox of the eschatological motif in social ethics in an illustration about a sinking ship:

> Nevertheless, the decent person is one who, though he knows that he is on a floundering ship doomed to a watery burial, refuses simply to think of saving himself by secretly escaping alone on a lifeboat. He ministers to the needy and for the welfare of all concerned, even though he may well realize that no hope remains for any of them. The Christian cannot do any less, and paradoxically the eschatological motive with its implication that there exists a righteous loving God in control of all things intensifies his desire to act in the way of his Lord Jesus Christ, who gave Himself not only for His friends but for His enemies.[84]

The argument, therefore, that a believer expecting the coming of the Lord and believing that our present world will vanish has no interest in people, their rights and their environment collapses. To the contrary, the believer with an insight into biblical eschatology knows that the God of love, justice, rightness, truth and morality is in control of history and this motivates the believer to live all the more responsibly, upholding and promoting the human rights of all people.

Also, the certainty of the Second Coming of Christ helps him create the right perspective and balance in prioritising his time and energy. The eschatological orientation helps him to see which things are really important. It brings priorities into the right focus. In expecting the end of the present age, some things become more vital than others. The life of the eschatological Christian must be dedicated to God in service for others. Just as in the parable of the sheep and the goats, which occurs in the context of the discourse on the Second Coming,[85] the Christian knows that his service to Christ now is expressed in the person of the poor, the prisoner, the disadvantaged, the needy and miserable.

Eschatology – an Additional Motif

Lastly, as Kubo observed, Christian social ethics does not rest directly and fundamentally on eschatology.[86] Godlikeness and the commandment of love are, in his opinion, the basic warrant for social action. Jesus did not allow his predictions of the future to affect the content of his moral teaching. His teaching is directed towards the need of the neighbour and not towards eschatology. The story of the Good Samaritan, for example, lacks an eschatological motif. Jesus' command is simply, 'Go and do likewise'.[87]

However, the eschatological motif is not entirely absent either. Although not the primary reason, Kubo argued that 'a kind of "eschatological" motive for ethics appears in the parable of the rich fool (Luke 12: 13–21), i.e., that death can overtake us by surprise.'[88] Although the eschatological factor is rarely the primary reason for social ethics, it is nevertheless given on occasions as an additional motif. For Kubo, the significant factor in the discussion of the theology of the Second Coming, especially in the context of social ethics, is that 'the eschatological motive is not an excuse to be unconcerned with ethics but an additional basis to be intensely more so'.[89] In other words, the Second Coming need not be an obstacle for the involvement in human rights but should become, although not necessarily the primary, at least an additional incentive for social ethics.

CONCLUSION

Seventh-day Adventists, together with other Christians, find a basis for human rights in the dignity and human worth found in the theology of creation, in the nature of human beings created in the image of God, and especially in the understanding of the Kingdom of God in terms of present reality as well as the future expectancy. Beside this common theological basis for human rights, Seventh-day Adventists contribute to the understanding of the theory of human rights through such aspects of theology as: the importance of the moral law in the present life of each believer; the equality which the theology of Sabbath offers to all creation regardless of culture, time or circumstances as a sign of the true liberation; the self-understanding of the prophetic community raised to bring the present truth to the contemporary world; and the Second Coming of Christ which may not be the primary but certainly is additional incentive for justice, equality and peace.

Other important aspects of Christian theology, such as soteriology and ecclesiology, would also throw a certain light on the subject but cannot be dealt with in the scope of this book. Suffice it to say that Christian theology, and Adventist thought within it, do make a substantial contribution to the understanding of the human rights.

For the Christian, this understanding is not an academic theory. When accepted, it becomes his way of life. For the Christian, theory and practice are two sides of the same coin interwoven together, since the Christian believes that his salvation occurs only in his relationship with God. In his relationship to his fellow man, this salvation is tested. John, in his first epistle, put this thought in a nutshell: 'We love because he first loved us. If anyone says, "I love God", yet hates his brother, he is a liar. For anyone who does not love his brother, whom he has seen, cannot love God, whom he has not seen. And he has given us this command: Whoever loves God must also love his brother' (1 John 4: 19–21). For the committed Christian, an understanding and practical application of human rights concepts are second nature. They are a natural consequence of his faith in a loving God, who desires that human beings love him and one another and even place the interests of others before their own (Matt 22: 37–9).

Conclusion

Throughout its history the Seventh-day Adventist Church has reacted to human rights in an inconsistent and on occasions even contradictory way. While the anti-slavery and abolitionist movements attracted the attention of the pioneers during the church's infancy, issues of race relations and women's rights, for example, have not been consistently dealt with in the twentieth century. While the church's great emphasis on health education and its insistence on religious liberty brought it into direct relations with human rights, its members failed to apply human rights principles in such other areas as nationalism, totalitarianism and gender equality.

These inconsistencies of Adventism in dealing with human rights issues can be attributed to the lack of a developed social theology and ethics of human rights. Since its humble beginnings, Adventism's primary concern was to define its role within the wider Christian community. For that it turned to particular doctrines, 'the present truth', which, as Seventh-day Adventists believed, the Christian church neglected or forgot to focus on. During the time of formulating its beliefs, concentrating on its organisation, clarifying its self-understanding and finding its mission, the Adventist church, like the early church at its beginning in history, had little time to concentrate on social action for the wider community. Only matters of human rights which directly affected its members attracted the church's response. It would be too harsh to describe such pragmatic responses to protect its believers as an ethic of self-interest, as some commentators have suggested.[1] However, the church has grown to the point where it realises that it cannot react to issues of social injustice only when its members are in trouble.[2] Wider non-sectarian issues should also be the church's concern. For this reason, the Seventh-day Adventist Church must establish a consistent social theology. The present volume is a contribution to that theology with its emphasis on human rights.

One cannot fail to notice that Seventh-day Adventist policies were in most cases reactive instead of proactive. They were apologetic rather than positively influencing, more often pragmatic in character than based on *a priori* principles. Such was the case, for example, with religious liberty issues, race relations and military involvement in the first half of the church's existence. More recently, the similar pragmatic and reactive pattern of decision-making is present in the scope of divisive issues of nationalism and the role of women in ministry.[3] The current Adventism has a choice to make between concentrating on the problems or exploring the possibilities of the church. Instead of an ever-present apologetic and defensive stand of attempting to justify its existence, the church should offer a more proactive lead in a number of fields of study, especially relating to the issues of human rights which are so basic to any authentic Christian life.

As many conservative Seventh-day Adventists perceive, the church should look back to its pioneers and learn from them. However, contrary to conservative Adventist understanding, the church should not concentrate on internal struggle and debate, but place its effort in the radical element of the pioneers' attempt to put their beliefs into effect in a practical, positive and caring way. As one writer put it:

> The radical Protestant element in our past teaches us this about Adventist identity: that through the witness and example of radical discipleship we are to transform human consciousness and thus transform society, and that in this special calling we are to address the other churches as well as the great mass of unbelievers. This advances the usual conception of Adventist identity ... by linking it unmistakably with the task of social transformation.[4] (emphasis in original)

The early SDAs were involved in moral, social, economic and even political dilemmas of their time in a considerably greater measure than their counterparts in the first half of the twentieth century. An apparent status quo in the area of the poverty, escalation in racial tensions and a rapid decline in the area of equal opportunities, examined in Part II, illustrate that there was a considerable change in the church's attitudes and response to injustice and inequality. Possibly radicalism was substituted by institutionalism. This trend was somewhat reversed in the late 1950s and is coming back in a form of Adventist social neo-orthodoxy. However, it has still a long way to go within the grass-roots of Adventism.

The 'new theology' has been identified as a leading factor in this reversal of Adventist attitudes towards certain human rights. More recently the church's theologians have become interested in the hitherto neglected study of social theology for two reasons: it is first a response to the general social climate, and second, a consequence of dialogue with scholars outside the church. Then, they began to address it and practically apply the principles. Hence, the new ideas of how equally to share in leadership positions regardless of race, the renewed emphasis on Adventist piety and the new 'discoveries' in the area of the role and equality of women.[5]

Since the 'new theology' is identified with the left wing of the church, it comes as no surprise that most of the input on social theology and ethics comes from the left-of-centre segment of the church's scholars. A great percentage of the articles dealing with human rights and social ethics are printed or sponsored by the liberal minded journal *Spectrum*. Some of the authors whose contributions we commented on earlier left the denominational employment, while others are regarded as a radical element in Adventist theological circles. While it has been argued that the 'new theology' is the way forward for a socially involved church,[6] it does not mean that 'traditionalists' have no place in the fight for justice, equality and freedom. Social concern must never become an easy option in order to avoid distinctive Seventh-day Adventist teachings. However, it should be an unavoidable option because it springs from general Christian, as well as the more particular Seventh-day Adventist, teachings. Traditional theological themes with which each Seventh-day Adventist could identify should encourage all members of the church to get involved in the struggle for human rights. Such are, for example, the themes of creation, the importance of God's moral law, the meaning of the Sabbath, the prophetic role, the two aspects of the Kingdom, and the certainty of the second coming of Christ.

Individual initiation of many Adventist programmes in the area of human rights is another important factor which must not pass unobserved. While many Seventh-day Adventists may have been overwhelmed with the needs of the world they live in, some decided to do whatever their limits would allow. Hence, a number of individuals started what later became official world-wide programmes of the church. From the house fellowship group in the home of Mrs Henry Gardner, several individuals formed 'Dorcas and Benevolent Association'.[7] John Harvey Kellogg's individual efforts and charisma led to the establishment of such institutions and schemes as the Chicago Medical Mission, the Life Boat Mission, Medical Missionary and Benevolent Association, and others.[8] The so-called 'Ingathering' programme 'originated with Jasper Wayne, a travelling salesman of nursery stock'.[9] Robert Bainum is another example of what an individual can accomplish with the strong desire to help others.[10] The Adventist Development and Relief Agency and smaller organisations such as Adventist Refugee Care, Croatian Relief Organisation and other similar schemes have all been initiated by individual Seventh-day Adventists. These individual initiatives and efforts have led to great results being accomplished for the poor, the refugees, the disadvantaged minorities and the needy. Other Seventh-day Adventists should learn from these individuals that no effort is too small when the right attitude is shown to the people whose rights are denied in one way or another, even if it means taking a serious political role such as in the case of Uganda's Prime Minister, Babi Mululu Kisekka.[11] But whatever role Seventh-day Adventists assume in the concern for human rights, it must be to protect and elevate others.

This selfless task of giving oneself for others, as Jesus most eloquently illustrated in his life, is the highest calling in any theory of human rights. It assumes the inner concern for another human being which is based on the common fatherhood of God and on common brotherhood with other people created in the image of God. The Christian is therefore primarily concerned for his neighbour and tries to protect his neighbours' rights. Only in this context can the doctrine of the second coming, the Sabbatical principal of both weekly and annual Sabbaths, the context of the ten commandments and the principles of the Kingdom of God be meaningful and relevant. All these doctrines must be understood through a realism too often lacking in human rights programmes. And Christian realism remembers that God, first and foremost, offered salvation to humankind through Jesus Christ. Out of this salvation, and love expressed through the Incarnate God, selfless compassion and interest in helping others must result. It must never be the other way around. The Christian cannot bring about the Kingdom of God through any kind of individual or social effort. Only as a response to the Kingdom already established by Jesus can the Christian take on all the aspects and responsibilities of the Kingdom. Hence, the social gospel becomes the gospel which affects social as well as individual life. And finally, regardless of the temporary outcome of the fight for human rights, the permanent and ultimate outcome is assured in the promise of the Kingdom of Glory still to be realised. So, the effects of realised eschatology here and now still need to be fulfilled in the future aspects of that same eschatology. Between the two phases, Jesus' command 'Occupy till I come' must be meaningfully accomplished.

Seventh-day Adventists need to explore further their methods of interpreting the Bible. Adventist hermeneutics is still in its infancy, especially in relation to social ethics. Too often literalistic approach has overshadowed questions of the historical, grammatical, syntactical, literary and sociological context. Also, aspects of cultural conditioning must be taken into account as well as the progressive revelation of God embodied in Adventism in the adopted phrase 'the present truth'. More emphasis on hermeneutics is paramount if the right adaptation of the revelation of God is applied to the contemporary understanding of Christian attitudes towards human rights.

Finally, Adventist theology must be dynamic and vibrant not only in regard to apocalyptic and eschatological aspects, however important they are for Adventism and its self-understanding, but also in regard to socio-ethical and socio-political interests which a number of Adventist doctrines point to. Instead of an apologetic look at the doctrine of Sabbath, Seventh-day Adventists should explore and develop its meaning further. Rather than defensively arguing on which day Christians should worship, Adventists should begin to influence the society by exploring what their belief in the true Sabbath brings to society at large. The questions of 'when' and 'how' should be exchanged for 'what' and 'why' in the future debate on the Sabbath. Such wonderful concepts as 'equality', 'dignity', 'Sabbatical way of life', 'liberation' and 'a day of freedom' have not only bearings on human rights but also on other more general rights, for example in regard to the earth and the environmental ethics. Adventists should explore the depth of the Sabbath well and enrich their community with the beauty of the Sabbath concept.

This balance between eschatological and social aspects of Adventist theology is supposed by both the role of a contemporary prophetic community which the SDA church assumes, and, especially, by the two phases of the Kingdom. The second coming of Christ, as a second phase of the Kingdom which is 'not yet', must be equated with the first phase of 'here and now', which began with the Christ event. Social aspects of these doctrines, mostly missing in Adventist thought, should be researched further and applied to human rights both in theory and in practice.

Ultimately, Seventh-day Adventist church, as a Christian denomination, will look at its founder and analyse his attitude to social action. And Jesus' work is unequivocally tied with preaching the good news to the poor, proclaiming freedom for the prisoners, restoring sight to the blind, releasing the oppressed and proclaiming the acceptable era of the Lord's favour (Luke 4: 18–19). He invites his followers to pursue a similar life of concern for others. Selfless ethics of feeding the hungry, providing for the thirsty, the naked and the foreigner, looking after the sick and the disadvantaged prisoner is a prerequisite for entering the Kingdom, both 'now' and 'not yet' (Matt 25: 31–46). The human rights concern is, therefore, the ultimate test on which a church stands or falls in its understanding of God's nature and his desire for created humankind. The Seventh-day Adventist church, like any other Christian church, is not exempted from this test.

Notes

INTRODUCTION

1. Human rights were closely tied in ancient Greece to the premodern natural law doctrines found in Greek Stoicism. See the classic example of Antigone who defended her defying of Creon's command by asserting that she acted in accordance with the immutable laws of the gods.

   Roman law may similarly be seen to have allowed for the existence of a natural law in the *jus gentium* ('law of nations'). According to the Roman jurist Ulpian, natural law was that which nature assures to all human beings, not the state.
2. Thomas Paine, *The Rights of Man* (1971), 8th edition, pp. 47–8.
3. Philosophers who wrote extensively on aspects of human rights include John Locke, Thomas Paine, Montesquieu, Voltaire, Rousseau, and later John Stuart Mill. At the level of practice, one can see the idea not only in theory but also in constitutional innovations such as the Magna Carta (1215), the Petition of Right (1628) and the Bill of Rights (1689) in England, the Declaration of Independence (1776) in the United States of America, and the Declaration of the Rights of Man and the Citizen (1789) in France.
4. About the preparatory stages of the text of the 1948 United Nations Universal Declaration of Human Rights and its origin and significance see: United Nations, Secretary-General, *Preparatory Study Concerning a Draft Declaration on the Right and Duties of States* (1948); Nehemiah Robinson, *The Universal Declaration of Human Rights: Its Origin, Significance, Application, and Interpretation* (1958); and United Nations General Assembly, *The International Bill of Human Rights: Universal Declaration of Human Rights, International Covenant on Economic, Social and Cultural Rights, International Covenant on Civil and Political Rights, and Optional Protocol* (Ottawa: Human Rights Program, 1980; originally published in New York: United Nations, Office of Public Information, 1978).
5. See, for example, Amnesty International's annual reports; David Hayes, *Human Rights* (Wayland, 1980); and *Collection of Decisions of the European Commission on Human Rights* [periodical], vols 1–46 (1960–74).

CHAPTER 1

1. An historical sketch of the whole period of the first half of the nineteenth century with specific references to the Millerite revivalism of the 1840s in the United States can be found in Everett N. Dick, 'The

Millerite Movement, 1830–1845', *Adventism in America*, ed. Gary Land (Grand Rapids, Michigan: William B. Eerdmans Publishing Company, 1986), pp. 1–35; for more extensive studies, see George R. Knight, *Millennial Fever and the End of the World: A Study of Millerite Adventism* (Boise, Idaho: Pacific Press Publishing Association, 1993); David Leslie Rowe, 'Thunder and Trumpets: The Millerite Movement and Apocalyptic Thought in Upstate New York, 1800–1845' (PhD dissertation, University of Virginia, 1974); Ruth Alden Doan, *The Miller Heresy, Millennialism, and American Culture* (Philadelphia: Temple University Press, 1987); Gerard Damsteegt, *Foundation of the Seventh-day Adventist Message and Mission* (Grand Rapids, Michigan: Wm. B. Eerdmans, 1977); and Arthur W. Spalding, *Origins and History of Seventh-day Adventists*, 4 vols. (Washington, D.C.: Review and Herald Publishing Association, 1962). For Millerite revivalism of the mid-nineteenth century in Great Britain, see Hugh Ivor Brian Dunton, 'The Millerite Adventists and Other Millenarian Groups in Great Britain, 1830–1860' (PhD dissertation, King's College, University of London, 1984).

2. Claude Welch, *Protestant Thought in the Nineteenth Century*. Volume I, *1799–1870* (New Haven and London: Yale University Press, 1972), p. 192.
3. Michael D. Pearson, 'Seventh-day Adventist Responses to Some Contemporary Ethical Problems' (DPhil dissertation, Oxford University, 1986), p. 340. Later this dissertation was published as *Millennial Dreams and Moral Dilemmas: Seventh-day Adventism and Contemporary Ethics* (Cambridge: Cambridge University Press, 1990).
4. A description of William Miller and his work can be found in LeRoy Edwin Froom, *Movement of Destiny* (Washington, D.C.: Review and Herald, 1971), pp. 64–5. The most accessible source of information on leading personalities of the advent awakening is Froom's encyclopaedic work *Prophetic Faith of Our Fathers*, 4 vols. (Washington, D.C.: Review and Herald, 1945–53).
5. About the Disappointment and its aftermath, see R. W. Schwarz, *Light Bearers to the Remnant: The Denominational History Textbook for Seventh-day Adventist College Classes* (Boise, Idaho: Pacific Press, 1979), pp. 53–71.
6. Damsteegt (1977), pp. 98–9.
7. Joseph Bates, *The Autobiography of Elder Joseph Bates* (Battle Creek, Michigan: Steam Press, 1868), p. 262; and *Life of Joseph Bates: An Autobiography* (Takoma Park, Washington D.C.: Review and Herald, 1927), p. 186.
8. Controversy around organisation of the church and difficulty in choosing the name is best described in Andrew G. Mustard, 'James White and the Development of Seventh-day Adventist Organization, 1844–1881' (PhD. dissertation, Andrews University, Michigan, 1987); and Godfrey T. Anderson, 'Sectarianism and Organization, 1846–1864', *Adventism in America* (1986), pp. 36–65. See also 'Organization, Development of, In SDA Church', *Seventh-day Adventist Encyclopedia*, ed. Don F. Neufeld (Washington, D.C.: Review and Herald, 1976), pp. 1042–54.

9. Janice Daffern wrote in 1986 about the Disappointment of Advent believers in 1844 and how it psychologically and sociologically must affect modern Seventh-day Adventists:

   > Because we survived that winter of 1844–45, confused and uncertain about what God was really saying to us, we can share in the painful doubts of those who sometimes do not hear His voice in the tones of triumph. ... But the people of the disappointment will reach out to those who bear the signs of human brokenness. Communities of disappointment are our communities: the native Americans whose land became the place of someone else's kingdom-building; the black Americans whose labor built the empire but were systematically excluded from sharing in the fruits of their labor; and refugees who have sacrificed family connections and the comfort of home for an apocalyptic dream of America – only to become families with a father who drives a taxi, a mother with two jobs and children who quickly pick up disruptive American values. Celebrating the Advent hope, while forgetting the disappointment, permits a shallow optimism about ourselves and a blindness to those around us. We must continue to wait in hopeful anticipation but remember that like the Lord who was himself hungry and thirsty, a stranger and a prisoner, we are the disappointed.

   Janice Daffern, 'Singing in a Strange Land', in Roy Branson (ed.), *Pilgrimage of Hope* (Takoma Park, Maryland: Association of Adventist Forums, 1986), pp. 96–7.
10. See below pp. 29–35.
11. John N. Andrews, 'Thoughts on Revelation XIII and XIV', *Review and Herald*, (19 May 1851): 83. Cf. Hiram Edson, 'The Times of the Gentiles', *RH*, (24 Jan 1856): 129; R. F. Cottrell, 'Should Christians Fight?', *RH*, (9 May 1865): 180–81.
12. Anderson, 'Sectarianism and Organization' (1986), p. 57.
13. Spalding, *Origins* vol. 2 (1962), p. 258.
14. Ibid., p. 253.
15. Cf. 'Public Affairs and Religious Liberty, Department of', *SDA Encyclopedia* (1976), pp. 1158–64.
16. Original reference from *Review and Herald* 61:16 (1 January 1884). Also quoted in 'Religious Liberty', *SDA Encyclopedia* (1976), p. 1198.
17. 'Sentinel Library', *SDA Encyclopedia* (1976), p. 1320.
18. As quoted in 'Religious Liberty', *SDA Encyclopedia* (1976), p. 1198.
19. The vast majority of articles in *Sentinel* are on the issue of Sunday legislation. Adventists also took an active part in the political struggle against Sunday laws. Cf. Ben McArthur, '1893 The Chicago World's Fair: An Early Test for Adventist Religious Liberty', *Adventist Heritage* 2 (Winter 1975): 11–21; Spalding, *Origins*, vol. 2 (1962), pp. 239–62; Everett Dick, 'The Cost of Discipleship: Seventh-day Adventists and Tennessee Sunday Laws in the 1890's, *Adventist Heritage* 11: 1 (Spring 1986): 26–32.
20. W. Johnsson, 'An Ethical People', *Adventist Review* (22 January 1981), p. 13; E. Vick, 'Against Isolationism: The Church's Relation to the

World', *Spectrum* 8: 3 (March 1977): 38–40; T. Dybdahl, 'We Should Be Involved in Politics', *Spectrum* 8: 3 (March 1977): 33–7.

21. Pearson (1986), p. 351.
22. Charles Teel, 'Withdrawing Sect, Accommodating Church, Prophesying Remnant: Dilemmas in the Institutionalization of Adventism' (unpublished manuscript of the presentation at the 1980 Theological Consultation for Seventh-day Adventist Administrators and Religion Scholars, Loma Linda University, 1980), p. 42.
23. In the last 20 years Adventists have established affiliated organisations such as ADRA (Adventist Development and Relief Agency), ARC (Adventist Refugee Care), SAWS (The Seventh-day Adventist World Service), COSIGN (Church of the Saviour – International Good Neighbours), etc. See below pp. 27 and 65–70.
24. On Kellogg's separation from the church, see Terje Jacobsen, 'Some Main Developments Leading Up to Dr. John Harvey Kellogg's Separation From the Seventh-day Adventist Church' (Andrews University, 1981); and Richard W. Schwarz, 'John Harvey Kellogg: American Health Reformer' (PhD dissertation, University of Michigan, 1964).
25. John Harvey Kellogg, *The Living Temple* (London, 1903).
26. Spalding, *Origins*, vol. 3 (1962), p. 335.
27. J. Wintzen, *Der Christ und der Krieg* (Berlin: Selbstverlag, 1915), p. 12. Cf. Johannes Hartlapp, 'Military Service – A Comparative Study Between the New Testament Teaching and the Attitude of German Adventists' (MA thesis, Andrews University, 1993)
28. 'Declaration of Principles of the Council of the European Division Committee', as quoted in Erwin Sicher, 'Seventh-day Adventist Publications and the Nazi Temptation', *Spectrum* 8: 3 (March 1977): 12.
29. Richard W. Schwarz, *Light Bearers* (1979), p. 425.
30. Sicher, *Spectrum* 8: 3 (March 1977): 13.
31. 'An unsere Gemeindeglieder in Deutschland', *Der Adventbote* 39: 17 (15 August 1933): 1–4, quoted in Sicher (1977), p. 15.
32. S. [Kurt Sinz], 'Der Retter', *Der Christliche Hausfreund*, vol. 2, no. 5 (1933), p. 67.
33. Otto Bronzio, 'Der Tatigkeitsbericht des Advent-Wohlfahrts-werkes', *Der Adventbote* 44: 16 (15 August 1938): 251.
34. Sicher (1977), p. 16.
35. W. K. Ising, 'Zur Lage in Palestina', *Der Adventbote* 41: 24 (15 December 1935): 377; 'Botenmeldung', *Der Adventbote* 43: 9 (1 May 1937): 128.
36. Jack M. Patt, 'Living in a Time of Trouble: German Adventists Under Nazi Rule', *Spectrum* 8: 3 (March 1977): 3.
37. W. Eberhardt, 'Der Gegenwartige Stand der Schulfrage', *Der Adventbote* 44: 21 (1 November 1938): 331.
38. Johannes Langholf, 'Arbeitsdienstpflicht', *Aller Diener* 7: 4 (1 October 1933): 84.
39. Patt (1977), p. 3.
40. *Der Adventbote* 40: 16 (15 August 1934): 256.
41. Otto Bronzio, *Was tun die Adventisten in der Wohlfahrts Pflege*, Tatigkeitsbericht für die Zeit vom 1. Januar bis zum Dezember 1937

(Hamburg: Adventverlag, n.d.). pp. 15–16, translated by Sicher in 'Adventist Publications' (1977), p. 19.

42. [Kurt Sinz], Editorial, *Der Adventbote* 44: 8 (15 April 1938): 128.
43. [Kurt Sinz], 'Im Strom der Zeit', *Der Adventbote* 45: 21 (1 November 1939): 305.
44. 'Wer da sat im Segen, der wird auch ernten im Segen', quoted in Sicher (1977), p. 21.
45. Charles Scriven, 'The Oppressed Brother: The Challenge of the True and Free Adventists', *Spectrum* 13: 3 (March 1983): 30.
46. Sicher (1977), p. 21.
47. E. Berner, 'Was schliesst die Heimatmission ein?', *Der Adventbote*, vol. 40, no. 21 (1 November 1934), p. 323.
48. Sicher (1977), p. 21.
49. J. Wintzen (1915), p. 12.
50. In 1981 Clifford Sorensen, President of Walla Walla College, travelled to the Soviet Union and met members of the True and Free Seventh-day Adventist Church. He expressed the above notion about the 1924 Conference in Moscow in an interview entitled 'The Oppressed Brother: The Challenge of the True and Free Adventists', *Spectrum* 13: 3 (March 1983): 28.
51. Sorensen points out to three primary reasons why the True and Free Adventists think the officially recognised church has distorted Adventist beliefs:

    > First, the apparent willingness, as they perceived it, of the official church to cooperate with military service requirements of the government – to the point even of bearing arms; second, the willingness of the church to cooperate with the government regarding prior approval of sermons and government supervision of the transfer of ministers from one congregation to another, and third, the apparent willingness of the church members to send their children to school on the Sabbath and to cooperate in government-enforced programs in the autumn, when young people are required to harvest crops on the Sabbath. (ibid., p. 27)

52. Ibid., p. 26.
53. The best example of this challenging and confrontational style can be observed in the leaders of the True and Free Seventh-day Adventists as described by Marite Sapiets in *True Witness: The Story of Seventh Day Adventists in the Soviet Union* (Keston: Keston College Publication, 1990).
54. Sapiets describes the life and work of Vladimir Shelkov focusing especially on his human rights endeavours in chapter 5 of her book *True Witness* (1990), pp. 68–92.
55. Sapiets, 'Shelkov and the True and Free Adventists', *Spectrum* 11: 4 (June 1981): 27.
56. *Chronicle of Current Events* (Russian edition), No. 53, p. 25, quoted in Sapiets (1978), p. 31.
57. Vladimir Shelkov sent the longest and most descriptive letter 'Facts on the flouting and violation of the Helsinki Agreement and all just laws by the dictatorship of state atheism'. In it he quoted the human

rights clauses of the Helsinki Final Act and contrasted them with the actual policy of the Soviet state towards religion in 70 individual cases of Seventh-day Adventists suffering under the regime because of their beliefs. Shelkov, 'Obrascheniye k pravitelyam gosudarstv – uchastnikam Belgradskogo soveshchaniya' [Appeal to the leaders of states participating in the Belgrade Conference] (Samizdat: June 1977), p. 1. See some sections of this letter reprinted in Sapiets (1990), pp. 3–15.

58. 'Amnesty International Asks Adventists to Help', *Spectrum* 13: 3 (March 1983): 27.
59. Ibid.
60. Sapiets (1981), pp. 31–2.
61. Scriven (1981), p. 29.
62. Cf. Sapiets (1981), p. 32, and *Religious Prisoners in the USSR: A Study by Keston College* (Keston College: Greenfire Books, 1987), pp. 121–4.
63. Keston News Service, 'Government Razes Romania's Largest Adventist Church', *Spectrum* 18: 1 (October 1987): 28–9.
64. Sidney Reiners, 'Catarama's Romanian Ordeal – Where was the Church?', *Spectrum* 18: 1 (October 1987): 26.
65. Ibid., p. 27.
66. Reiners suggested that the church received oral assurances that Adventists will be able to renovate two buildings to house a church and conference headquarters. Reiners, (1986), p. 31. The question, however, remains about the ethical implications of such a compromise.
67. Another example of misuse of the official position for giving misinformation about the church situation in Eastern Europe can be demonstrated by the example of Hungarian Adventists. The situation of the Seventh-day Adventist Church in Hungary is complex and, for an outside observer, difficult to understand. However, one thing is clear. The registered church has made a number of administrative mistakes in the past and about 1300 believers were disfellowshipped without any apparent reason. The Western leaders have tried to resolve the tension and make compromises several times, but without success. There might be more success in the future since the Hungarian Union has been transferred to the Trans-European Division with its headquarters in England. See an excellent exposition about problems within Hungarian Adventism in Sidney Reiners, 'Betrayal in Budapest', *Adventist Currents* (September 1986): 10–15.
68. About the organisational structure of the SDA Church, see 'Division' and 'Organization, Development of, in SDA Church', in *SDA Encyclopedia* (1976), pp. 393–4, and 1042–54.
69. Ray Dabrowski, 'Voicing Church's Concerns', *Northern Light* (April 1987): 3.
70. Ibid.
71. Bob Nixon, 'Neal C. Wilson on Religious Liberty Issues in the Soviet Union', *Northern Light* (April 1987): 4.
72. Roy Branson, 'College Student Leaders Meet *Spectrum*, Amnesty International', *Forum Newsletter* (July 1988): 2.
73. Adventist Refugee Care, For Active Assistance to Refugees (Huizen, Holland: Stichting Adventist Refugee Care, n.d.); Cf. Jurrien den

Hollander, 'New Opportunities for Mission in Europe', *Newbold Forum* 4 (Winter 1989): 12.

74. Cf. 'SDA World Service, Incorporated', *SDA Encyclopedia* (1976), pp. 1335–6. In recent years ADRA International has taken over the work of SAWS.
75. Roy Branson, 'Massacre at Sea', *Spectrum* 12: 3 (April 1982): 23.
76. Ibid., p. 24.
77. D. D. N. Nsereko, 'Adventist Revolutionary Leads Uganda', *Spectrum* 17: 4 (May 1987): 12.
78. Gene Daffern, 'Adventist Layman Helps Indochinese Refugees', *Spectrum* 12: 4 (April 1982): 31.
79. Branislav Mirilov, 'An Examination of the Response of the Seventh-day Adventist Church to Some Contemporary Socio-Political Issues in the Light of the Two Distinctive Adventist Doctrines: A Comparison of North America and Former Yugoslavia' (PhD dissertation, University of Birmingham, 1994), pp. 250–67. Mirilov's contribution is also significant in the wider context of the Adventist response to socio-political issues in the former Yugoslavia from its beginnings until the present day. See ibid., pp. 146–279.
80. This situation somewhat resembles to what was being said about the German Adventism during the Third Reich. See above, pp. 17–21.
81. Miroslav Vukmanic, '... U Ratnim Uvjetima', *Odjek* (July/August 1991): 11. Also the official Adventist statement against participating in a war was published in Roberto Vacca, 'Pred Problemima Svijeta', *Adventisticki Pregled* 1 (January/February 1993): 10.
82. Although somewhat cautiously, Mirilov brings out both these points (1994, pp. 257, 261).
83. 'What is ADRA?', *Bulletin of the Humanitarian Agency*, no. 8 (May–August 1992), p. 4.
84. Ivan Halozan, 'Rad "ADRE" u Ratnim Uvjetima' ('ADRA's Work in the War Conditions'), *Bilten Humanitarne Organizacije ADRA*, no. 8 (November/December 1991): 5.
85. John Arthur, 'ADRA Delivers 17,000 letters and 4,500 Food Parcels to Sarajevo', *ADRA Advertiser*, 4: 1.
86. Cf. Tihomir Kukolja, 'People Whose Needs Ought to be Our Priority!', *Bulletin of the Humanitarian Agency ADRA*, no. 10 (May–August 1992), pp. 20–1; Ray Dabrowski, 'Slike iz Europske Hirosime', *Bulletin of the Humanitarian Agency ADRA*, no. 10, pp. 8–9; 'More Aid for Croatia', *Bulletin of the Humanitarian Agency ADRA*, no. 10, p. 19, reprinted from *CROPaper*, the official publication of the Croatia Relief Organization established by Croatian Adventists in Australia in June 1992; section 'Rat u Hrvatskoj i BiH' ['War in Croatia and Bosnia and Herzegovina'], *Adventpress* (January–February 1993), pp. 6–7, for an eye-witness account of the horribly destructive war against Croatia and how the local church congregation tried to cope with it see Mirta Didara, 'Osijecka Stvarnost', *Odijek* (Nov–Dec. 1991), pp. 8–9; Tihomir Kukolja, 'Sarajevo 1993', *Adventisticki Pregled*, no. 3 (May–June 1993), pp. 1–5; Josip Takac, 'Adventisti u Ratu' ['Adventists in the War'], ibid., pp. 26–7; etc.

87. Mirilov (1994), p. 258.
88. Kukolja, Adventpress Newsfax to Christain Schaffler, APD Basel, Zagreb, 21 January 1992. See also Zdenko Hlisc-Bladt, Letter to Jan Paulsen, Zagreb, 9 September 1991.
89. Lorencin, Letter to Zdenko Hlisc, Belgrade, 3 September 1991, p. 1.
90. Zdenko Hlisc-Bladt, Letter to Dr. Jan Paulsen, Zagreb, 10 October 1991, p. 2.
91. Ibid.
92. 'TED Approves New Structure Changes in Former Yugoslavian Union', *Adventist News Review* (8 July 1992); 4; Jan Paulsen, Letter to Zdenko Hlisc-Bladt, St Albans, 17 June 1992.; K. C. van Oossanen, Letter to Zdenko Hlisc-Bladt, St Albans, 17 July 1992. See also recommendations of the West Conference that led to the separation in Kukolja, *Adventpress Releases* of 11 May 1992 and 8 June 1992; and Martin Anthony, 'Report on Situation in West Yugoslavian Conference as at September 18, 1991', p. 5.

    In August 1992, the first Constituency Session was held for Croatian-Slovenian Conference at the Marusevec Adventist Seminary, Croatia, where the constituency formally approved the new conference status linking it directly with the Trans-European Division and elected Zdenko Hlisc-Bladt as president. See 'First Constituency Session Held for Croatia-Slovenia Conference', *Adventist News Review* (11 September 1992): 2–3.
93. 'Change of Name for Yugoslavian Union', *Adventist News Review* (10 June 1992): 4.
94. See, for example, 'Stradalo desetak adventistickih crkava' ['Ten Adventist Churches Ruined'], *Vjesnik* (10 December, 1991); 'Zabreh Zagrebu', *Vjesnik* (30 November 1991); 'Jos jedna zrtva' ['Yet Another Dead'], *Vecernji List* (30 December 1991); 'ADRA pomaze' ['ADRA helps'], *Vjesnik* (11 November 1991); Biserka Lovric, 'Dobri duh Marusevca' ['Marusevec's Good Spirit'], *Vecernji List* (17 November 1991); 'ADRA obnavlja Vocin' ['ADRA Restores Vocin'], *Vecernji List* (19 May 1992); etc.
95. *Spectrum, ADRA, Outlook.*
96. This lack of interest is illustrated by the fact that in the course of two and a half years of the war in former Yugoslavia, not one article in the official church publications appeared against or even about the war, not one special collection for members of the church in the affected areas was organised, not one official prayer meeting was called for in order to pray for peace and for the members of the church in Croatia or Bosnia.
97. Christian B. Schaffler, 'Letter to Mr. Kukolja' (Basel, 5 September 1991), p. 1. [A copy of the letter available from the Adventist Press Service file and from the author's personal file.]
98. Jovan Lorencin, 'Circular Letter to be Read Before the Church' (Belgrade, 27 May 1992).
99. Ibid., p. 2.
100. Jovan Slankamenac, 'Otvoreno Pismo' ['An Open Letter'] (Varazdin, Croatia, 18 May 1992).

101. Zdenko Hlisc-Bladt, 'Letter to Ministers Where the Circular Letter Had Been Sent' (Zagreb, Croatia, 10 June 1992), p. 2.
102. Zdenko Hlisc-Bladt, 'Letter to Dr. Jan Paulsen on behalf of the Executive Committee of the West Conference' (Zagreb, Croatia, 9 September 1991), p. 3.
103. Cf. Martin L. Anthony, 'Report on Situation in West Yugoslavian Conference as at September 18, 1991' (unpublished report done by the Trans-European Division representative after the visit to Croatia, St Albans, England, 1991), p. 5.
104. Zdenko Hlisc-Bladt, 'Letter to Dr. Jan Paulsen', (Zagreb, Croatia, 9 September 1991), p. 1.
105. The President of the Trans-European Division significantly said after leading the meetings in Republic of Macedonia: 'When feelings of nationalism and ethnic consciousness rise to the fore, as is regrettably the case in much of former Yugoslavia, it has devastating consequences for relationships between peoples. Sadly, the church is not sheltered from this. And these sentiments are at the root of the rebellious upheaval by the small group of anarchists in our church in Macedonia', in 'Church Services Disrupted in Former Yugoslav Republic of Macedonia', *Adventist News Review* (16 February–4 March 1993): 2. See also on the issue of Macedonian Adventism 'Church Structure Reorganisation for the Former Yugoslav Republic of Macedonia', *Adventist News Review* (1–15 December 1992): 2; 'Church in Macedonia Organised Into a Mission', *Adventist News Review* (21–30 June 1993): 2; Ray Dabrowski, 'Separatist Movement in Macedonia Disrupts Church', *Far Eastern Division Outlook* (April 1993); and Stefan Mitrov, 'The Macedonia Mission Executive Committee Report Prepared for the TED Session in November 1993'.
106. Mirilov (1994), p. 265.
107. John Arthur, 'Croats, Muslims and Serbs Appreciate ADRA's Helping Hand!', *ADRA Advertiser* 4: 2.
108. Zdenko Hlisc-Bladt, 'Letter to Dr. Jan Paulsen' (Zagreb, Croatia, 9 September 1991), p. 2.
109. Ibid., p. 1.
110. See 'Lifeline for a Besieged City', *European* (28 May 1993); Goran Rosic and Vesna Radivojevic, – 'Najvazniji je – Covek, "Adra", humanitarna organizacija Adventisticke crkve, heroj rata' [The Most Important is – Man, ADRA, Humanitarian Organisation of Adventist Church, the Hero of the War'], *Borba* (3–4 April 1993); 'Adra hvala ti!' ['Thank You ADRA'], *Borba*, (3–4 April 1993); ALFA, 'Istrazivanje Javnog Mijenja' ['Examination of Public Opinion'], *Dani* (10 September 1993), p. 15; 'Morali smo pomoci ljudima' ['We Had to Help People'], *Sarajevske Srpske Novine* (7 September 1993), p. 7; and 'Sinonim humanosti', *Oslobodenje* (26 April 1993).
111. In October 1996 at its Annual Council in Costa Rica, the church released positive and timely statements which give lead and direction in the area of social ethics and human rights. 'A Statement on Human Relations', 'A Statement on Smoking & Tobacco, ' 'A Statement

Regarding Smoking and Ethics', 'A Statement on Stewardship of the Environment', 'A Statement on the Environment', 'Caring for Creation – A Statement on the Environment', 'Family Violence', 'A Statement on Abuse and Family Violence', and 'Homelessness and Poverty', are among number of other statements and guidelines published by the Communication Department of General Conference of Seventh-day Adventist Church under the title *Statements, Guidelines and Other Documents: A Compilation*, ed. Ray Dabrowski (Hagerstown, MD: Review and Herald, 1996).

112. Joe Mesar, 'Sakharov and Solzhenitsyn: Dialogue on the Good Society', *Spectrum* 8: 3 (March 1977). 32.
113. John Stott, *Issues Facing Christians Today: A Major Appraisal of Contemporary Social and Moral Questions* (Basingstoke: Marshalls, 1984), p. 14.
114. *Evangelism and Social Responsibility: An Evangelical Commitment* (Lausanne Committee for World Evangelization and the World Evangelical Fellowship, 1982), p. 61.

CHAPTER 2

1. Slavery, which directly opposed justice, freedom and equality – the greatest notions of democracy – was apparently the only human right violation condemned by the pioneers of Adventism which did not incorporate some self-interest or direct benefit. Racism, as a separate issue, is discussed in Chapter 4.
2. By the beginning of the twentieth century the Adventist mission developed in such measure that Adventism became an international denomination. Human rights and in particular religious liberty concepts based on 'American democracy' assumptions were challenged and differently explained and applied in European countries, the Middle and Far East, Australia and later in Latin America. See, for example, pp. 17–25 and 29–35.
3. About the Millerite movement and its leaders' 'blessed hope' in the second coming of Christ, see R. W. Schwarz, *Light Bearers* (1979), pp. 24–52; and Wayne R. Judd, 'William Miller: Disappointed Prophet', in *The Disappointed: Millerism and Millenarianism in the Nineteenth Century*, ed. Ronald L. Numbers and Jonathan M. Butler (Bloomington and Indianopolis: Indiana University Press, 1987), pp. 17–35.
4. The Millerites calculated the 2300 evening/mornings of Daniel 8: 14 from 457 BC to 1844 AD.
5. At least three major groups stemmed from the post-Disappointment Millerites: (1) those who repeatedly set times for Christ's return; (2) those who continued in the Advent hope but differed little from other Protestants; (3) those who became eventually Seventh-day Adventists. Cf. Schwartz, *Light Bearers* (1979), pp. 56–8; T. Housel Jemison, *A*

Prophet Among You (Mountain View, California: Pacific Press, 1955), pp. 197–9; and Everett N. Dick, 'The Millerite Movement, 1830–1845', *Adventism in America*, ed. Gary Land (1986), pp. 31–5.

6. See Fundamental Belief 24 in Ministerial Association, General Conference of Seventh-day Adventists, *Seventh-day Adventists Believe ... A Biblical Exposition of 27 Fundamental Doctrines* (Hagerstown, Maryland: Review and Herald, 1988), p. 332.
7. In the book *Seventh-day Adventists Answer Questions on Doctrine* (Washington D.C.: Review and Herald, 1957) a number of prominent Adventist theologians and administrators elaborate on this doctrine: 'In summation: Seventh-day Adventists believe that Christ's Second Advent will be personal, visible, audible, bodily, glorious, and premillennial, and will make the completion of our redemption. And we believe that our Lord's return is imminent, at a time that is near but not disclosed' (p. 463) This visible coming of Jesus Christ is believed to be in the very close future. Therefore sometimes it is called the 'soon' Second Coming of Jesus. Cf. Lawrence Maxwell, 'Christ Coming Soon', in *Signs of the Times* (January 1971).
8. Quoted in Spalding, (1962), 1: 29, n. 4.
9. Joseph Bates, *Life of Joseph Bates* (1927), p. 186.
10. Cf. E. S. Gaustad, *Rise of Adventism* (New York: Harper & Row, 1974).
11. This self-awareness of being a movement with the message of proclamation came somewhat later after the initial 'shut-door period' through which the Advent believers thought that God's mercy is closed and salvation is not available to those who were not part of the pre-1844 Advent movement. See, for example, 'Open and Shut Door', in *SDA Encyclopedia* (1976), pp. 1034–6; Spalding, (1962), 1: 158–65; Schwarz, *Light Bearers*, (1979), pp. 55, 69–71; Arthur L. White, 'Ellen G. White and the Shut Door Question' (unpublished paper, 1971); Ingemar Lindén, *1844 and the Shut Door Problem* (Uppsala and Stockholm: Libertryck Stockholm, 1982); and Ingemar Lindén, *The Last Trump: An Historico-Genetical Study of Some Important Chapters in the Making and Development of the Seventh-day Adventist Church* (Frankfurt-am-Main, Bern and Las Vegas: Peter Lang, 1978), pp. 85–105.
12. Damsteegt, *Foundations* (1977), pp. 263–308.
13. Emmett K. Vandevere, 'Years of Expansion, 1865–1885', *Adventism in America* (1986), p. 66.
14. See in *SDAs Believe* (1988), p. 248.
15. Everett Dick, 'The Cost of Discipleship: Seventh-day Adventists and Tennessee Sunday Laws in the 1890's', *Adventist Heritage* 11: 1 (Spring 1986): 26–32.
16. Cf. 'Liberty', 'Sabbath Sentinel' and 'Sentinel of Christian Liberty', *SDA Encyclopedia* (1976), pp. 785, 1264–5 and 1320.
17. Jonathan Butler, 'The Seventh-day Adventist American Dream', *Adventist Heritage* 3: 2 (Summer 1976): 9.
18. Ibid.
19. As quoted in Ben McArthur, '1893 The Chicago World's Fair: An Early Test for Adventist Religious Liberty', *Adventist Heritage* 2 (Winter 1975): 17.

20. Ellen G. White, Ms. 16, 1890. Published in part in Ellen G. White, *Evangelism* (Washington, D.C.: Review and Herald, 1946), p. 179.
21. International Religious Liberty Association, Association Internationale pour la Défense de la Liberté Religieuse, Council on Religious Freedom, International Academy for Freedom of Religion and Belief, Public Affairs and Religious Liberty Department of General Conference of Seventh-day Adventists, etc. See also the very important magazine *Liberty* and its European counterpart *Conscience and Liberty* published in several European languages. These publications would be very important in the context of human rights discussion but for the fact that they are almost exclusively concerned with one issue – namely, religious liberty. Again, the church becomes involved only when and where its members religious liberty is at stake. See discussion above, pp. 14–16.
22. Cf. Timothy L. Smith, *Revivalism & Social Reform: American Protestantism on the Eve of the Civil War* (Baltimore and London: Johns Hopkins University Press, 1980), pp. 151–8 and 221–37.
23. See *SDAs Believe* (1988), p. 362.
24. *A Sociological Yearbook of Religion in Britain 7*, ed. Michael Hill (London: SCM Press, 1974), p. 127.
25. *Evangelism and Social Responsibility* (1982), pp. 37–8.
26. See below discussion on the Kingdom of God, pp. 168–84.
27. (Grand Rapids: William B. Eerdmans, 1978), p. 153. Cf. Walter Eichrodt, *The Theology of the Old Testament*, vol. I (Philadelphia: The Westminster Press, 1961); F. C. Fensham, 'Covenant, Promise and Expectation in the Bible', in *Theologishe Zeitschrift* 23 (1967): 305–22; and D. R. Hillers, *Covenant: The History of a Biblical Idea* (Baltimore: 1969).
28. (Mountain View, California: Pacific Press, 1982), pp. 16–17.
29. Roy Branson, 'Covenant, Holy War, and Glory: Motifs in Adventist Identity', in *Spectrum* 14: 3 (December 1983): 21; and Michael Pearson, 'Covenant and Ethics', in *Righteous Remnant Series: Adventist Themes for Personal and Social Ethics* (unpublished article, 1987); this has been published in Charles W. Teel, Jr (ed.), *Remnant & Republic: Adventist Themes for Personal and Social Ethics* (Loma Linda University Center for Christian Bioethics, 1995).
30. Over 110 articles can be found in *Review and Herald* alone on the theme of 'Covenants' between 1850 and 1900. Cf. 'Covenants from 1850–1900' (Review and Herald Research, April 16, 1975. Stored in EGW Centre, Europe).
31. Ellen G. White, Letter 16, 1892.
32. Pearson, 'Covenant and Ethics' (1987) p. 2.
33. 'Covenant', in Siegfried H. Horn, *Seventh-day Adventist Bible Dictionary*, rev. edn (Washington: D.C.: Review and Herald, 1979), p. 243.
34. 'Ellen G. White Statements of Possible Service in a Study of the Covenants' (unpublished material stored in EGW Centre, Europe).
35. Ellen G. White, 'Our Covenant Relation not Realized by Many', *General Conference Bulletin* (1 April 1903).
36. White, 'God's Covenant with Israel', Ms 64, 1903.
37. White, 'Compact Between God and Christ', Ms 16, 1890.

38. White, 'God's Covenant with Israel', Ms 64, 1903.
39. White, 'Conditions of Salvation the Same', Letter 216, 1906; and 'Ratification of the Sinaitic Covenant', in Ms 126, 1901.
40. White, *Counsels on Stewardship* (Washington D.C.: Review and Herald, 1940), pp. 74, 257.
41. White, *Ministry of Healing* (Washington, D.C.: Review and Herald, 1905), p. 396.
42. White, *Testimonies to the Church* 2 (Mountain View, California: Pacific Press, 1948), p. 273.
43. White, *Evangelism* (1946), p. 618.
44. White, *Testimonies* 7 (1948), p. 243.
45. Pearson (1987), p. 2.
46. Ibid., p. 3.
47. Branson, 'Covenant, Holy War, and Glory: Motifs in Adventist Identity', in *Spectrum* 14: 3 (December 1983): 21–4.
48. Pearson (1987), pp. 6–7.
49. Ibid., p. 5.
50. Ibid.
51. Ibid.
52. Lev 20: 2.
53. Pearson (1987), p. 6.
54. Deut 24: 19–21. Cf. Joe Mesar, 'Income-Sharing in the Local Church', *Spectrum* 16: 2 (1985): 24–8.
55. Pearson (1987), p. 6.
56. There is a sense, especially in Western Europe and the Third World countries, where Adventism may be influenced too much by American values and opinions. 'Westoxification' is a term sometimes used to describe the influx of Western values and practices to other non-Western cultures. In this case American Adventism could be said to be guilty of 'Westoxification' of world-wide Adventism. Cf. Borge Schantz, 'The Development of Seventh-day Adventist Missionary Thought: Contemporary Appraisal' (PhD dissertation, Fuller Theological Seminary, 1983)
57. Pearson (1987), p. 7.
58. Ibid., p. 4.
59. Ibid., p. 9.
60. For a very good exposition of the origin, development and contemporary approaches to the concept of remnant in Seventh-day Adventism, see Stephen Paul Mitchell, '"We are the Remnant": A Historical, Biblical, and Theological Analysis of Seventh-day Adventist Ecclesiological Self-Understanding' (MA thesis, Loma Linda, California: Loma Linda University, September 1988). Also see a very significant contribution on the remnant theme by Jack Provonsha, *A Remnant in Crisis* (Hagerstown: Review and Herald, 1993).
61. Pearson, 'Seventh-day Adventist Responses' (1986), p. 6. Cf. Pearson, 'Covenant', (1987) p. 4.
62. William G. Johnsson, 'Seventh-day Adventism: A Profile' (unpublished paper presented to the Conference of Secretaries of Christian World Communions, London, 21–24 October 1985, pp. 18, 20.

63. Edward W. H. Vick, 'Against Isolationism: The Church's Relation to the World', *Spectrum* 8: 3 (March 1977): 40.
64. Adventists often tend to create nuclei or communities in which they feel protected and secure. These 'ghettos' are often around church's institutions such as schools, hospitals or food factories.
65. Cf. Pearson, *Millennial Dreams* (1990), pp. 23–6.
66. Dybdahl, 'We should be Involved in Politics', *Spectrum* 8: 3 (March 1977): 37.
67. Pearson (1986), p. 351.
68. Adventists have never elaborated or clarified their understanding of pragmatism as a philosophical concept. It only affected them as a way of practical thinking and decision-making which one could also call adaptability or flexibility. For more about the Kantian concept of *pragmatisch* and American application of pragmatism, see Bruce Kuklick, *The Rise of American Philosophy: Cambridge, Massachusetts, 1860–1930* (New Haven and London: Yale University Press, 1977), pp. 49–54, 121–5 and 266–74; Robert Handy, 'Pragmatism', *A New Dictionary of Christian Ethics*, ed. John Macquarrie and James Childress (London: SCM Press, 1986), pp. 491–4; and H. S. Thayer, 'Pragmatism', *The Encyclopedia of Philosophy* 8 vols, ed. Paul Edwards (New York: Macmillan and The Free Press, and London: Collier Macmillan Publishers, 1967) 6: 430–6.
69. Some observed that Adventist moral teaching constituted a 'fine-tuning' of traditional Christian morality. The highly specific prohibitions, or as one author labelled them, 'taboos', included the consumption of tea, coffee, alcohol beverages, spices, meat (especially pork), the use of tobacco, cosmetics, the wearing of immodest dress and jewellery, card-playing, gambling, theatre-going, etc. See Pearson, *Millennial Dreams* (1990), pp. 43–4; and Gary Schwartz, *Sect Ideologies and Social Status* (Chicago: University of Chicago Press, 1970), pp. 116–36. See also original references in Ellen White writings, *Education* (1903), p. 202; *Ministry of Healing* (1905) pp. 327–30; *Messages to Young People* (Nashville, Tennessee: Southern Publishing Association, 1930), pp. 380, 398–400; *Counsels on Diet and Foods* (Takoma Park, Washington: Review and Herald, 1938), pp. 373–416, and 420–31; *Counsels on Health* (Mountain View, California: Pacific Press, 1951), p. 114; and *The Adventist Home* (Nashville, Tennessee: Southern Publishing Association, 1952), pp. 517–18.
70. Theobald, 'From Rural Populism to Practical Christianity: The Modernization of the Seventh-day Adventist Movement', *Archives de Sciences Sociales des Religions* 60: 1 (July–September 1985): 114.
71. Jonathan Butler, 'The World of E. G. White and the End of the World', *Spectrum* 10: 2 (August 1979): 7.
72. Pearson (1990), p. 51.
73. See below, chapters 4 and 5.
74. For a good article about the concept of individualism in Christian ethics see Roger L. Shinn, 'Individualism', *A New Dictionary of Christian Ethics* (1986), pp. 295–7.

    Shinn points out that Jesus' teachings that, for example, God numbers the hairs on the heads of persons, and that there is more joy in heaven over one repentant sinner that over 99 people who need no repentance, and that Jesus was also the solitary man as representative person, might have influenced what is commonly called 'Protestant individualism'.

75. Ibid., p. 297.
76. E. Chellis, 'The Review and Herald and Early Adventist Response to Organized Labor', *Spectrum* 10: 2 (August 1979): 25; and Pearson (1990), pp. 40–1.
77. Ellen White, *Desire of Ages* (Mountain View, California: Pacific Press, 1898), p. 509.
78. Pearson (1990), p. 42.
79. Shinn, 'Individualism' (1986), p. 297.

CHAPTER 3

1. Elmer T. Clark, an influential sect-typologist is a typical example in his *The Small Sect in America* (New York, 1949) as cited in Ronald Graybill, 'Millennarians and Money: Adventist Wealth and Adventist Beliefs', *Spectrum* 10: 2 (August 1979): 32. See also David F. Aberle, 'A Note on Relative Deprivation Theory as Applied to Millennarian and Other Cults', in Sylvia L. Thrupp (ed.), *Millennial Dreams in Action* (New York, 1970), pp. 209–14. Most modern scholars, however, argue that millennial and other sectarian groups rise out of the middle-class society. See, for example, Bryan Wilson, *Religious Sects: A Sociological Study* (London: Weidenfeld & Nicolson 1970).
2. Ronald Graybill, 'Millennarians and Money' (1979): 32.
3. Walter R. Goldsmith, 'Class Denominationalism in Rural California Churches', *American Journal of Sociology* 49 (January, 1944): 351; Gary Schwartz, *Sect Ideologies and Social Status* (Chicago: Chicago University Press, 1970), pp. 9–17, 90–136, 194–202; and John M. Donahue, 'Seventh-day Adventism and Social Change Among the Aymara of Southern Peru' (unpublished paper, Columbia University, 1972).
4. Ellen G. White, *Welfare Ministry* (Washington, D.C.: Review and Herald, 1952), p. 270; originally published in Manuscript 11, 1892.
5. Ibid., p. 189; originally written in the 'Australian ministry period' between 1891 and 1900.
6. Ibid., pp. 45–6; first published in *Review and Herald* (1 January 1895).
7. Calvin B. Rock, 'Did Ellen White Downplay Social Work?', *AR* (5 May 1988), p. 6.
8. Ibid.
9. See numerous entries on 'Stewards(s)' and 'Stewardship' in *Comprehensive Index to the Writings of EGW*, vol. 3 (Mountain View, California: Pacific Press, 1963), pp. 2635–6.
10. White's major aspects of the concept of stewardship were published in *Counsels on Stewardship* (1940).
11. Cf. White, 'The Principle of Stewardship', *RH* (12 September 1899).

12. White, 'We Must Care', *AR* (5 May, 1988), p. 38. Cf. White's article from *RH* (26 June 1894) reprinted in *Welfare Ministry* (1952), p. 16.
13. White, 'We Must Care' (1988), p. 38.
14. Jan Paulsen, 'Social Service/Social Action: Is That Also God's Mission?' (Presentation to the Institute of Missiology, Newbold College, Bracknell, 1988), pp. 4–5. Later this presentation was published with the same title in *Adventist Missions Facing the 21st Century: A Reader*, ed. Hugh I. Dunton, Baldur Ed. Pfeiffer and Borge Schantz (Frankfurt am Main: Peter Lang, 1990), pp. 142–3.
15. Calvin B. Rock, 'Did Ellen White Downplay Social Work?' (1988): 6; White, 'We Must Care' (1988), p. 38.
16. Letter, Ellen G. White to Dr. John H. Kellogg (3 February 1895).
17. White, Letter (3 February 1895).
18. *RH* 16 (30 October 1860): 192.
19. 'Community Services', *SDA Encyclopedia* (1976), p. 343.
20. 'Dorcas Welfare Societies', *SDA Encyclopedia* (1976), p. 399.
21. Ibid.
22. Ibid.
23. Ellen G. White, *Ministry of Healing* (1903), pp. 195–6.
24. Richard William Schwarz, *John Harvey Kellogg, M. D.* (Nashville, Tennessee: Southern Publishing Association, 1970), p. 163.
25. *SDA Daily Bulletin*, IV (10 March 1891): 114–15, quoted in Schwarz, 'John Harvey Kellogg' (1964), p. 324.
26. Richard W. Schwarz, 'Adventism's Social Gospel Advocate John Harvey Kellogg', *Spectrum* 1: 2 (Spring 1969): 19.
27. Ibid.
28. Many Seventh-day Adventist churches today do similar work on a local church level. For example, in 1990 the Youth Federation of Seventh-day Adventists in London organised 'Walkathon for Homeless 1990', a sponsored walk to raise money for the homeless of London. There are other similar programmes on a weekly basis which attempt to help the poor, the hungry and the homeless.
29. White, Letter to J. H. Kellogg, 14 June 1895. The meaning of 'soul' in this (evangelistic) SDA context is a spiritual dimension of each person.
30. White, Letter to J. H. Kellogg, 15 July 1895.
31. Jonathan Butler, 'Ellen G. White and the Chicago Mission', *Spectrum* 2: 1 (Winter 1970): 47.
32. *The Life Boat* 5 (Febuary 1902): 33, quoted in Butler, 'White and the Chicago Mission', p. 47.
33. Schwarz, 'John Harvey Kellogg' (1964), p. 333.
34. Richard Rice, 'Adventists and Welfare Work: A Comparative Study', *Spectrum* 2: 1 (Winter 1970): 57.
35. White, 'Our Compassionate Saviour', *The Life Boat* (September 1909): 263, quoted in Butler, 'White and the Chicago Mission', p. 47. See above note 29.
36. Cf. 'City Missions', in *SDA Encyclopedia* (1976), pp. 305–6.
37. Schwarz (1964), p. 13.
38. Schwarz (1970), p. 153.

39. Schwarz (1964), p. 340.
40. Ibid., p. 336.
41. Hereafter MMBA.
42. Schwarz (1970), p. 162.
43. Schwarz (1964), pp. 318–19.
44. Ibid., p. 85.
45. Ibid.
46. See Terje Jacobsen, 'Some Main Developments Leading Up to Dr. John Harvey Kellogg's Separation From the Seventh-day Adventist Church' (unpublished paper, Andrews University, 1981).
47. Cf. 'Kellogg, John Harvey', *SDA Encyclopedia* (1976), p. 723.
48. International MMBA, *The Medical Missionary* 9 (May 1899), p. 16, quoted in Schwarz, 'Adventism's Social Gospel Advocate', *Spectrum* 1: 2 (Spring 1969): 61.
49. Gary Land (ed.), *Adventism in America* (1986), p. 146.
50. Keld J. Reynolds, 'The Church under Stress, 1931–1960', *Adventism in America* (1986), p. 170.
51. 'SDA World Service, Incorporated', *SDA Encyclopedia* (1976), p. 1335.
52. Ibid., p. 1336.
53. Ray Tetz, 'The Adventist Development and Relief Agency (ADRA)', *AR* (5 May 1988): 23.
54. *SDA Encyclopedia* (1976), p. 645.
55. Ibid., p. 646.
56. Monte Sahlin, 'Adventist Community Services', *AR* (5 May 1988): 21.
57. Ibid.
58. Tetz, '(ADRA)' (1988): 23.
59. Heikki J. Luukko, *ADRA – TED Update*, (11 April 1989): 3.
60. Tetz (1988): 23.
61. Ralph S. Watts, 'ADRA – Partners With the Poor', *AR* (5 May 1988): 10.
62. Ibid.
63. 'Render Effective Aid to Children', *REACH Report* (December 1988): 12.
64. Jasmine E. Jacob, 'REACH International Helps Needy Children', *AR* (17 May 1979): 18.
65. Ibid., p. 17.
66. 'More Aid for Croatia', *Bilten Humanitarne Organizacije ADRA* 10 (May–August 1992): 19.
67. 'Organizing for Success', *CROPaper* 1 (June 1992): 3.
68. 'Krscanska Jednakost u Raznolikosti', *Nas Glas* 9: 32 (1993): 8.
69. 'More Aid for Croatia', *CROPaper* 1 (June 1992): 1.
70. 'Krscanska Jednakost u Raznolikosti', *Nas Glas* 9: 32 (1993): 8.
71. 'Organizing for Success', (1992): 3.
72. Ibid.
73. *World Development Report* (World Bank, Washington, D.C., 1978), p. iii, as quoted in Stott, (1984), p. 213. See also a report on poverty in David B. Barrett (ed.), *World Christian Encyclopedia* (Oxford: Oxford University Press, 1982).
74. Stott (1984), p. 213.
75. H. J. Luukko. 'ADRA's Role', *Light* 37 (February 1987): 2.

76. *ADRA Annual Report 1983–84*, chaired by Kenneth J. Mittleider (Washington, D.C.: University Printers, 1984), p. 1.
77. Ibid., pp. 3–4.
78. Ibid., p. 14; and Luukko, 'ADRA's Role' (1987): 2.
79. 'Adventists are Peacemakers, International Year of Peace 1986', *Light* 36 (April 1986): 1.
80. Stott (1984), p. 212.
81. Poverty and the Churches, *Newsletter No. 112 of the Church of England General Synod's Board for Social Responsibility* (January 1983), p. 3.
82. Andrew Purvis, 'No Particular Place to Go', *Midweek* 17 (March 1988): 10–11.
83. Margaret Robertson, 'People Helping People', *Communicator* (December 1987): 3.
84. Ibid.
85. William G. Johnsson, 'Seventh-day Adventism: A Profile', Paper presented to the Conference of Secretaries of Christian World Communions, (London, 21–24 October 1985), p. 20.
86. 'Safari Leads Student to Sobering Conclusions on Poverty and Injustice', *AR* (13 October 1988): 20.
87. William G. Johnsson, 'Christians in a Needy World', *AR* (5 May 1988): 5.

CHAPTER 4

1. Although women in the church have not been in a minority, they have received a minority status. A significant contribution on the subject of race, gender and other relationships has been published in Human Relationship Series: Sakae Kubo, *The God of Relationships: How to Reach Across Barriers such as Race, Culture, and Gender* (Hagerstown, MD: Review and Herald, 1993).
2. Joseph Bates, *The Autobiography* (1868), p. 236.
3. Joseph Bates, *Life of Joseph Bates* (1927), p. 186 and *The Autobiography* (1868), p. 277.
4. As cited in Jonathan Butler, 'Race Relations In the Church, Part I, The Early Radicalism', *Insight* (30 January 1979), p. 9.
5. Ibid., pp. 8–9.
6. Ibid., p. 10; cf. Malcom Bull and Keith Lockhart,, *Seeking a Sanctuary: Seventh-day Adventism & the American Dream* (San Francisco: Harper & Row Publishers, 1989), pp. 193–4.
7. Cf. Butler, *Insight* 30 (January 1979), p. 9.
8. Bull and Lockhart, *Seeking a Sanctuary* (1989), p. 194.
9. Butler, *Insight* (30 January 1979), p. 10.
10. Ellen G. White, *Testimonies 1* (1948), pp. 359, 360.
11. Ibid., p. 264 and White, *Early Writings* (Washington, D.C.: Review and Herald, 1882), pp. 275, 276.
12. White, *Early Writings* (1882), p. 275.
13. White, *Testimonies 1* (1948), p. 264.

14. White, *Testimonies 7* (1948), p. 225.
15. White, *Testimonies 9* (1948), p. 206–8, 214.
16. Roy Branson, 'Ellen G. White – Racist or Champion of Equality?', *RH* (9–23 April 1970).
17. White, *Testimonies 9* (1948), p. 214.
18. Cf. Ellen G. White, Letter 136, 1898 (to J. E. White and his wife, 14 August 1898), Ellen G. White, Letter 156, 1900 (to James Edson White, 10 December 1900), J. E. White, *The Southern Work* (Washington, D.C.: Review and Herald, 1966), p. 84.
19. White, *Testimonies 9* (1948), p. 207 (original date of the statement is 19 October 1908). Cf. Ronald D. Graybill, *Ellen G. White and Church Race Relations* (Washington, D.C.: Review and Herald, 1970), pp. 70–87.
20. James Edson White, 'Labor for the Two Races', *Gospel Herald* III (January 1901), p. 4.
21. Ibid.
22. Ibid.
23. Cf. Ellen G. White, Letter 5, 1895 (to 'My Brethren in Responsible Positions in America', 24 July 1895).
24. White, Manuscript 7, 1896 ('The Colored People').
25. Ibid.
26. White, Letter 26 1900 (to W. S. Hyatt, 15 February 1900).
27. For additional information about formation of black conferences see Benjamin Reeves, 'The Call for Black Unions', *Spectrum* 9: 3 (July 1978): 2–3; Penelope Kellogg Winkler, 'Black Adventists Hold Ministry Meeting' *Spectrum* 14: 4 (March 1984): 61; and Bull and Lockhart (1989), pp. 193–206.
28. Jonathan Butler, 'Race Relations in the Church, Part 3–Black Adventists Protest', *Insight* (13 February 1979), pp. 15, 16; see also Joe Mesar and Tom Dybdahl, 'The Utopia Park Affair and the Rise of Northern Black Adventists', *Adventist Heritage*, vol.1, no.1 (January 1974), pp. 34–41, 53–6. A somewhat different view on Humphrey as 'a leader far in advance of his time' is given by W. W. Fordham in *Righteous Rebel: The Unforgettable Legacy of a Fearless Advocate for Change* (Washington, D.C.: Review and Herald, 1990), pp. 71–2.
29. A phrase used by one of the activists and leaders of the Oakwood student strike of 1931. See a participants description in Fordham (1990), p. 27.
30. Ibid., p. 30.
31. Ibid., p. 29.
32. Ibid., p. 73.
33. Ibid.
34. Black workers were not permitted to eat in the Review and Herald cafeteria with other workers until the 1950s.
35. Fordham suggested that in some instances the salary of a white intern was larger than the salary of an ordained black pastor.
36. Such as when one of the prominent leaders of the General Conference remarked in a black church in Detroit, after listening to the choir

singing, 'When I get to heaven I'm coming over on your side to enjoy again this beautiful singing by the choir.' Cited in Fordham (1990), p. 75.

37. For example, Lucy Byard, a fair-skinned member of the Seventh-day Adventist church in Brooklyn, was admitted without hesitation to the Washington Sanatorium in 1943. However, before her treatment begun, her admission slip was reviewed. When Byard's racial identity was discovered, she was informed that there was mistake in her admission and she was wheeled out into the corridor and transferred by car to the state hospital without examination or treatment. She died soon afterwards of pneumonia.
38. Cf. Butler, *Insight* (13 February 1979), p. 16, and Fordham, (1990), pp. 78–83.
39. Bull and Lockhart (1989), pp. 202, 203.
40. Robert Kennedy, 'Gender and Race in the Church', *Spectrum* 2: 2 (March/April 1994): 9.
41. Bull and Lockhart (1989), p. 204.
42. Ibid.
43. Cf. Reeves, 'The Call for Black Unions' (1978): 2–3.
44. In this capacity he automatically became a vice-president of the General Conference, the highest organisational body of the Church. Also, North American Division is, by far, the greatest contributor to the finances of the church, cf. *Seventh-day Adventist Year book 1981* (Washington, D.C.: Review and Herald, 1981), p. 4.
45. Winkler, 'Black Adventists' (1984): 60.
46. Ibid., p. 61.
47. Cf. Reeves, (1978): 2–3.
48. Timothy L. Smith, 'Four Great Ideas In Adventism – An Evangelical's Testimony', *Spectrum* 14: 3 (December 1983): 4.
49. White, Letter 80-a, 1895 (to J. E. White, 16 August 1895).
50. White, Manuscript 7, 1896 ('The Colored People').
51. White, *Testimonies 7* (1948), p. 225.
52. Roy Branson, *RH* (16 April 1970), p. 9.
53. White, Letter 80-a, 1895, to J. E. White and wife, 16 August 1895.
54. White,*Testimonies 7* (1948), p. 223.
55. Branson, *RH* (16 April 1970), p. 9.
56. White, Manuscript 107, 1908 ('The Color Line').
57. White, *Testimonies 7* (1948), p. 223.
58. Talbert O. Shaw, 'Racism and Adventist Theology', *Spectrum* 3: 4 (Autumn 1971): 29.
59. Ibid., p. 33.
60. Ibid.
61. Ibid.
62. Ibid., pp. 34–5.
63. Ibid., p. 35.
64. Ibid.
65. Ibid., p. 36.
66. Ibid., p. 37.
67. Emory J. Tolbert, *Spectrum* 2: 2 (Spring 1970), p. 51.

68. Ibid.
69. Johnson A. Adeniji, *Of One Blood* (Grantham, Lincolnshire: The Stanborough Press, 1980), p. 30.
70. Ibid., p. 31.
71. 'A Christian Declaration On Race Relations', *Spectrum* 2: 2 (Spring 1970): 53–5.
72. 'SDA Church Issues Statement on Human Relations', *Communicator* (1988).
73. Ibid.
74. Ibid.
75. (London: Scripture Union, 1968), p. 83.
76. Cf. *Yazoo City Sentinel* (7 June 1900), and ibid. (1 June 1900), quoted in James Edson White, 'The Southern Field Closing to the Message', in *Gospel Herald* II (October 1900), pp. 86 and 88.
77. Fordham (1990), p. 82.
78. As cited by Fordham (1990), p. 115.

CHAPTER 5

1. Cf. Ronald D. Graybill, 'The Power of Prophecy: Ellen G. White and the Women Religious Founders of the Nineteenth Century' (DPhil. dissertation, Johns Hopkins University, Baltimore, Maryland, 1983), p. iii.
2. Pearson probably rightly suggests that James White, M. W. Howard, G. W. Morse and others primarily defended Ellen White's special role as a messenger favoured by the Lord above others rather than call for equal opportunities at this stage (1990), pp. 144–5.
3. James White, 'Unite and Gifts of the Church', *RH* (7 January 1858): 69.
4. D. Hewitt, 'Let Your Women Keep Silence in the Churches?', *RH* (15 October 1857): 190.
5. See for example, S. C. Welcome, 'Shall Women Keep Silence in the Churches?' *RH* (23 February 1860): 109–10; J. N. Andrews, 'May Women Speak in Meeting?', *RH* (2 January 1879); James White, 'Women in the Church', *RH* (29 May 1879); and G. C. Tenney, 'Woman's Relation to the Cause of Christ', *RH* (24 May 1892).
6. Bull and Lockhart, *Seeking a Sanctuary* (1989), p. 182.
7. John G. Beach, 'The Role of Women in Leadership Positions within the Seventh-day Adventist Church' (unpublished paper, Andrews University Theological Seminary, 1971), p. 33.
8. Ibid., p. ii.
9. Ibid.
10. Bull and Lockhart (1989), p. 180.
11. Beach (1971), p. 33.
12. Ellen White, Letter 231, 1899.
13. White, Letter 77, 1898.
14. White, Manuscript 43a, 1898.
15. White, Letter 13, 1893.
16. White, Manuscript 47, 1898; Manuscript 149, 1899; Letter 137, 1898.

17. White, Letter 137, 1898.
18. Bull and Lockhart (1989), p. 183. Cf. a chart of women workers and administrators in 'Adventist Women in Leadership', *AR* (4 February 1988): 16.
19. Bertha Dasher, 'Leadership Positions: A Declining Opportunity?', *Spectrum* 15: 4 (December 1984): 35.
20. Reprinted from Dasher, 'Leadership Positions', *Spectrum* 15: 4 (December 1984): 36–7.
21. Robert Pierson, 'True Christian Woman Power', *RH* (4 February 1971): 2.
22. Ibid.
23. Ibid.
24. Cf. M. McLeod, *Betrayal* (Loma Linda, California: Mars Hill Publications, Inc., 1985).
25. See, for example, Tom Dybdahl, 'Merikay and the Pacific Press: Money, Courts and Church Authority' *Spectrum* 7: 2 (1975): 44–53; T. Dybdahl, 'Merikay and the Pacific Press: An Update' *Spectrum* 8: 1 (1975): 44–5; Robert H. Pierson, 'When the Church is Taken to Court', *RH* (24 March 1977): 6–8; N. C. Wilson, 'Pacific Union Settles Litigation', *RH* (5 January 1978): 17–18; N. C. Wilson, 'Pacific Press Suit Settled out of Court', *RH* (30 March 1978): 32; a series of articles in *Spectrum* 8: 4 (1977): 2–36.
26. Pearson (1990), p. 161.
27. Brenda Butka, 'Women's Liberation', *Spectrum* 3: 4 (Autumn 1971): 22–8.
28. Leona Running, 'The Status and Role of Women in the Adventist Church', in *Spectrum* 4: 3 (Summer 1972): 61; N. Vymeister, 'Women of Mission', *Spectrum* 15: 4 (December 1984): 38–43.
29. *RH* (28 November 1974): 19.
30. About the significance of the scholarly endeavour at the Camp Mohaven in defining the role of women in the church and discussions on the question of women ordination see below, pp. 97–100 and 104–11.
31. Bull and Lockhart (1989), p. 189.
32. Ibid., p. 190. Cf. 'The Original Camp Mohaven Document' *The Adventist Woman* 12: 4–5 (September–October 1993): 6.
33. Cf. Kit Watts, 'Standing on the Verge of Jordan', *The Adventist Woman* 12: 4–5 (September–October 1993): 3; Leona Glidden Running, 'Careful Study and Common Sense', ibid., 12: 4–5 (September–October 1993): 3; Elisabeth Wear, 'Mohaven Council on the Role of Women in the Church: The Final Grade is Pending', ibid., 12: 4–5 (September–October 1993): 2. The whole issue of 12: 4–5 (September–October 1993) is entitled 'Remember Mohaven!: A Special Issue Commemorating the 20th Anniversary of the Council on the Role of Women in the Church, Sept. 16–19, 1973'. Also, 'The 1973 Annual Council's Response to the Mohaven Report' can be found.
34. *Symposium on the Role of Women in the Church* ed. Julia Neuffer (Biblical Research Institute Committee, General Conference of Seventh-day Adventists, 1984).
35. Rebecca F. Brilhard, 'Directory of Groups Addressing Concerns of Women in the Adventist Church', in *Spectrum* 19: 5 (July 1989): 46.

36. Ibid., pp. 46–50.
37. Elwyn Platner, 'SECC Constituents Urge GC Study Commission to Ordain Women', *The Adventist Woman* (June/July 1989): 3.
38. Jocelyn Fay, 'Ordination Issue Squelched; Commission on Justice Established', *The Adventist Woman (*December 1990), p. 1.
39. Roy Branson, 'Doing What is Right is Doing What is Wise' (letter to Potomac Conference Committee members, 24 August 1995), reprinted in *Spectrum* 25:1 (September 1995): 49 – 51.
40. Charles Scriven, 'World Votes No to Women's Ordination', *Spectrum* 25:1 (September 1995): 30–2, Stella Ramirez Greig, 'Conference Within a Conference', *Spectrum* 25:1 (September 1995): 20–4, and Roy Branson, 'Utrecht 1995: Editor's Notebook', *Spectrum* 25:1 (September 1995): 8–12.
41 'Action of Sligo Church in Business Session, August 1, 1995', *Spectrum* 25:1 (September 1995): 39; 'Sligo's Action: The Documents: Towards a Documented History of How and Why Sligo Chose to Ordain Women to Gospel Ministry', *Spectrum* 25:1 (September 1995): 37–62; Bryan Zervos, 'A Sacred Moment at Sligo', *Spectrum* 25:1 (September 1995): 33–6
42 Emily Tillotson, 'College Church Pursues Equality in Ministry', *Adventist Today* 4:5 (September/October 1996): 24 and 'Adventist Women Confer Regarding "Crossroads"', *Adventist Today* 4:6 (November/December 1996): 9. See also on La Sierra University Church's action in 'Why should the La Sierra University Church ordain women for gospel ministry?', prepared by a subcommittee of the La Sierra University Church Board, (La Sierra University Church, Riverside, California, November 1995).
43 As quoted in Bryan Zervos, 'A Sacred Moment at Sligo', *Spectrum* 25:1 (September 1995): 33.
44. James White, 'Women in the Church', *RH* (29 May 1879).
45. Ibid.
46. G. C. Tenney, 'Woman's Relation to the Cause of Christ', *RH* (24 May 1892).
47. Ibid.
48. Ibid.
49. Ibid.
50. Ibid.
51. J. N. Andrews, 'May Women Speak in Meeting?', *RH* (2 January 1879).
52. Ibid.
53. White, *Welfare Ministry* (1952), p. 143.
54. Ibid., p. 145, White, *Evangelism* (1946), pp. 464–6, 493.
55. Ibid., p. 492.
56. White, Letter 138, 1909; and in *RH* (18 May 1911), p. 1.
57. Roger W. Coon, 'Ellen G. White's View of the Role of Women in the S.D.A. Church' (unpublished manuscript, Washington, D. C.: Ellen G. White Estate, General Conference of SDAs, 1986), p. 7.
58. White, 'The Duty of the Minister and the People', *RH* (9 July 1895): 2.
59. Pearson (1990), pp. 148–9.
60. See 'Appendix H'in Roger W. Coon (1986), p. 24.

61. White, Manuscript 43a, 1898; *Testimonies 6* (1948), p. 322; and *Testimonies 8* (1948), p. 230.
62. Coon (1986), p. 12.
63. See above, pp. 94–7.
64. The historical outline which led to the meeting in Ohio is described in Bert Haloviak, 'The Long Road to Mohaven: A Look at the People, Events and Historical Circumstance that Moved the Church Toward Action', in *The Adventist Woman* 12: 4–5 (September–October 1993): 1–2.
65. Cf. 'The Camp Mohaven Papers', *The Adventist Woman* 12: 4–5 (September–October 1993): 6.
66. Only 20 years later was the original Camp Mohaven document published as 'The Original Camp Mohaven Document', *The Adventist Woman* 12: 4–5 (September–October 1993): 6.
67. Pearson (1990), p. 161.
68. Leona Running, 'Study of the Role of Women in Israel, in the Background of the Contemporary Near East' (unpublished manuscript, 1973).
69. Kit Watts, 'The Role of Women in the Seventh-day Adventist Church' (unpublished manuscript, 1972).
70. Raoul Dederen, 'The Role of Woman Today: A Theology of Relationship – Man to Woman' (unpublished manuscript, 1972).
71. Gerhard F. Hasel, 'Man and Woman in Genesis 1–3', *Symposium* (1984), pp. 10–27; also published in a shorter form as 'Equality From the Start: Woman in the Creation Story', *Spectrum* 7: 2 (1975): 21–8.
72. Ibid., p. 14.
73. Ibid., p. 26.
74. Ibid., p. 21.
75. Ibid., p. 26.
76. Ibid., p. 27.
77. Kenneth L. Vine, 'The Legal and Social Status of Women in the Pentateuch', *Symposium* (1984), p. 44.
78. Ibid.
79. Jerry A. Gladson, 'The Role of Women in the Old Testament Outside the Pentateuch', *Symposium* (1984), p. 60.
80. Walter F. Specht, 'Jesus and Women', *Symposium* (1984), p. 79.
81. Ibid.
82. Ibid., p. 82.
83. Ibid., p. 89.
84. Ibid., p. 90.
85. J. Sot. iii. 4 19a, 7 cited in Specht (1984), p. 90.
86. Specht (1984), p. 96.
87. Sakae Kubo, 'An Exegesis of 1 Timothy 2: 11–15 and its Implications' *Symposium* (1984), p. 97.
88. Ibid., p. 101.
89. On Kubo's 'principles of interpretation' see below, p. 118.
90. Kubo (1984), p. 105.
91. Ibid., pp. 105–6.
92. Ibid., p. 106.

93. Frank B. Holbrook, 'A Brief Analysis and Interpretation of the Biblical Data Regarding the Role of Women', *Symposium* (1984), pp. 107–7.
94. Betty Stirling, 'Society, Women and the Church', *Symposium* (1984), p. 163.
95. Raoul Dederen, 'A Theology of Ordination', *Symposium* (1984), p. 183.
96. Ibid., p. 184.
97. Ibid., p. 195.
98. Wadie Farag, 'Women's "Distinctive Duties"', *The Ministry* (October 1973): 10.
99. James Londis, *Spectrum* 15: 4 (December 1984): 52–8.
100. Ibid., p. 54.
101. Ibid., p. 55.
102. Ibid., p. 56.
103. Ibid., p. 57.
104. James Londis, 'The Gospel Demands Equality *Now*', *Spectrum* 19: 5 (July 1989): 41.
105. Richard Davidson and Skip MacCarty, 'Biblical Questions On Women and Ministry', *Spectrum* 19: 5 (July 1989): 29.
106. Ibid., p. 31.
107. Beatrice S. Neall, 'A Theology of Woman', *Spectrum* 19: 5 (July 1989): 14–28.
108. Ibid., p. 15.
109. Ibid.
110. Ibid., p. 16.
111. Ibid.
112. Ibid.
113. Ibid., p. 17.
114. Ibid.
115. Ibid., p. 19.
116. Ibid., p. 23.
117. Ibid.
118. Ibid.
119. Ibid.
120. Ibid., p. 24.
121. Samuel Bacchiocchi, 'Ministry or Ordination of Women?', *Spectrum* 17: 2 (December 1986): 20–5. and 'Bacchiocchi Responds to Criticism', *Spectrum* 17: 2 (December 1986): 34–5. See also his *Women in the Church* (Berrien Springs, Michigan: Biblical Perspectives, 1987).
122. Bryan Ball, 'The Ordination of Women: A Plea for Caution', *Spectrum* 17: 2 (December 1986): 39–43.
123. Sakae Kubo, 'An Exegesis of 1 Timothy 2: 11–15 and Its Implications', *Symposium* (1984), p. 106. 106.
124. Sakae Kubo, 'The Bible and the Ordination of Women: A Bibliographical Essay', *Spectrum* 7: 2 (1975): 32.
125. Ibid., p. 33.
126. Ibid.
127. Sakae Kubo, 'An Exegesis' (1984), p. 102.
128. Ibid.
129. Ibid., p. 106.

130. Gladson (1984), p. 60.
131. Ibid.
132. Ibid., p. 61.
133. Holbrook (1984), p. 118.
134. Beatrice Neall, 'A Theology of Woman', *Spectrum* 19: 5 (July 1989): 14.
135. Ibid., p. 15.
136. Ibid.
137. See, for example, several articles printed in *Adventist Today* (January/February 1996) such as Ivan Blazen: 'Women, Culture and Christ: Hearing Scripture Yesterday and Today', David Larson, 'What Adventists Can Learn from John Wesley: The Wesleyan Quadrilateral', Leon Mashchak, 'God Means What He Says What He Means'. Also see Fritz Guy, 'The Moral Imperative to Ordain Women in Ministry' (unpublished paper, La Sierra University, California, 1995).

CHAPTER 6

1. Francis D. Nichol, 'The Church and Social Reform' *RH* (15 April 1965), p. 13.
2. George Colvin, 'Social Conscience at the General Conference', *Adventist Currents* (September 1986), p. 34.
3. Colvin points out that Wilson did not 'obtain any assistance on these statements from anyone educated in specific areas related to the topic of the statements', ibid.
4. Bull and Lockhart (1989), p. 80; Cf. Bull and Lockhart, 'The Intellectual World of Adventist Theologians', *Spectrum* 18: 1 (1987): 33–4.
5. Jack W. Provonsha, *God Is With Us (*Washington D.C.: Review and Herald, 1974), p. 45.
6. Provonsha, 'The Health of the Whole Person' (cassette tape, Loma Linda University, March 1985).
7. Bull and Lockhart (1989), p. 80.
8. Don Hawley, *Come Alive Feel Fit – Live Longer* (Washington D.C.: Review and Herald, 1975), p. 144.
9. 'A Distinctive World View', *AR* (24 June 1982), p. 12.
10. Roy Branson, 'Celebrating the Adventist Experience', *Spectrum* 12: 1, p. 3.
11. Ibid., p. 4.
12. Ibid.
13. Ibid., p. 5. The evil of alcohol use and abuse is described in a chapter on 'Alcohol and Society' in Ellen White's compilation *Temperance As Set Forth in the Writings of Ellen G. White* (Mountain View, California: Pacific Press, 1949), pp. 23–54.
14. See, for example, Schwarz, *John Harvey Kellogg* (1964); Schwartz, 'Adventism's Social Gospel Advocate' (1969): 15–28.; 'A Distinctive World View' *AR* (24 June 1982): 12–14.; Roy Branson, 'Celebrating the Adventist Experience', *Spectrum* 12: 1 (September 1981): 2–5.

15. W. G. Johnsson, 'An Ethical People', *AR* (22 January 1981): 13.
16. Roy Branson, 'Celebrating', (1981), p. 5.
17. G.C. [editorial], 'The Social Gospel versus Christ's Gospel', *AR* (7 June 1979): 14.
18. Fritz Guy, 'The Church and its Future: Adventist Theology Today', *Spectrum* 12: 1 (September 1981), p. 11.
19. Andrew Gordon Mustard, 'James White and the Development of Seventh-day Adventist Organization, 1844–1881' (PhD dissertation, Andrews University, 1987), p. 201.
20. James Walters, 'Toward an Adventist Ethic', *Spectrum* 12: 2 (December 1981): 4.
21. Ibid., p. 2.
22. Something which is attempted below, pp. 198–206.
23. Waltors (1981) p. 4.
24. Pearson (1990), p. 21.
25. Ibid.
26. Ibid., p. 22.
27. James J. Londis, 'Waiting for Messiah: The Absence and Presence of God in Adventism', *Spectrum* 18: 3 (February 1988): 8.
28. Ibid., p. 9.
29. Ibid., p. 10.
30. Ibid.
31. See earlier discussion on pragmatic approach of SDAs in the nineteenth century, above, pp. 48–9.
32. Pearson (1990), p. 50.
33. Ibid., p. 51.
34. George Colvin, 'Social Conscience at the General Conference'*Adventist Currents* (September 1986), p. 40.
35. Ibid.
36. Walters, 'Toward an Adventist Ethic' (1981), p. 3.
37. Johnsson, 'An Ethical People' (1981), p. 13.
38. Branson, 'Celebrating' (1981), p. 5.
39. Kent D. Seltman, 'Christian Brotherhood: The Foundation of the Church', *Spectrum* 12: 1 (September 1981): 16.
40. Ibid., p. 17.
41. Guy, 'The Church and its Future' (1981), p. 11.
42. An increased interest in a Biblical concept of remnant can be found in shortened and revised doctoral dissertation on the remnant motif in the Old Testament in Gerhard Hasel, *The Remnant: The History and Theology of the Remnant Idea From Genesis to Isaiah* (Berrien Springs, Michigan: Andrews University Press, 1974). The remnant idea, as a self-examining concept can be found in an increasing number of studies in the late 1980s. For example, Stephen Paul Mitchell, 'We are the Remnant' (1988); the whole issue of *Adventists Affirm* 2: 2 (Fall 1988); Kit Watts, 'The Remnant Is as the Remnant Does', *AR* (3 September 1992): 5; Provonsha, *A Remnant in Crisis* (1993); and recent examination of the remnant concept in the context of socio-political activity of the church in Mirilov, 'An Examination of the Response' (1994).
43. 'A Distinctive World View', *AR* (24 June 1982): 12.

44. Bryan Wilson, 'Sect or Denomination: Can Adventism Maintain Its Identity?', *Spectrum* 7: 2 (Spring 1975), p. 41.
45. See below (pp. 139–41) for discussion on *Questions on Doctrine* and Adventists–Evangelicals Dialogue.
46. Charles Scriven, 'Radical Discipleship And the Renewal of Adventist Mission', *Spectrum* 14: 3 (December 1983): 11; Scriven, *The Transformation of Culture: Christian Social Ethics After H. R. Niebuhr* (Scottdale: Herolds Press, 1988); W. Leslie Emmerson, *The Reformation and the Advent Movement* (Washington D.C.: Review and Herald, 1983). Also see Walter Klaassen, 'Anabaptist Ethics' and 'Mennonite Ethics', *A new Dictionary of Christian Ethics* (1986), pp. 20–1 and 377–8; and Charles W. Teel, 'The Mennonites and Social Responsibility', in *Spectrum* 1: 3 (Summer 1969): 58.
47. Scriven, 'Radical Discipleship' (1983), p. 18.
48. Ibid.
49. Scriven (1983), p. 11.
50. Ibid.
51. Colvin, 'Social Consciences (1986)', p. 40.

CHAPTER 7

1. Adventism has often been regarded by other Christian denominations as a cult or religious innovation. See, for example, Anthony A. Hoekema, *The Four Major Cults: Christian Science, Jehovah's Witnesses, Mormonism, Seventh-day Adventism* (Grand Rapids, Michigan: William B. Eerdmans, 1963); Jan Karel Van Baalen, *The Chaos of Cults* (London, Glasgow: Pickering and Inglis, 1979), pp. 228–56; J. Paul Williams, *What Americans Believe and How They Worship* (New York, Evanston: Harper and Row Publishers, 1962), pp. 427– 452; and Josh McDowell and Don Stewart, *The Deceivers: What Cults Believe and How They Lure Followers* (Amersham-on-the-Hill: Scripture Press, 1992), pp. 297–9.
2. Joseph Bates, *A Seal of the Living God* (1849); James White, 'Editorial', *Present Truth* 1: 1 (July 1849), reprinted in 'The Present Truth & The Spirit of Prophecy', *The Sabbath Sentinel* 45: 8 (August 1993): 4–7; and White, *Testimonies 6* (1948), p. 291.
3. Cf. 'Present Truth [2]' and 'Review and Herald', *SDA Encyclopedia* (1976), pp. 1149 and 1207.
4. Cf. 'Education, SDA Philosophy of', *SDA Encyclopedia* (1976), pp. 416–18; and White, *Education* (1903).
5. Cf. Schwarz, *Light Bearers*, (1979), pp. 204–6; and E. Cadwallader, *A History of Seventh-day Adventist Education* (Lincoln, Nebraska: Union College Press, 1958).
6. In America this happened in the 1920s and 1930s. Cf. Schwarz (1979), pp. 524–5. In England this is in the process of happening only in the last few years.
7. The *SDA BC* was 'long in planning by the Review and Herald Publishing Association, with the knowledge of the General

Conference, but as an enterprise of the publishing house'. Keld J. Reynolds, 'The Church under Stress, 1931–1960', *Adventism in America*, (1986), p. 182.

8. *Questions on Doctrine* (1957).
9. Ibid., pp. 7–8.
10. See Froom, *Movement of Destiny* (1971), pp. 476–80; and T. E. Unruh, 'The Seventh-day Adventist Conferences of 1955–1956', *Adventist Heritage* 4 (Winter 1977): 35–46.
11. Reynolds (1986), p. 186.
12. Walter R. Martin, *The Truth About Seventh-day Adventists* (Grand Rapids, Michigan: Zondervan Publishing House, 1960).
13. Schwarz (1979), p. 545.
14. I am indebted for this classification to Geoffrey J. Paxton, suggested in his book *The Shaking of Adventism* (Wilmington: Zenith Publishers, 1977).
15. Edward Heppenstall, 'Is Perfection Possible?', *Sings of the Times*, December 1963.
16. Paxton (1977), p. 113.
17. See in *Spectrum* 9: 3 (July 1978): 28–57; Fritz Guy, 'A View From the Outside'; Herbert E. Douglass, 'Paxton's Misunderstanding of Adventism'; Desmond Ford, 'The Truth of Paxton's Thesis', Hans LaRondalle, 'Paxton and the Reformers'.
18. Robert Brimsmead, under the powerful influence of Ford, LaRondelle and Heppenstall, changed his 'perfectionistic' view and adopted the doctrine of justification by faith as taught by Reformation theology.
19. Gary Land, 'Coping With Change, 1961–1980', in *Adventism in America* (1986), p. 228.
20. (Victoria, Australia: published by the authors, 1976).
21. Colin D. Standish and Russell R. Standish, *Deceptions of the New Theology* (Hartland Publications, 1989), p. 8.
22. Desmond Ford, *Sings of the Times*, Australian edn, 1 August 1967.
23. Desmond Ford, 'Daniel 8: 14 and the Day of Atonement', *Spectrum* 11: 2 (November 1980): 31.
24. The review of this meeting can be found in Raymond F. Cottrell, 'The Sanctuary Review Committee and its New Consensus', *Spectrum* 11:2 (November 1980): 2–26.
25. Desmond Ford, 'Daniel 8: 14, The Day of Atonement, and The Investigative Judgement' (a position paper), 1980. Later it was printed as *Daniel 8: 14. The Day of Atonement, and the Investigative Judgement* (Casselberry, FL.: Euangelion Press, 1980).
26. Cottrell stated that in his 'personal acquaintance, both at Glacier View and over a period of many years, with the thinking of approximately three fourths of the Bible scholars present, indicated that four-fifths of this number (24% of the 115 delegates) acknowledge the same problems in interpreting Daniel and Hebrews to which Ford has called attention.' Cottrell, 'Sanctuary Consensus', *Spectrum* 11: 2 (November 1980): 19.
27. Ford, *Daniel 8: 14* (1980), pp. 215–21.
28. Ibid., p. A-269.

29. It is reported that 76 workers of the Adventist church in Australasion Division alone withdrew from church service by 1985. The exact number of lay people is not known but it can be counted in thousands. Cf. Desmond Ford, 'Five Years After Glacier View', *Good News For Adventists* (Good News Unlimited, 1985): 6–9; and Land, *Adventism in America* (1986), p. 225.
30. Ford, *Good News* (1985), p. 9.
31. Cf. Mitchell, 'We Are the Remnant' (1988); Hasel, *The Remnant* (1974), p. 403. See also recent treatise which changes the traditional Adventist understanding of the remnant concept in order to accommodate the socio-ethical responsibility of the church in Mirilov, 'An Examination of the Response' (1994), pp. 90–3.
32. William Fagal, 'Whatever Happened to the Remnant', *Adventists Affirm* 2: 2 (Fall 1988): 3–4; C. Mervyn Maxwell, 'The Remnant in SDA Theology', 13–20; and Laurel Damsteegt, 'The Remnant's Vision: Getting Foggy?', ibid: 21–28.
33. See 'Biography' to Colin D. Standish and Russell R. Standish, *Keepers of the Faith* (Rapidan, VA: Hartland Publications, 1988).
34. 'Spirit of Prophecy' is how traditional Adventists call Ellen G. White and her writings.
35. Standish and Standish, *Deceptions* (1989), p. 32.
36. See, for example, Ralph Larson, 'Heresies Will Come In', in *Our Firm Foundation* 6: 2 (February 1991): 16–20.
37. Ibid., p. 77.
38. Cf. Neal Wilson, 'Statement Regarding Hope International/Ron Spear' (2 April 1992), p. 4. Reprinted in *Issues: The Seventh-day Adventist Church and Certain Private Ministries* (North American Division, [1992]), pp. 288–9; D. Douglas Devnich, 'Dissident Groups: The Threat and The Truth', *Ministry* (April 1992): 25–26; and 'Objectives of Hope International and *Our Firm Foundation*', *Issues* ([1992]), pp. 102–11.
39. *Issues* ([1992]), pp. 8–9.
40. Standish and Standish, *Keepers of the Faith* (1988), p. 250.
41. Ibid., p. 251.
42. Cf. 'The Definition of Chalcedon', and 'The Creed of Nicea', *Creeds of the Churches: A Reader in Christian Doctrine From the Bible to the Present*, ed. John H. Leith (Garden City, N.Y.: Anchor Books, Doubleday & Company, Inc., 1963), pp. 35–36 and 30–31. An understanding of the nature of Christ was the major achievement of the early Christian church. This development has received enormous scholarly attention. For an account of the major issues involved see J. N. D. Kelly, *Early Christian Doctrines*, rev. edn (San Francisco: Harper & Row Publishers, 1960), pp. 138–162 and 280–343.
43. Woodrow Whidden, 'Essential Adventism or Historic Adventism?' *Ministry* (October 1993): 5–9.
44. Kenneth R. Samples, 'The Recent Truth About Seventh-day Adventism', *Christianity Today* (5 February 1990).
45. Alvin L. Kwiram, 'Our Once and Future Church', *Spectrum* 20: 3 (April 1990): 5.

46. Fred Veltman cited in Gary Land, 'Coping With Change, 1961–1980', *Adventism in America* (1986), p. 227.
47. Ibid., p. 226.
48. Pearson (1990), pp. 277–8.

CHAPTER 8

1. Jan Milic Lochman, 'Ideology or Theology of Human Rights?', *The Church and the Rights of Man* (New York: The Seabury Press, 1979).
2. Carlos Santiago Nino, *The Ethics of Human Rights* (Oxford: Clarendon Press, 1991); Harlan Cleveland, 'The Chain Reaction of Human Rights', *Human Dignity: The Internationalization of Human Rights* ed. Alice H. Henkin (New York: Aspen Institute for Humanistic Studies, 1979), pp. IX–XII; Charles E. Wyzanski, Jr, 'The Philosophical Background of the Doctrine of Human Rights', in *Human Dignity* (1979), pp. 9– 13; James W. Nickel, *Making Sense of Human Rights: Philosophical Reflections on the Universal Declaration of Human Rights* (Berkeley: University of California Press, 1987); Elaine Pagels, 'The Roots and Origins of Human Rights', *Human Dignity* (1979).
3. From a Protestant perspective see Torleiv Austad, 'The Theological Foundations of Human Rights', *A Lutheran Reader on Human Rights*, ed. Jorgen Lissner and Sovik Arne (The Lutheran World Federation, 1978); from Catholic perspective see Jack Mahoney, 'The Basis of Human Rights', *Moral Theology: Challenges for the Future*, ed. Charles E. Curran (New York/Mahwah: Paulist Press, 1990), pp. 313–33.
4. Nino (1991), p. 1.
5. Pagels (1979), p. 6.
6. Roy Jenkins, *What the Churches Can Do About Human Rights* (London: British Council of Churches, 1989); Richard Harries, 'Human Rights in Theological Perspective', *Human Rights for the 1990s*, ed. Robert Blackburn and John Taylor (London and New York: Mansell, 1991), pp. 1–13; R. J. Henle, 'A Christian View of Human Rights: A Thomistic Reflection', *The Philosophy of Human Rights: International Perspectives*, ed. Alan S. Rosenbaum (London: Aldwych Press, 1989), pp. 87–94; Lochman (1979).
7. Harries (1991), p. 1.
8. Ibid.
9. The American Bill of Rights.
10. The French Declaration of the Rights of Man.
11. Pagels (1979), p. 7.
12. Harries (1991), p. 8.
13. Ibid.
14. A phrase from 2 Peter 1: 12 taken by Adventist pioneers to mean 'truth applicable to that present time'. James White, one of the founders of the SDA church wrote: 'The Church have ever had a present truth. The present truth now, is that which shows present

duty, and the right position for us. ...' Quoted in 'Present Truth', in *SDA Encyclopedia* (1976), p. 1149.

15. A Catholic theologian R. J. Hanle pointed to that fact when he observed that 'human rights are prior to society and the state, although positive refinements and additions can be made by human law'. Henle (1989), pp. 88–9.
16. Alan S. Rosenbaum (ed.)*The Philosophy of Human Rights* (1989), p.IX.
17. Jürgen Moltmann, *The Experiment Hope* (London: SCM Press, 1975), p. 152.
18. Lochman (1979), pp. 18–19.
19. David Little, 'Human Rights', *A New Dictionary of Christian Ethics* (1986), p. 279.
20. Douglas MacLean, *Review of Human Rights*, ed. Eugene Kamenka and Alice Erh-Soon Tay, *Universal Human Rights* vol. 2, no. 2 (April–July 1980), p. 90.
21. Ibid., pp. 90–1.
22. Wellman, 'A New Conception of Human Rights', *A Lutheran Reader on Human Rights* (1978).
23. Cf. Joseph Raz, 'Right-based Morality', *Theories of Rights*, ed. Jeremy Waldron (Oxford: Oxford University Press, 1984), pp. 186–90; and S. Lukes, *Individualism* (Oxford, 1973).
24. Bert B. Beach, *Bright Candle of Courage* (Boise, Idaho: Pacific Press, 1989), pp. 13, 47.
25. David Lyon (ed.), *Rights* (Belmont, California: Wadsworth Publishing Company, 1979), p. 11.
26. Ibid.
27. Joel Feinberg, 'The Nature and Value of Rights', *Rights*, (1979), p. 85.
28. Ronald Dworkin, *Taking Rights Seriously* (London: Duckworth, 1978), pp. 171–2.
29. Ibid., p. 171.
30. John L. Mackie, 'Can There Be a Right-based Moral Theory?', *Theories of Rights* (1984), pp. 168–81.
31. Jeremy Waldron, 'Introduction', *Theories of Right* (1984), p. 12.
32. Ibid., p. 13.
33. Raz, 'Right-based Moralities', *Theories of Rights* (1984), p. 182.
34. Jo Renee Formicola, *The Catholic Church and Human Rights: Its Role in the Formulation of U.S. Policy 1945–1980* (New York & London: Garland Publishing, 1988), p. 3.
35. Jürgen Moltmann, *On Human Dignity: Political Theology and Ethics* (Philadelphia: Fortress Press, 1984), p. 8.
36. See above, pp. 126–8.
37. Patrick J. O'Mahony, *The Fantasy of Human Rights* (Great Wakering: Mayhew-McCrimmon, 1978), p. 65.
38. John Stott put it in this way: 'Human rights are the rights of human beings, and the nature of human rights depends on the nature of the human beings, whose rights they are.' In *Issues Facing Christians Today* (1984), p. 144.
39. O'Mahony, *The Fantasy of Human Rights* (1978), p. 63.

40. Two main classical discussions on self-identity are John Locke's discussion of identity in Book 2, Chapter 27 of the *Essay Concerning Human Understanding*, ed. Campbell Fraser (Oxford, 1894), and David Hume's *Treatise of Human Nature*, published in various editions including that of A. D. Lindsay (Everyman's Library, 1964). For a good summary of the philosophical aspects of personhood see Terence Penelhum, 'Personal Identity', in *The Encyclopedia of Philosophy* vols. 5 & 6, ed. Paul Edwards (New York: Macmillan & The Free Press and London: Collier Macmillan Publishers, 1967), pp. 95–107; and P. A. Minkus, *Philosophy of the Person* (Oxford, 1960).
41. Some of the most important theological writings of this century have been concerned with the doctrine of man. See, for example, Emil Brunner, *Man in Revolt: A Christian Anthropology* (Philadelphia: The Westminster Press, 1939); Reinhold Niebuhr, *The Nature and Destiny of Man*, 2 vols. (New York: Charles Scribner's Sons, 1941, 1943); Marianne H. Micks, *Our Search for Identity: Humanity In the Image of God* (Philadelphia: Fortress Press, 1982); and Wolfhart Pannenberg, *What Is Man? Contemporary Anthropology in Theological Perspective*, trans. Duane Priebe (Philadelphia: Fortress Press, 1970). For the aspect of dignity, see R. C. Sproul, *In Search of Dignity* (Basingstoke: Pickering & Inglis, 1984).
42. Gregory Vlastos, 'Justice and Equality', *Theories of Rights* (1984), p. 47.
43. Alan Gewirth, 'Are There Any Absolute Rights?', *Theories of Rights* (1984), p. 91.
44. Ibid., p. 92.
45. Ibid., p. 100.
46. See, for example, H. L. A. Hart, 'Are There Any Natural Rights?', *Theories of Rights* (1984), pp. 77–90.
47. O'Mahony, *The Fantasy of Human Rights* (1978), p. 63.
48. As cited by Lochman, 'Ideology or Theology of Human Rights?' (1979), pp. 13–14.
49. Cf. Church of Norway Working Paper, 'Theological Notes on Human Rights', *A Lutheran Reader on Human Rights* (1978), pp. 12–14.
50. Jenkins, *What the Churches Can Do* (1989), p. 6.
51. Lochman (1979), p. 14.
52. Ibid., p. 17.
53. The United Evangelical Lutheran Church in the GDR, 'The Theological Relevance of Human Rights', *A Lutheran Reader on Human Rights* (1978), p. 30.
54. Moltmann, *The Experiment Hope* (1975), p. 152.
55. Moltmann, *The Power of the Powerless* (London: SCM Press, 1983), p. 47.
56. Lyons (ed.) *Rights* (1979), p. 11.
57. For the purpose of this work, the expression 'natural rights' should be taken to mean moral rights to life, to freedom (to free speech, religious freedom, freedom of association, etc.), to safety. Although these and other such moral rights are not identified with legal rights, they are often indistinguishable.
58. Elaine Pagels, 'The Roots and Origins of Human Rights', *Human Dignity* (1979), pp. 3–4.

59. Garrett Barden, 'A Dialectic of Right', *Understanding of Human Rights: An Interdisciplinary and Interfaith Study*, ed. A. D. Falconer (Dublin: Irish School of Ecumenics, 1980), pp. 68–9.
60. Nathan Glazer criticises John Rawls for ignoring the problem of justice for groups in his *A Theory of Justice*. See N. Glazer, 'Individual Rights Against Group Rights', *A Lutheran Reader on Human Rights* (1978), pp. 90.
61. Moltmann, *On Human Dignity* (1984), p. 5.
62. N. Goodall (ed.) *The Uppsala Report 1968: Official Report of the Fourth Assembly of the World Council of Churches* (Geneva: World Council of Churches, 1968), pp. 5–6.
63. O'Mahony (1978), p. 8.
64. Cf. John Rawls, *A Theory of Justice* (London: Oxford University Press, 1972).
65. Martti Lindqvist, 'Human Life Within Limits', *Understanding of Human Rights* (1980), p. 88.
66. Lochman (1979), p. 18.

CHAPTER 9

1. See fundamental belief 6 in *SDAs Believe* (1988), p. 68.
2. *Seventh-day Adventist Church Manual* (General Conference of Seventh-day Adventists, revised 1995), p. 8.
3. *SDAs Believe* (1988), p. 71.
4. An exception is a more recent study of equality between men and women on the basis of Genesis 1–3, in Hasel, 'Man and Woman in Genesis 1–3, *Symposium* (1984), pp. 10–27. Also published as 'Equality from the Start', *Spectrum* 7: 2 (1975): 21–8.
5. Harries (1991), pp. 2–3.
6. Rice (1985), p. 100.
7. *SDAs Believe* (1988), p. 74.
8. In Adventist writings, unlike in some other Christian circles, 'likeness' and 'image of God' bear the same meaning.
9. Pannenberg, *What is Man?* (1970), p. 15.
10. See above Hasel's conclusion, for example, pp. 105–6.
11. Rice (1985), pp. 112–13.
12. For the notion of stewardship in relation to the image of God, see Douglas John Hall, *Imaging God: Dominion as Stewardship* (Grand Rapids, Michigan: Wm. B. Eerdmans, 1986). Other works on biblical aspects of stewardship have been published by Friendship Press in the Library of Christian Stewardship.
13. Jenkins, *What the Churches Can Do* (1989), p. 6.
14. Moltmann (1975), p. 149.
15. Moltmann (1984), p. 9.
16. Ibid., pp. 8–9.
17. See, for example, the philosophical treatise on rights in Lyons, (ed.), *Rights* (1979).
18. Dworkin (1979), p. 105.

19. Harries, *Human Rights for the 1990s* (1991), p. 2.
20. For a good exposition of the concept of the image of God see Hall, *Imaging God* (1986); David Cairns, *The Image of God in Man* (London: SCM Press, 1953); and G. C. Berkouwer, *Man: The Image of God*, trans. Dirk W. Jellema (Grand Rapids: Wm. B. Eerdmans, 1962).
21. The idea elaborated in Kamenka and Tay (eds.), *Human Rights* (1978), p. 91.
22. Whenever a term 'man' appears in the text, its meaning is 'mankind' as in Genesis 1: 27.
23. *SDA Church Manual* (1990), p. 24.
24. Rice (1985), p. 126.
25. Ibid.
26. Moltmann (1975), p. 149.
27. A number of excellent discussions on the effects of the Fall on humanity and restoration of the image of God in Christ have appeared since the early 1970s. See, for example, David E. Jenkins, *What Is Man?* (London: SCM Press, 1970), pp. 71–88; Brunner, *Man in Revolt* (1939); and G. C. Berkouwer, *Sin* (Grand Rapids, Michigan: Wm. B. Eerdmans, 1971). From the Adventist perspective on the Fall and its effects on man, see Rice (1985), pp. 123–38; and 'Fall of Man', in *SDA Encyclopedia* (1976), pp. 448–9.
28. A concise discussion on Ritschl's contribution in the theology of the Kingdom of God is found in Claude Welch, *Protestant Thought in the Nineteenth Century*, Vol. 2, *1870–1914* (New Haven and London: Yale University Press, 1985), pp. 1–25.
29. In English, 'Dominion of God' being Ritschl's own translation of 'Basileia tou Teou', in *Die christlische Lehre von Rechtfertigung und Versohnung*, Vol. II, 4th edition (Bonn, 1900).
30. Ibid., p. 31, as cited by Gosta Lundstrom, *The Kingdom of God in the Teaching of Jesus: A History of Interpretation from the Last Decades of the Nineteenth Century to the Present Day* (Edinburgh and London: Oliver and Boyd, 1963), p. 4.
31. *Rechtfertigung und Versohnung*, Vol. III, 3rd edition (Bonn, 1888) p. 271. This work has been translated as *The Christian Doctrine of Justification and Reconciliation. The Positive Development of the Doctrine*, trans. H. R. Mackintosh and A. B. Macaulay (Edinburgh, 1900).
32. Lundstrom, pp. 6–7. See also A. C. Ewing and J. F. Childress, 'Kantian Ethics', in *A New Dictionary of Christian Ethics* (1986), pp. 334–7.
33. Lundstrom, p. 25.
34. (London: SCM Press, 1971), p. 4.
35. Ibid., p. 133.
36. Ibid., pp. 82, 113–15, 132–5.
37. Ibid., p. 132.
38. Ibid., pp. 73ff.
39. See discussion in Hiers and Holland, 'Introduction', in Johannes Weiss, *Jesus' Proclamation* (1971), pp. 15–22.
40. In the Foreword to Weiss's *Jesus' Proclamation*, Rudolf Bultmann wrote that Weiss is 'one of the founders of the eschatological movement in critical theology', and that 'despite numerous rejoinders and attempts

to distort it, Johannes Weiss's judgement on the matter has prevailed triumphantly'. (p. XI).
41. Lundstrom, p. 232.
42. Hiers and Holland (1971) p. 27.
43. (Philadelphia: Westminster, 1964), pp. 139–43. G. E. Ladd in *The Presence of the Future* (1974) and W. G. Kümmel in *Promise and Fulfilment* (1957) believe similarly that the arrival of the Kingdom is in two stages: the 'fulfilment' and the 'consummation' of the Kingdom.
44. (Welwyn: James Nisbet and Company, 1935, rev. 1936), p. 49.
45. Ibid., p. 51.
46. Moltmann, *Theology of Hope* (London: SCM Press; New York: Harper, 1967).
47. Moltmann, *The Power of the Powerless* (1983), pp. 45–6. Cf. Moltmann, *The Experiment Hope* (1975).
48. Moltmann, *The Power of the Powerless* (1983), p. 50.
49. Bruce Chilton (ed.) *The Kingdom of God in the Teaching of Jesus* (Philadelphia: Fortress Press and London: SPCK, 1984).
50. Ibid., p. 26.
51. Ellen G. White, *The Great Controversy Between Christ and Satan During the Christian Dispensation* (Mountain View, California: Pacific Press, 1888), p. 323.
52. Ibid., p. 322.
53. Ibid., p. 323.
54. Weiss's first edition of *Die Predigt Jesu vom Reiche Gottes* was published in 1892 and the second in 1890.
55. *Great Controversy* (1888), pp. 347, 322–3, 416, 427; *Thoughts From the Mount of Blessing* (Washington, D.C.: Review and Herald, 1896), pp. 107–9; *Testimonies 5* (1948), p. 732.
56. *Desire* (1898), p. 130, 138; *Testimonies 9* (1948), p. 218; *Thoughts* (1896), p. 110.
57. *Desire* (1898), p. 299; *The Story of Patriarchs and Prophets: As Illustrated in the Lives of Holy Men of Old* (Mountain View, California: Pacific Press, 1890 (1958), p. 207; *Fundamentals of Christian Education: Instruction for the Home, the School, and the Church* (Nashville, Tennessee: Southern Publishing Association, 1923), p. 398.
58. *Thoughts* (1986), p. 8; *Fundamentals* (1923), p. 142; *Desire* (1898), p. 727; *Christ's Object Lessons* (Washington, D.C.: Review and Herald, 1900), p. 397.
59. *GC* (1888), pp. 345–7; *Desire*, (1898), p. 34.
60. *GC* (1888), p. 347.
61. Ibid., p. 416; cf. *The Acts of the Apostles, In the Proclamation of the Gospel of Jesus Christ* (Mountain View, California: Pacific Press, 1911), p. 228.
62. *GC* (1888), p. 347.
63. Ibid., p. 348.
64. *Questions on Doctrine* (1957). About significance of the book in the development of Adventist theology see above, pp. 139–40.
65. *Questions on Doctrine* (1957), p. 213.
66. Ibid.
67. Ibid., p. 215.

68. Ibid.
69. Promises to David and Solomon were also conditional (1 Chron 28: 6–8; 1 Kings 9: 3–9; 2 Chron 7: 16–22); as well as the threat of captivity (Jer 17: 21–7).
70. *Questions on Doctrine* (1957), p. 222.
71. Ibid., pp. 224–5.
72. Ibid., p. 226.
73. Ibid., p. 228.
74. Ibid., pp. 233–4.
75. Ibid., pp. 236–7.
76. Rice (1985).
77. 'Responding to the Delay' and 'Adventists Between the Times: The Shift in the Church's Eschatology', in *Pilgrimage of Hope*, ed. Roy Branson (Takoma Park, Maryland: Association of Adventist Forums, 1986), pp. 8–17 and 41–63.
78. *Now and Not Yet: How Do People Waiting for the Second Coming Respond to Poverty, Lawsuits, Hunger, Political Oppression, Sexuality, and Sin?* (Washington, D.C.: Review and Herald, 1987); cf. John Brunt, 'Going About Our Daily Business', in *Pilgrimage of Hope* (1986), pp. 26–40.
79. Rice (1985), p. 13.
80. Ibid.
81. George Eldon Ladd, *Journal of Biblical Literature* 81 (1962): 236, quoted in Rice (1985), p. 14.
82. Ibid., p. 146.
83. Ibid., pp. 146–7.
84. Ibid., p. 147.
85. Ibid., p. 267.
86. Ibid.
87. Ibid., pp. 278–9.
88. Ibid., pp. 270–1.
89. Ibid., p. 271.
90. Branson (1986), p. 59.
91. Ibid.
92. Ibid., p. 61.
93. Ibid., p. 14.
94. Ibid.
95. Ibid., p. 42.
96. Ibid., p. 19.
97. Ibid., p. 27.
98. Cf. Eph 1: 14, 18.20–22; Eph 2: 1–7; Rom 12: 1.2; Jn 5: 24–9; Jn 6: 53–4; Rev 2: 7; Rev 5: 9–10.
99. Brunt, *Now and Not Yet* (1987), p. 81.
100. Ibid., p. 32.
101. Ibid., p. 33; cf. John Brunt, 'Daily Business' (1986), p. 34.
102. Brunt (1987), p. 44.
103. Brunt (1986), p. 28.
104. Brunt (1987), p. 47.
105. Ibid.
106. Ibid., p. 48.
107. Ibid., p. 62.

108. Ibid., pp. 62–3.
109. Ibid., p. 70.
110. Ibid., p. 73.
111. Ibid., p. 74.
112. Ibid., p. 77.
113. Ibid., p. 81.
114. Brunt (1986), p. 28.
115. Although written at different times and with very different standpoints, Synoptics and John give us the *ipsissima vox* of Jesus' sayings on the Kingdom of God.
116. Cf. Mk 14: 23; Matt 24: 30–31; Matt 10: 7; Lk 10: 9; Matt 25: 34, 46; Lk 11: 2; Lk 17: 21; Jn 3: 3, 5; Jn 14: 1–3.
117. Brunt (1987), p. 73.
118. Ibid., p. 16.

CHAPTER 10

1. See 'Fundamental Belief 18', in *SDAs Believe* (1988), p. 232.
2. See, for example, C. H. Dodd, *Gospel and Law: Bampton Lectures in America* (Cambridge: Cambridge University Press, 1951), pp. 62–3.
3. Matt 5: 19.
4. Matt 22: 37–9; cf. Deut 6: 4–5.
5. See 'Fundamental Belief 19', in *SDAs Believe* (1988), p. 248.
6. Adventists believe that the Sabbath commandment is 'a perpetual memorial of Creation' (Ex 20: 11–12) and that it points to the worship of the Creator as a special sign of loyalty (Rev 14: 7–12). Cf. *SDAs Believe* (1988), pp. 255–8.
8. For example, see, Sakae Kubo, *God Meets Man: A Theology of the Sabbath and Second Coming* (Nashville, Tennessee: Southern Publishing Association, 1978); Samuele Bacchiocchi, *Divine Rest for Human Restlessness: A Theological Study of the Good News of the Sabbath for Today* (Rome: The Pontifical Gregorian University Press, 1980); and Rice, *The Reign of God* (1985).
9. Kubo (1978), p. 7.
10. Philo, *On the Creation*, XXX, cited in Kubo (1978), p. 19.
11. See, for example, how Jack Provonsha illustrates this point by the use of 'a black rock in the midst of the garden' as an inadequate sign for human beings in *A Remnant in Crisis* (1993), p. 86.
12. Kubo (1978), p. 24.
13. Kubo (1978), p. 27.
14. Provonsha (1993), p. 87.
15. Bacchiocchi (1980), pp. 194–5.
16. Rice (1985), p. 370.
17. Ibid.
18. Charles E. Bradford, 'The Sabbath and Liberation: With the Sabbath, No One Can Keep Us Down', in *Anchor Points* (Hagerstown, MD: Review and Herald, 1993), p. 28.
19. Ibid., pp. 29, 31.

20. Ibid., p. 28.
21. Ibid., p. 30.
22. Ibid.
23. Ibid., p. 31.
24. Ezek 20: 10–12. 20.
25. Bradford (1993), p. 32.
26. Kubo (1978), p. 46. Cf. Sakae Kubo, 'The Experience of Liberation', in *Festival of the Sabbath*, ed. Roy Branson (Takoma Park: Association of Adventist Forums, 1986), pp. 43–54.
27. Ibid.
28. See above, chapter 4.
29. Kubo (1978) p. 46.
30. This suggests also certain environmental rights.
31. Rice (1985), p. 370.
32. On Seventh-day Adventism's self-understanding as 'Prophetic Minority', see Teel, 'Withdrawing Sect' (1980).
33. Gen 20: 7.
34. Deut 34: 10.
35. Deut 18: 15ff.
36. For this division into four elements of prophetic ethics I am indebted to Walter Harrelson. See his 'Prophetic Ethics' in *A New Dictionary of Christian Ethics* (1986), pp. 508–12.
37. See, for example, Deut 30: 15–20.
38. Exod 23: 3, and Deut 16: 19–20.
39. Is 5: 8.
40. Deut 7: 6–11.
41. Cf. 1 John 4: 9–10.
42. Provonsha (1993), p. 50.
43. Ibid., pp. 50–1.
44. Though the theme of social concern is reflected throughout all prophets, three Major Prophets (Isaiah, Jeremiah and Ezekiel) and seven Minor Prophets (Hosea, Amos, Micah, Habakkuk, Zephaniah, Zechariah and Malachi) illustrate this most emphatically.
45. Amos pointed to the following sins of the nation: exploitation and oppression of the poor (4: 1; 5: 11; 8: 4–6); corrupt and degenerate religious practice (2: 4, 6); corruption of justice and righteousness (5: 7. 10; 6: 12); unnecessary riches (6: 4); and neglect of God's law (2: 8; 8: 5). He saw a solution to these sins in repentance (4: 12, 13; 5: 4–13) and consequently, if sins were not repented, in punishment and judgment (2: 5, 13–16; 3: 2; 5: 25–7).

    Hosea termed prostitution (4: 11–18), lying (4: 2; 7: 1), violence and murder (4: 2; 6: 8–9), robbery (7: 1; 4: 2), drunkenness (4: 11; 7: 5), idolatry (4: 12; 8: 4; 13: 2), and rebellion against God (9: 15; 13: 16) as the greatest sins of his time. His proposed solution was again repentance or destruction in God's judgment (5: 1–14; 8: 1–9; 14: 1).

    Isaiah marked the sins of God's people of his time as idolatry (2: 8), injustice (5: 7; 59: 8), bloodshed (59: 7), rebellion (1: 5; 57: 4), neglect of widows (1: 23; 10: 2), heavy drinking (5: 11; 28: 1–7) and oppression of the poor (3: 14–15; 10: 2). Again, like other prophets,

Isaiah saw the solution either in repentance and God's forgiveness, or in facing judgement, punishment and destruction. Inevitably, Isaiah emphasised, Messiah will come and establish social justice in His millennial kingdom.

46. Luke 7: 22b.
47. Mirilov deals with the relationship of religious minorities from the perspective of the book of Revelation, comparing it with the experience of the Seventh-day Adventist Church in 'An Examination of the Response' (1994).
48. Cf. Rev 2: 2, 9–10, 13, 21–2; 12: 1–7; and 13: 4, 15–16.
49. Luke 4: 18–21. Cf. Karl Barth, *Deliverance to the Captives*, translated by Marguerite Wieser with Preface by John Marsh (London: SCM Press, 1961).
50. Matt 4: 23; 15: 30.
51. O'Mahony, *The Fantasy of Human Rights* (1978), p. 139.
52. Rice (1985), p. 311.
53. Ibid.
54. John T. Robinson, *In the End God* (New York: Harper & Row Publishers, 1968), pp. 22, 47.
55. Rice (1985), p. 312.
56. Bacchiocchi, *The Advent Hope for Human Hopelessness: A Theological Study of the Meaning of the Second Coming for Today* (Berrien Springs, Michigan: Biblical Perspectives, 1986), p. 398.
57. Ibid., p. 399.
58. Kubo (1978), p. 105.
59. Max Warren, *The Truth of Vision: A Study in the Nature of the Christian Hope* (London and Edinburgh: The Canterbury Press, 1948), p. 53.
60. Bacchiocchi (1986), p. 399.
61. Kubo (1978), p. 98.
62. Ibid.
63. Ibid., p. 99. Cf. Rice (1985), p. 312.
64. Bacchiocchi (1986), pp. 399–400.
65. Cf. Kubo (1978), pp. 97–104.
66. G. C. Berkouwer, *The Return of Christ* (Grand Rapids, Michigan: Wm. B. Eerdmans, 1972), p. 84.
67. Kubo (1978), pp. 102–3.
68. Ibid., p. 103.
69. Rice (1985), p. 346.
70. Kubo (1978), p. 91.
71. Ibid.
72. See 1 Cor 15: 22.
73. Rom 3: 23.
74. Rom 5: 12.
75. Kubo (1978), p. 92.
76. Ibid., p. 93.
77. Ibid.
78. J. E. Fison, *The Christian Hope: The Presence and the Parousia* (New York: Longmans, Green, and Co., 1954), p. 221.
79. Ibid., p. 4.

81. Emil H. Brunner, *Eternal Hope*, translated by Harold Knight (Philadelphia: Westminster, 1954), p. 30, as cited by Kubo, (1978), p. 93.
82. Colin Morris, *The Hammer of the Lord* (Nashville and New York: Abingdon Press, 1973), pp. 137–8.
83. Robert McAfee Brown, '"Eschatological Hope" and Social Responsibility' *Christianity and Crisis* (16 November 1953): 147.
84. Kubo (1978), p. 108.
85. Cf. Matt 24 and 25.
86. Kubo (1978), p. 106–11.
87. Luke 10: 37.
88. Kubo (1978), p. 107.
89. Ibid.

CONCLUSION

1. See above, p. 15. Cf. James Walters, 'Towards an Adventist Ethic', in *Spectrum* 12: 2 (December 1981): 2.
2. Cf. Pearson, *Millennial Dreams* (1990), pp. 9, 24–5; Jan Paulsen, 'Social Service/Social Action' (1990), pp. 139–48; W. Johnsson, 'An Ethical People', *RH* (22 January 1981): 13.; and E. Vick, 'Against Isolationism', *Spectrum* 8: 3 (March 1973): 38–40.
3. George R. Knight, *Anticipating the Advent: A Brief History of the Seventh-day Adventists* (Boise, Idaho and Oshawa, Ontario: Pacific Press, 1993), pp. 126–7.
4. Charles Scriven, 'Radical Discipleship and the Renewal of Adventist Mission', *Spectrum* 14: 3 (December 1983): 18.
5. See above, pp. 104–21.
6. See above, pp. 148–50.
7. 'Dorcas Welfare Societies', *SDA Encyclopedia* (1976), p. 399.
8. See above, pp. 59–62.
9. 'Ingathering', *SDA Encyclopedia* (1976), p. 645.
10. See above, pp. 28–9.
11. See above, pp 27–8.

Further Reading

All works cited in the text are listed in the notes. In addition I referred to the following works while preparing this book.

BOOKS

Armstrong, Douglas, and Dworaczek, Marian, *A Selective Bibliography On Human and Civil Rights* (Toronto, Ontario: Ministry of Labour Research Library, 1973).

Beals, Art, *Beyond Hunger: The Compassion of Christ in a Needy World* (Eastbourne: Kingsway Publications, 1985).

Boerma, Conrad, *Rich Man, Poor Man – and the Bible*, trans. John Bowden (London: SCM Press, 1979).

Bonhoeffer, Dietrich, *The Cost of Discipleship* (London: SCM Press, 1959).

Bowden, John and Richmond, John (eds), *A Reader in Contemporary Theology* (London, SCM Press, 1967).

Byron, William (ed.), *The Cause of World Hunger* (New York: Paulist Press, 1982).

Childress, James F. and Macquarrie, John (eds.), *A New Dictionary of Christian Ethics* (London: SCM Press, 1986).

Christian, Lewis Harrison, *Prophecies of Race and Religion* (Washington, D.C.: Review and Herald, 1944).

Colemann, Richard J., *Issues of Theological Conflict: Evangelicals and Liberals* (Grand Rapids, MI: Wm. B. Eerdmans Publishing Company, 1972).

Cullmann, Oscar, *Christ and Time*, trans. F. V. Filson, rev. edn (Philadelphia: Westminster, 1964).

Daily, Steven Gerald, *The Irony of Adventism: The Role of Ellen White and Other Adventist Women in Nineteenth Century America* (Ann Arbor, MI: University Microfilms, 1985).

Dalrympe, Gwynne, *The Fight for Freedom* (Takoma Park, D.C.: Review and Herald, 1941).

Devetak, Silvo, *Manjine, Ljudska Prava, Demokracija: Medunarodna Zastita Ljudskih i Etnickih Prava*. (Sarajevo: Oslobodenje, 1989).

Donnelly, Jack, *The Concept of Human Rights* (London and Sydney: Croom Helm, 1985).

Donovan, Oliver, *Resurrection and Moral Order: An Outline for Evangelical Ethics* (Leicester: Inter-Varsity Press and Grand Rapids, MI: Wm. B. Eerdmans, 1986).

Dudley, Roger L and Hernandez, Edwin I., *Citizens of Two Worlds: Religion and Politics Among American Seventh-day Adventists* (Berrien Springs, MI: 1992).

Dumbrell, William J., *Covenant and Creation: An Old Testament Covenant Theology* (Exeter: The Paternoster Press, 1984).

Elliot, Elisabeth, *Let Me Be a Woman* (London, etc.: Hodder and Stoughton, 1979).
Falcones, Alan D. (ed.), *Understanding Human Rights: An Interdisciplinary and Interfaith Study*. (Dublin: Irish School of Ecumenics, 1980).
Ferm, Robert L. (ed.), *Issues in American Protestantism: A Documentary History From the Puritans to the Present* (Gloucester, MA: Peter Smith, 1976).
Ford, Desmond, *Daniel 8:14, the Day of Atonement, and the Investigative Judgment*. (Casselberry, Fl: Euangelion Press, 1980).
Fuchs, Josef, *Personal Ethics & Christian Morality* (Washington, D.C.: Georgetown University Press and Dublin: Gill and Macmillan, 1983).
Garling, Marguerite (compiler), *The Human Rights Handbook* (London: Macmillan, 1979).
Gasper, Louis, *The Fundamentalist Movement* (The Hague, Paris: Mouton & Co., 1963).
Ginger, Ann Fagan (ed.), *Human Rights Organizations and Periodicals Directory, 1973* (Berkeley, CA: Meiklejohn Civil Liberties Institute, 1973).
Gutierrez, Gustavo, *The Power of the Poor in History* (Maryknoll, NY: Orbis Books, 1983).
Hanks, Thomas D., *God So Loved the Thirld World (The Biblical Vocabulary of Oppression) – The Bible, the Reformation, and Liberation Theologies*, trans. James C. Dekker (Maryknoll, NY: Orbis Books, 1983).
Harrelson, Walter, *The Ten Commandments and Human Rights* (Philadelphia: Fortress Press, 1980).
Haselden, Kyle, *The Racial Problem in Christian Perspective* (London: Lutterworth Press, 1960).
Henry, Carl F. C., *A Check List of Significant Books On Christian Personal Ethics* (Pasadena: Fuller Theological Seminary/Fuller Library Bulletin, 1955).
Hopkins, Charles Howard, *The Rise of the Social Gospel in American Protestantism 1865–1915* (New Haven, CT: Yale University Press, 1940).
Howse, Ernest Marshall, *Saints in Politics: The 'Clapham Sect' and the Growth of Freedom* (London: George Allen & Unwin, 1953).
Issues: The Seventh-day Adventist Church and Certain Private Ministries (North American Division of Seventh-day Adventists, 1992).
Iyer, V. R. Krishna, *Human Rights and Inhuman Wrongs* (Delhi: B.R. Publishing Corporation, 1990).
Jesop, T. E., *Social Ethics: Christian and Natural* (London: The Epworth Press, 1952).
Keylor, R. David, *Paul's Covenant Community: Jew and Gentile in Romans* (Atlanta GA: John Knox Press, 1988).
Knight, George R., *Anticipating the Advent: a Brief History of Seventh-day Adventists* (Bois, ID: Pacific Press, 1992).
Knott, Ronald A., *The Makings of a Philantropic Fundraiser: The Instructive Example of Milton Murray* (San Francisco: Jossey-Bass Publishers, 1992).
Lanares, Pierre, *La Liberté Réligieuse* (Ambilly – Annemasse: Presses de Savole, 1964).
Levin, Leah, *Human Rights Questions and Answers* (New York: UNESCO, 1981).
Lincoln, A. T., *Paradise Now and Not Yet: Studies in the Role of the Heavenly Dimensions in Paul's Thought with Special Reference to His Eschatology. Society*

of the New Testament Studies Monograph Series (Cambridge: Cambridge University Press, 1981).

Linden, Ingemar, *The Last Trump: An Historico-genetical Study of Some Important Chapters in the Making and Development of the Seventh-day Adventist Church* (Frankfurt-am-Main, Bern and Las Vegas: Peter Lang, 1978).

Lissner, Jorgen and Arne, Sovik (eds.), *A Lutheran Reader on Human Rights* (The Lutheran World Federation, 1978).

Longenecker, Bruce W., *Eschatology and the Covenant: A Comparison of 4 Ezra and Romans 1–11*. Supplements to J.S.N.T., vol. 57 (Sheffield: Sheffield Academic Press, 1991).

Maimela, Simon., *Proclaim Freedom to My People* (Braamfontein: Skotaville Publishers, 1987).

Marquardt, Manfred, *John Wesley's Social Ethics: Praxis and Principles* (Nashville, TN: Abingdon Press, 1992).

Martin, Walter R., *The Truth About Seventh-day Adventism* (London & Edinburgh: Marshall Morgan and Scott, 1969).

McCarthy, Dennis J., *Old Testament Covenant: A Survey of Current Opinions* (Oxford: Basil Blackwell, 1973).

McCormick, Richard A., S. J., *Notes on Moral Theology 1965 through 1980* (University Press of America, 1981).

McLeod, Merikay, *Betrayal: The Shattering Sex Discrimination Case of Silver vs Pacific Press Publishing Association* (Loma Linda, CA: Mars Hill Publications, 1985).

Mealand, David L., *Poverty Expectation in the Gospel* (London: SPCK, 1980).

Mill, John Stuart, *On Liberty* (London: Penguin Books, 1974).

Miller, Allen O. (eds.), *Christian Declaration on Human Rights* (Grand Rapids, MI: Wm. B. Eerdmans Publishing Company, 1977).

Milles, Robert, and Phizacklea, Annie (eds), *Racism and Political Action in Britain* (London: Henley and Boston: Routledge & Kegan Paul, 1979).

Moore, Basil, *Black Theology: The South African Voice* (London: C. Hurst & Company, 1973).

Niebuhr, Reinhold, *Moral Man and Immoral Society: A Study in Ethics and Politics* (New York: Charles Scribner's Sons, 1960).

Numbers Ronald L. and Butler, Jonathan M. (eds), *The Disappointed: Millerism and Millennarianism in the Nineteenth Century* (Bloomington and Indianopolis: Indiana University Press, 1987).

Pilgrim, Walter E., *Good News to the Poor, Wealth and Poverty in Luke-Acts* (Minneapolis, MN: Augsburg Publishing House, 1981).

Provonsha, Jack W., *A Remnant in Crisis.* (Hagerstown, MD: Review and Herald, 1993).

Rad, Gerhard von, *The Message of the Prophets* (London: SCM Press, 1968).

Rauschenbusch, Walter, *A Theology For the Social Gospel* (Nashville, TN: Abingdon, 1978).

Religious Prisoners in the USSR (Keston College: Greenfire Books, 1987).

Renteln, Alison Dundes, *International Human Rights: Universalism Versus Relativism* (Newbury Park, CA: Sage Publications, 1990).

Rosado, Caleb, *The Role of Women and the Nature of God: A Socio-Biblical Study.* (Loma Linda, CA: Loma Linda University Press, 1989).

Rouner, Leroy S. (ed.), *Human Rights and the World's Religions.* (Notre Dame, In: University of Notre Dame Press, 1988).
Schmidtke, Leah, (compilor), *The Need for an Orphan's Home* (Mentone, CA: Leah's Press, n.d.).
Sider, Ronald J., *Rich Christians in an Age of Hunger* (London, etc.: Hodder and Stoughton, 1978).
Sidorsky, David. (ed.), *Essays on Human Rights: Contemporary Issues and Jewish Perspectives* (Philadelphia: The Jewish Publication Society of America, 1979).
Snow, Charles Miles, *Religious Liberty in America* (Takoma Park, D.C.: Review and Herald, 1914).
Stegemann, Wolfgang *The Gospel and the Poor*, trans. Dietlinde Elliott. (Philadelphia: Fortress Press, 1984).
Taylor, John V., *Enough is Enough* (London: SCM Press, 1975).
The Role of Women in the Church (Washington, D.C.: General Conference of Seventh-day Adventist Church, 1984).
United Nations, *Human Rights: Questions and Answers* (New York: United Nations, 1987).
United Nations Centre for Human Rights and United Nations Institute for Training and Research (UNITAR), *Manual of Human Rights Reporting.* (New York: United Nations, 1991).
Veenhoven, Willem A. (ed.), *Case Studies on Human Rights and Fundamental Freedoms: A World Survey, Vol. 1* (ed.), (The Hague: Martinus Nijhoff, 1975).
Waldron, Jeremy (ed.), *Theories of Rights* (New York: Oxford University Press, 1984).
Wallenkamph, Arnold, *The Apparent Delay: What Role Do We Play in the Timing of Jesus' Return?* (Hagerstown, MD: Review and Herald, 1994).
Weiss, Johannes, *Jesus' Proclamation of the Kingdom of God.* trans., ed. and intro. Richard H. Hiers and David L. Holland (London: SCM Press, 1971).
Wilson, John F. (ed.), *Church and State in American History* (Boston: Health and Co., 1965).
Winter, Gibson. (ed.), *Social Ethics: Issues in Ethics and Politics* (London: SCM Press, 1968).
Wirt, Sherwood Eliot, *The Social Conscience of the Evangelical* (London: Scripture Union, 1968).
Wright, David (ed.), *Essays in Evangelical Social Ethics* (Exeter: The Paternoster Press, 1978).
Wright, N. T., *The Climax of the Covenant: Christ and the Law in Pauline Theology* (Edinburgh: T&T Clark, 1991).
Wright, Robert Ernest Midddleton (compilor), *Human Rights: A Booklist* (Worthing: Worthing College of Further Education/College Library, 1968).
Year Book On Human Rights (New York: United Nations, 1946).

SEVENTH-DAY ADVENTIST ARTICLES

Allen, Edward Martin. 'Rest as a Spiritual Discipline: The Meaning and Manner of Sabbath Observance', D. Min. dissertation (Fuller Theological Seminary, 1991)

Anderson, Eric, Butler, Jonathan, Couperus, Jonathan and Zytkoskee, Adrian, 'Must the Crisis Continue?', *Spectrum*, vol. 11, no. 3 (March 1981): 44–52.
Anderson, E. Marcella, 'The Roles of Women in the Seventh-day Adventist Church: Significance of Ellen G. White Counsels', *Symposium on the Role of Women in the Church* (Biblical Research Institute Committee of General Conference of Seventh-day Adventists, 1984), pp. 138–55.
Anderson, Yvonne D. 'The Bible, the Bottle and the Ballot: Seventh-day Adventist Political Activism 1850–1900', *Adventist Heritage*, vol. 7, no. 2 (Fall 1982): 38–52.
Andreasen, Niels-Erik, 'Jubilee of Freedom and Equality', *Spectrum*, vol. 9, no. 1 (December 1977): 43–7.
Anfenson-Vance, Deborah, 'The Kingdom At Hand', *Insight* (25 February 1984): 30.
'A Service Experience', *REACH Report* (December 1988): 2–4.
Bacchiocchi, Samuele, 'Living the Remnant Lifestyle', *Adventists Affirm*, vol. 2, no. 2 (Fall 1988): 44–53.
Baker, Delbert W., 'From War to Peace: Suggestions for Solving Conflict', *Adventist Review*, vol. 166 (16 February 1989): 12–13.
Ball, Bryan, 'The Ordination of Women: A Plea for Caution', *Spectrum*, vol. 17, no. 2. (December 1986): 39–54.
Barkun, Michael, '"The Wind Sweeping over the Country": John Humphrey Noyes and the Rise of Millerism', in *The Disappointed: Millerism and Millenarianism in the Nineteenth Century*, ed. Ronald L. Numbers and Jonathan M. Butler (Bloomington and Indianopolis: Indiana University Press, 1987), pp. 153–72.
Benton, Josephine, 'The High Ground of Hope', *The Adventist Woman*, vol. 12, nos 4–5 (September–October 1993): 5.
Bradford, Charles E. 'Hunger and the Caring Church', *Adventist Review* (5 May 1988): 17.
——'To Preserve the Remnant: God's Historic Purpose for His Chosen', *Adventist Review*, vol. 166 (4 May 1989): 9–11.
Branson, Roy, 'Beyond the Wall – a Special Moment', *Spectrum*, vol. 22, no. 1 (March 1992): 2.
——'Two Years After the Revolution: Germany and Czechoslovakia', *Spectrum*, vol. 22, no. 1 (March 1992): 30–48.
Brunt, John, 'Adventists against Ordination: a Critical Review', *Spectrum*, vol. 17, no. 2 (December 1986): 55–62.
Butler, Jonathan, 'The Making of a New Order: Millerism and the Origins of Seventh-day Adventism', in *The Disappointed: Millerism and Millenarianism in the Nineteenth Century* ed. Ronald L. Numbers and Jonathan M. Butler (Bloomington and Indianopolis: Indiana University Press, 1987), pp. 189–208.
Campolo, Anthony Jr, 'A Christian Perspective on Civil Disobedience', in *Insight* (5 November 1988): 8–10.
Campolo, Tony, 'Which Jesus Do You Believe In?', *Adventist Review*, vol. 166 (20 April, 1989): 9–11.
Casey, Barry L., 'Needles Hunger in a Bountiful World', *Adventist Review* (6 November 1986): 8–10.
——'Today's H-Bombs: Hunger and Homelessness', *Adventist Review* (5 May 1988): 16–17.

——'Winners and Loosers', *Insight* (8 June 1982): 5–8.

Clouse, Robert G., 'The New Christian Right, America, and the Kingdom of God', *Liberty* (July–August 1984): 8–10.

Colvin, George Wood. Jr, 'The Women, the Church, and the Courts: Sex Discrimination and the First Amendment', PhD dissertation (Claremont Graduate School, 1986).

Colson, Charles, 'A Different King', *Insight* (5 November 1988): 16.

——'Kingdoms in Conflict', *Insight* (5 November 1988): 4–6.

Cook, Joan Marie, 'Let's Sabotage the Enemy Poverty', *These Times* (October 1965): 25–6.

Daily, Steven Gerald, 'The Irony of Adventism: The Role of Ellen White and Other Adventist Women in Nineteenth Century America' D. Min. dissertation (School of Theology at Claremont, 1985).

Damsteegt, Laurel, 'The Remnant's Vision: Getting Foggy?', *Adventists Affirm*, vol. 2, no. 2 (Fall 1988): 21–8.

Damsteegt, P. Gerard, 'Seventh-day Adventist Doctrines and Progressive Revelation', *Journal of the Adventist Theological Society* vol. 2 (1991) 77–92.

Dewees, Curt, 'Whites and Blacks Unite in South Africa', *Spectrum*, vol. 22, no. 1 (March 1992): 3–8.

Dickinson, Loren, 'Milton Murray's Dream', review of *The Makings of a Philanthropic Fundraiser: The Instructive Example of Milton Murray* by Ronald A. Knott, *Spectrum* vol. 22, no. 5 (January 1993): 58.

Douglass, Herbert, 'Movement Unclear about Message', review of *A Remnant in Crisis* by Jack Provonsha, *Adventist Today* (November–December 1993): 19.

Dunn, H., 'Reality and Truth in the Seventh-Day Adventist Church', PhD dissertation University of Nottingham, 1987).

Dybdahl, Tom, 'How to Wait for the Second Coming', in *Pilgrimage of Hope*, ed. Roy Branson (Takoma Park, MD: Association of Adventist Forums, 1986).

——'We Should Be Involved', *Insight* (5 November 1988): 11.

——'What Causes World Hunger?', *Adventist Review* (5 May 1988): 9–10.

Dyer, Mercedes, 'Mexico Mission', *REACH Report* (December 1988): 8–9.

'Ellen G. White Statements Concerning the Church', (unpublished material stored in Ellen G. White Research Centre Europe, Newbold College, Bracknell, England).

'Ellen G. White's Use of the Term "Remnant Church"' (unpublished material stored in Ellen G. White Research Centre Europe, Newbold College Bracknell, England)

Eva, Willmore D. 'Should Women Ministers Desire Ordination?', *The Adventist Woman*, vol. 8, nos 3–4 (June–July 1989): 6.

Evans, Harrison S., 'Every Person is Significant', *These Times* (1 September 1965): 10–12.

Fagal, William, 'Whatever Happened to the Remnant?', *Adventists Affirm*, vol. 2, no. 2 (Fall 1988): 3–4.

Fiedler, Dave, 'Adventism and Walter Martin', *Our Firm Foundation* (February 1990): 20–1 and 30–1.

Flowers, Karen, 'Women and the Church: The Role of Women in the Church', *Adventist Review*, vol. 166 (28 September 1989): 14–18.

'Food for Everyone', *Adventist Review* (5 May 1988): 15.
Forsyth, Diane Dunlap, 'The 1990 GC Session: Prayers of Manipulation and of Praise', *Adventist Woman* (September–October 1990): 4.
Fowler, John W., 'Preaching "Present Truth"', *Adventists Affirm*, vol. 2, no. 2. (Fall 1988): 29–34.
General Conference, 'Business Proceedings', *Review and Herald*, vol. 58, no. 25 (20 December 1881): 392.
Geraty, Lawrence T. 'The Church and Prejudice in a Biblical View: Breaking Down the Barriers in the Shadow of the Cross', *Adventist Review*, vol. 166 (9 February 1989): 14–15.
Graham, R. E., 'Ellen G. White: An Examination of Her Position and Role in the Seventh-Day Adventist Church', PhD dissertation – (University of Birmingham, 1978).
Graybill, Ronald D. 'The Abolitionist–Millerite Connection', in *The Disappointed: Millerism and Illenarianism in the Nineteenth Century* ed. Ronald L. Numbers and Jonathan M Butler. (Bloomington and Indianopolis: Indiana University Press, 1987), pp. 139–52.
Grieg, Stella Ramirez, 'Women Elders: The Education of Pioneer Memorial Church', *Spectrum*, vol. 17, no. 2 (December 1986): 14–19.
'Gulley's Christology Offers False Christ as Basis for Unity of Church', (unpublished manuscript, Adventist Layman's Foundation. Stored at Ellen G. White Research Centre Europe, Newbold College, Bracknell, England).
Guy, Fritz, 'Dynamics of the Advent Hope', in *Pilgrimage of Hope* ed. Roy Branson. (Takoma Park, MD: Association of Adventist Forums, 1986), pp. 109–21.
——'Why "Special Ordination" For Women is a Bad Idea', *The Adventist Woman*, vol. 8, nos 3–4. (June–July 1989): 8.
Hackleman, Douglas, 'Keeping a World Church Together', *Adventist Currents*, vol. 2, no. 4 (March 1987): 3.
Haenni, Viviane and Watts, Kit, 'Seventh-day Adventists and Women's Ordination: a Bibligraphy for 1972–1989', *The Adventist Woman*, vol. 8, nos 3–4 (June–July 1989): 10–11.
Haldeman, Madelynn Jones, 'A Watershed in Adventist History', *The Adventist Woman*, vol. 12, nos 4–5 (September–October 1993): 4.
Halovak, Bert, 'Route to the Ordination of Women in the S.D.A. Church: Two Parts' (unpublished manuscript, 1985).
——'The Adventist Heritage Calls for Ordination of Women', *Spectrum*, vol. 16, no. 2 (August 1985): 52–60.
Hasel, Gerhard F., 'The Remnant in Scripture and the End Time', *Adventists Affirm*, vol. 2, no. 2 (Fall 1988): 5–12 and 62–4.
Hernandez, Edwin Ivan, 'Religious Commitment and its Political Consequences Among Seventh-day Adventists in the United States', PhD dissertation (University of Notre Dame, 1989).
Hill, H. Ward, 'Response to Charles Teel's Withdrawing Sect, Accommodating Church, Prophesying Remanant: Dilemmas in the Institutionalization of Adventism' (unpublished manuscript, Ellen G. White Research Centre Europe, Newbold College, Bracknell, England, 1980).

Hirsch, Charles B, 'Religion and Politics From an Adventist View', in *Review and Herald* (30 September 1976): 6–8.
Holmes, Shirley S., 'Remnant Pilgrimage', *Adventists Affirm*, vol. 2, no. 2 (Fall 1988): 35–43.
Jenkins, Gary C., 'Mrs. Almira S. Steele and the Steele Home for Needy Children', *Adventist Heritage* vol. 11, no. 2 (Fall 1986): 26–9.
Johnsson, William G. 'Christian in the Needy World', *Adventist Review* vol. 165 (5 May 1988): 2–5.
——'Committees Vote Recommendations on Women's Roles, Global Strategy', *Adventist Review*, vol. 166 (3 August 1989): 6–7.
——'Christians in a Needy World: Does the Bible Teach That We Have a Duty to the Poor and the Homeless?', *Adventist Review* (5 May 1988): 3–5.
Kearnes, John, 'Ethical Politics: Adventism and the Case of William Gage', *Adventist Heritage*, vol. 15, no. 1 (Summer 1978): 3–15.
Knight, George R. 'Adventists and Change', *Ministry* (October 1993): 10–15.
Larson, Ralph, 'A Tale of Two Books: Will This Be the End of an Era?', *Our Firm Foundation* (September 1988): 8–11.
'Letter From the Union Executive Committee to Erich Honecker', *Spectrum*, vol. 22, no. 1 (March 1992): 34–5.
Levenson, Sam, 'Royal Treatment: Any Kid Who Lives in Such a Home Is Lucky', *Insight* (10 May 1986): 6–9.
Luukko, Heikki J., 'ADRA's Role', *Light*, vol. 37 (February 1987): 2.
Marter, Nancy, 'The 1990 GC Session: Women More Visible, Look More Initiative', *Adventist Woman* (September–October 1990): 4.
Maxwell, C Mervyn, 'The Remnant in SDA Thought', *Adventists Affirm*, vol. 2, no. 2 (Fall 1988): 13–20.
Mazrui, Ali, 'The Burden of Underdevelopment', *The Listener* (29 November 1979): 729.
McGarrell, Roy Israel, 'The Historical Development of Seventh-day Adventist Eschatology, 1884–1895', PhD dissertation (Andrews University, 1990).
Moore, Roberta J., 'Fact and Fiction About Women at Work', *Spectrum*, vol. 7, no. 2 (Spring 1975): 34–9.
Morgan, Doug, 'Apocalyptic Anti-Imperialists', *Spectrum*, vol. 22, no. 5 (January 1993): 20–7.
——'The Millennium and Dr. King', *Adventist Review* (22 February 1990): 18–19.
Mowatt, J. A. 'Women as Preachers and Lecturers', *Review and Herald*, vol. 18, no. 9 (30 July 1861): 65–6.
Mutch, Patricia B., 'Ordination: A Cultural or Moral Issue?', *The Adventist Woman*, vol. 8, nos 3–4 (June–July 1989): 6.
Neall, Beatrice S. 'Major Chinks in Bacchiocchi's Armor', *Spectrum*, vol. 18, no. 1 (October 1987): 54–6.
Neall, Ralph E., 'The Nearness and the Delay of the Parousia in the Writings of Ellen G. White', PhD dissertation (Andrews University, 1982).
Neff, LaVonne, 'The Role of Women in American Protestantism, 1975', *Symposium on the Role of Women in the Church* (Biblical Research Institute Committee of General Conference of Seventh-day Adventists, 1984): 156–62.

Nyantakyi, Odomse, 'Are the Reasons of the Seventh-day Adventist Church for Non-membership to the World Council of Churches Valid?' (unpublished essay, Newbold College, Bracknell, England, 1990)
Ochoa, Mario, 'Ethiopia: The Tragedy of Chronic Hunger', *Adventist Review* (5 May 1988): 12.
Olsen, Janet, 'REACH Needs You', *REACH Report* (December 1988): 10–11.
'Ordaining Women: Andrews Faculty Responds', *Spectrum*, vol. 17, no. 2 (December 1986): 20–38.
Pettis, Jerry L., 'An Adventist in Congress', *Spectrum*, vol. 22, no. 1 (Winter 1970): 36–51.
'Protest Letter from the Czech Union Constituency', *Spectrum*, vol. 22, no. 1 (March 1992): 40.
Provonsha, Jack, 'The Church as a Prophetic Minority', in *Pilgrimage of Hope* ed. Roy Branson. (Takoma Park, MD: Association of Adventist Forums, 1986), 98–107.
'Real Christians', *Adventist Review* (15 August 1985): 2.
Reid, George, 'A Birth of a Giant', *Adventist Review* (13 February 1985): 18–20.
Rhoads, Karl, 'Forty Eight Hours with Adventists in Zagreb', *Spectrum*, vol. 22, no. 1 (March 1992): 56–7.
Rittenhouse, Carlos O., 'Labor Unions and SDAs: The Formative Years 1877–1903', *Adventist Heritage*, vol. 4, no. 2 (Winter 1977): 11–19.
Rock, Calvin B., 'Institutional Loyalty Versus Racial Freedom: The Dilemma of Black Seventh-day Adventist Leadership', PhD dissertation (Vanderbilt University, 1984).
Rodor, Amin A., 'The Concept of the Poor in the Context of the Ecclesiology of Liberation Theology', *Andrews University Seminary Studies*, vol. 27 (Summer 1989): 135–6.
'Role of Women in the Seventh-day Adventist Church: Biblical and Spirit of Prophecy Principles' (unpublished manuscript, n.d., filed in Ellen G. White Research Centre Europe, Newbold College, Bracknell, England).
Ross, Gary M., 'Alarmingly Good News', *Adventist Review*, vol. 165 (9 June 1988): 22.
——'SDAs: Conservative and Liberal', review of *Citizens of Two Worlds: Religion and Politics Among American Seventh-day Adventists* by Roger Dudley and Edwin I. Hernandez, *Spectrum*, vol. 22, no. 5 (January 1993):5–7.
Rupert, James, 'Sarajevo's SDA Postal Service – 'Nobody's and Everybody's', *Spectrum*, vol. 23, no. 3 (October 1993): 4.
Russell, Gary, 'Boomers Call for a Socially Conscious Church', *Adventist Today* (November–December 1993): 9.
Scriven, Charles, 'God's Justice, Yes; Penal Substitution, No', *Spectrum*, vol 23, no. 3 (October 1993): 31–8.
——'Jesus and the Role of Women', *Adventist Review*, vol. 166 (2 February 1989): 12–14.
Sinclair, Maurice. 'Evangelical and Radical Christians', *Sally Oak Journal*, no. 10 (Spring 1989): 21–3 and 26–9.
Singleton, H. D., 'Inequality, Civil Rights, and Women's Ordination', *The Adventist Woman*, vol. 8, nos 3–4 (June–July 1989): 4.
Siqueira, Marcus C., 'Ellen White and the Oppressed Poor', *Adventist Review* (22 May 1980): 9–11.

Spangenberg, James L., 'The Ordination of Women: Insights of a Social Scientist', *Spectrum*, vol. 6, nos 1–2 (March–June 1974): 67–73.
Standish, Colin D. and Standish, Russel R., 'The Human Nature of Christ and the New Theology', *In Our Firm Foundation* (September 1988): 20–30.
Takac, Josip, 'Lipik, Croatia – Where Armageddon Began', *Spectrum*, vol. 22, no. 1 (March 1992): 49–51.
Taylor, Ervin, 'Remnant an Apologetic for Historic Adventism', review of *A Remnant in Crisis* by Jack Provonsha, *Adventist Today* (November–December 1993): 18.
Teel, Charles. Jr, 'The Apocalypse as Liturgy', in *Pilgrimage of Hope*, ed. Roy Branson. (Takoma Park, MD: Association of Adventist Forums, 1986), pp. 122–141.
'The BRI Papers', *The Adventist Woman*, vol. 12, nos 4–5 (September–October 1993): 7.
'The Caudills' Private War On Poverty', In *These Times* (October 1965): 26–8.
'The Church and Social Reform', (editorial), *Review and Herald* (15 April 1965).
'The Social Gospel Versus Christ's Gospel' (editorial) *Adventist Review* (7 June 1979): 14.
Theobald, Robin, 'The Seventh-Day Adventist Movement: a Sociological Study, With Particular Reference to Great Britain', PhD. dissertation (London School of Economics, University of London, 1979).
Trefz, Bob, 'Liberty of Conscience and the Everlasting Gospel', *Our Firm Foundation* (February 1990): 16–18.
Wade, David, 'What are You ... Rich or Poor?' *Insight*, vol. 20 (14 January 1989): 13.
Warden, Ivan Leigh, 'Cities – The Fourth World', *Adventist Review* (5 May 1988): 13.
'War On Poverty?', *These Times* (December 1964): 34.
Watts, Kit, 'Men Evaluate Mohaven's Significance, Theology', *The Adventist Woman*, vol. 12, nos 4–5. (September–October 1993): 7.
'What Can I Do?', *Adventist Review* (5 May 1988): 30.
'What Can My Church Do?', *Adventist Review* (5 May 1988): 31.
Whidden, Woodrow, 'Essential Adventism or Historic Adventism?' *Ministry* (October 1993): 5–9.
——'Words to Lay Members', *Review and Herald* (26 August 1902): 7–8.
White, Ellen G. to J. H. Kellogg, Letter 23 October 1985.
White, James, 'The Present Truth and The Spirit of Prophecy', *The Present Truth*, vol. 1, no. 1 (1849): 1.
White, William G., 'Lieutenant Governor George A. Williams: An Adventist in Politics', *Adventist Heritage*, vol. 5, no. 1. (Summer 1978): 24–39.
White, W. C., Robinson, D. E. and White A. L., 'The Spirit of Prophecy and Military Service' (unpublished manuscript, 1956. Stored in Ellen G. White Research Centre Europe, Newbold College, Bracknell, England).
Widmer, Myron, 'The Faces of Grinding Poverty', *Adventist Review* (27 August 1987): 4.
——'The Faces of Poverty – Part II', *Adventist Review* (10 September 1987): 4–5.
——'What the Adventist Church is Doing About Poverty', *Adventist Review* (5 May 1988): 19–25.

Wilson, Neal C., 'Global Strategy and the Poor', *Adventist Review* (5 May 1988): 5.
'Women Licensed as Ministers, 1878–1975', *Spectrum*, vol. 16, no. 3 (November 1985): 60
Yamagata, Masao, 'Ellen G. White and American Premillennialism', PhD dissertation (The Pennsylvania State University, 1983).
Yob, Iris, 'God's Feminine Roles', *Spectrum*, vol. 23, no. 3. (October 1993): 19–30.
Zackrison, Edwin Harry, 'Seventh-day Adventists and Original Sin: A Study of the Early Development of the Seventh-day Adventist Understanding of the Effect of Adam's Sin on His Posterity', PhD dissertation (Andrews University, 1984).

OTHER ARTICLES

Allen, Joseph L., 'Social Ethics', in *A New Dictionary of Christian Ethics*, ed. James F. Childress and John Macquarrie (London: SCM Press, 1986).
Arthur, D. F. 'Come out of Babylon: a Study of Millerite Separation and Denominationalism, 1840–1865', PhD dissertation, (University of Rochester, 1970).
Augsburger, Myron S., 'Overconsumption in the Developed Nations', in *The Cause of World Hunger* ed. William J. Byron (New York: Paulist Press, 1982): 232–253.
Bascio, Patrick Anthony, 'Black Theology. Its Critique of Classical or Scholastic Theology', PhD dissertation (Fordham University, 1987).
Benjamin, Marlene, 'Rights of Persons, Duties of States: Philosophical Justifications of Human Rights in the International Arena', PhD dissertation (Brandies University, 1986).
Berlin, Isaiah, 'Two Concepts of Liberty', *Four Essays on Liberty*. (Oxford: Oxford University Press, 1969).
Boven, Theo Van, 'The International System of Human Rights: An Overview', in *Manual on Human Rights Reporting by United Nations Centre for Human Rights and United Nations Institute for Training and Research (UNITAR)* (New York: United Nations, 1991): 3–10.
Brady, Edward J., 'Theological Underdevelopment and Ethical Insensitivity', in *The Cause of World Hunger*, ed. William J. Byron (New York: Paulist Press, 1982): 38–54.
Byron, William J., 'The Causes of World Hunger', in *The Cause of World Hunger*, ed. William J. Byron (New York: Paulist Press, 1982): 5–15.
Calhoun, John C., 'The Unequal Distribution of Wealth and Income in the World', in *The Cause of World Hunger*, ed. William J. Byron (New York: Paulist Press, 1982): 220–31.
Carle, Robert Dwight, 'Theological Critiques of Human Rights Theory: the Contributions of Jacques Maritain and Gustavo Gutierrez', PhD dissertation (Emory University, 1989).
Cooper, John Wesley, 'Democratic Pluralism and Human Rights: the Political Theologies of Jacques Maritain and Reinhold Niebuhr', PhD dissertation (Syracuse University, 1982).

Cowdin, Daniel Martin, 'Religious Liberty and the Unity of the Human Person: a Philosophical Reflection on Religion, Liberalism, and Human Dignity', PhD disertation (Yale University, 1991).

Cronin, K. J., 'The Value of the Language of Rights in Christian Ethics, With Particular Reference to Reproductive Rights', PhD dissertation (University of Edinburgh, 1989).

Cullity, G., 'The Limits of Obligation: On the Extent of our Obligations to Help the Starving', BPhil dissertation (Oxford University, 1989).

Donnely, Jack, 'What are Human Rights?: An Historical and Conceptual Analysis', PhD dissertation (Berkeley, University of California, 1981).

Dushnyck, Walter, 'Yugoslavia', in *Case Studies on Human Rights and Fundamental Freedoms: a World Survey vol. 1*, ed. Willem A. Veenhoven (The Hague: Martinus Nijhoff, 1975): 430–8.

Egan, Eileen, 'Refugees: the Uprooting of Peoples as a Cause of Hunger', in *The Cause of World Hunger*, ed. William J. Byron (New York: Paulist Press, 1982): 173–95.

Ewing, A. C. and Childress, J. F., 'Kantian Ethics', *A New Dictionary of Christian Ethics* ed. John Macquarrie and James Childress (London: SCM Press, 1986), pp. 334–7.

Fishbane, Michael, 'The Image of the Human and the Rights of the Individual in Jewish Tradition', in *Human Rights and the World's Religions*, ed. Leroy S. Rouner (Notre Dame, IN: University of Notre Dame Press, 1988): 17–32.

Freudenberger, C. Dean, 'The Land Does Not Lie' in *The Cause of World Hunger*, ed. William J. Byron (New York: Paulist Press, 1982): 90–105.

Giles, Kevin, 'The Biblical Argument for Slavery: Can the Bible Mislead? A Case Study in Hermeneutics' in *The Evangelical Quarterly*, vol. 66, no. 1 (January 1994): 3–17.

Glenny, Misha, 'The Massacre of Yugoslavia', *Spectrum*, vol. 22, no. 1 (March 1992): 52–62.

Gumbleton, Thomas J., 'Toward a Solution: Bread for the World', *The Cause of World Hunger*, ed. William J. Byron (New York: Paulist Press, 1982): 241–53.

Gunderson, Gil, review of *Human Dignity: the Internationalization of Human Rights*, ed. Alice H. Henkins (New York: Aspen Institute for Humanistic Studies, Oceana Publications and The Netherlands: Sitjthoff and Noordhoff, Alphen aan den Rijn, 1979), in *Universal Human Rights*, vol. 2, no. 2 (April–June 1980): 97–9.

Hayward, T. P., 'Philosophy and Human Rights', PhD dissertation (University of Sussex, 1989).

Hehir, J. Bryan, 'Population and Poverty: Exploring the Relationship', in *The Cause of World Hunger* ed. William J. Byron (New York: Paulist Press, 1982): 207–19.

Himes, Kenneth Robert, 'Freedom and Self-realization: Toward a Theology of Human Rights', PhD dissertation (Duke University, 1981).

Holleman, Warren Lee, 'A Theological Analysis of the Role of Western Values and American Foreign Policy in the Movement For Universal Human Rights', PhD dissertation (Rice University, 1986).

Hooker, M. A., 'A Philosophical Study of the Meaning, Justification and Scope of Personal and Individual Human Rights in the Contemporary

World, and Their Social Context', PhD dissertation (Manchester University, 1987).

Huber, Wolfgang, 'Human Rights: A Concept and its History', in *The Church and the Rights of Man* ed. Alois Muller and Norbert Greinacher (New York: The Seabury Press, 1979): 1–10.

Kelly, Arthur James, 'The Response of the Episcopal Church to Social Change and Social Issues, 1860–1978: How These Changes Have Affected the Life and Mission of the Church as Reflected in the Diocese of Long Island', PhD dissertation (New York University, 1981).

Kymlicka, W., 'Liberal Equality and Cultural Community', DPhil dissertation (Oxford University, 1987).

Lee, S. K., 'Election and Ethics in the Prophecy of Amos', PhD dissertation (University of Bristol, 1990).

Markovic, Mihailo, 'Political Rights Versus Social Rights' in *Human Rights and the World's Religions*, ed. Leroy S. Rouner. (Notre Dame, IN: University of Notre Dame Press, 1988): 46–62.

Martenson, Jan, 'Foreword' in *Human Rights: Questions and Answers* (New York: United Nations, 1987).

Matthews, A. D., 'The Doctrine of Creation and the Ethics of Life and Death' MA thesis (University of Durham, 1986).

McGrath, Alister E., 'The Church's Response to Pluralism' in *Evangelical Review of Theology*, vol. 18, no. 1. (January 1994): 4–19.

Mealand, David L., 'Poverty as a Social Problem' in *A New Dictionary of Christian Ethics*, ed. James F. Childress and John Macquarrie (London: SCM Press, 1986): 488–9.

Millar-Wood, Jayne, 'Food Insecurity: the Inadequacy and Unreliability of Reserves', in *The Cause of World Hunger*, ed. William J. Byron (New York: Paulist Press, 1982): 121–37.

Moo, Douglas J., 'Paul and the Law in the Last Ten Years', *Scotish Journal of Theology* vol. 40 (1986): 287–307.

Ndungane, W. N., 'Human Rights and the Christian Doctrine of Man', MTh Thesis (University of London, 1979).

Rendtorff, Trutz, 'Christian Concepts of the Responsible Self', in *Human Rights and the World's Religions*, ed. Leroy S. Roune (Notre Dame, IN: University of Notre Dame Press, 1988): 33–45.

Ripp, Rudolph K., 'Transnationalism and Human Rights: The Case of Amnesty International', PhD dissertation (City University of New York, 1982).

Schmidt, Robert Frederick, 'The Legitimacy of Revolution: the World Council of Churches' Grants to Liberation Movements in Southern Africa', PhD dissertation, (University of Washington, 1983).

Simon, Arthur, 'The Basic Cause: Poverty', in *The Cause of World Hunger*, ed. William J. Byron (New York: Paulist Press, 1982): 16–27.

Traer, Robert A., 'Human Rights: A Global Faith', PhD dissertation (Graduate Theological Union, 1988).

Turner, Jack David, 'A Rhetorical Analysis of Liberation Theology', PhD dissertation (Ohio University, 1987).

Ward, James Garcia, 'Comparison of Two Liberation Thinkers: Enrique Dussel From Latin America and Michael Novak From the United States (Argentina)', PhD dissertation (Depaul University, 1985).

Wollaston, Isabel, 'Faith and Fratricide: Christianity, Anti-Semitism, and the Holocaust in the Work of Rosemary Radford Ruether', in *Modern Churchman*, vol. 33, no. 1 (1991): 8–14.

'World Conference on Human Rights to be Held in 1993', *Human Rights Newsletter*, vol. 4, no. 4 (January 1992): 1–2.

Ziesler, J. A., 'Anthropology of Hope', *Expository Times*, vol. 90 (1979): 104–9.

Index

Adam–Christ theology 144
ADRA 5, 31–3, 35, 67–72
advent *see* Second Coming
Adventist Refugee Care 27, 29, 68–9
Amnesty International 22, 24–6
Anabaptists 134–5
Anderson, R. Allan 79, 140
Andreasen, M. L. 141
Andrews, John N. 13, 75–6, 100, 102
apotelesmatic principle 145
ARC, *see* Adventist Refugee Care

Bacchiocchi, Samuel 117, 190, 199–201
Bainum, Robert 28–9, 211
Barnhouse, Donald Gray 139–40
Barth, Karl 170
Bates, Joseph 12, 39, 75, 89, 138
Biblical Research Institute 110
Black Conferences, *see* Regional Conferences
Bradford, Charles 81, 191–3
Branson, Roy 27, 44–5, 77, 83–4, 127–8, 133, 135, 177, 179–80
BRIAD *see* Biblical Research Institute
Brimsmead, Robert 142–3
brotherhood 35, 83–4, 89–90, 120, 133, 164–5, 169, 211
Brunt, John 177, 180–5
Bull, Malcolm, *see* Bull and Lockhart
Bull and Lochkart 5, 94, 127
Bultman, Rudolf 170
Butler, Jonathan 41, 75

Camp Mohaven, *see* Symposium at Camp Mohaven
Chicago Medical Mission 59–61, 211
Collectivism 49
Colvin, George 126, 132, 135–6
Community Services 58–9, 65, 68
COSIGN 28
covenant 43–7, 175–7, 196
creation 1, 4, 36, 76, 83–90, 101, 105–8, 113, 117, 121, 130, 144, 150, 153, 163–8, 196, 206, 209–10
CRO *see* Croatia Relief Organisation
Croatia 1, 30–5
Croatia Relief Organisation 69–70, 211
Cullman, Oscar 171

Davidson, Richard 113
Decalogue, *see* Ten Commandments
Dederen, Raoul 104, 110
delay 129–31, 137, 200, 202
dignity *see* human dignity
doctrinal purity 133
Dodd, C. H. 171, 177, 180
Dorcas Welfare Society 57–8, 210
Douglas, Herbert 142–3
duty 15, 28, 36, 54–5, 59, 72–3, 75, 129–30, 138, 155–8, 160–1, 167
Dworkin, Ronald 156, 166

egoism 129, 133
ends-oriented ethic 129–30
equality 6–7, 38, 54, 56, 75–80, 82–6, 89–90, 93, 98, 100, 105–6, 108, 110, 112–13, 120, 125, 128, 150, 161, 164–5, 167, 188, 191–4, 204, 206, 209–10, 212
eschatology 7, 75, 83, 86–7, 129, 144–5, 169–71, 179–84, 196, 198–9, 204–6, 211–12
ethic of duty 130
ethical egoist 129, 133

Farag, Wadie 111
Ford, Desmond 142–6
Fordham, W. W. 79–80

Formicola, Jo Renee 157
Froom, LeRoy E. 140

Gewirth, Alan 158–9
Gladson, Jerry 106–7, 118–19
Graybill, Ronald 53
Great Disappointment 12, 39–40

Harnack, Adolf 169
Harris, Richard 154, 164, 166
Hasel, Gerhard 43–4, 105–6
Heppendstall, Edward 142–3
Holbrook, Frank 110, 119–20
holism 26, 126–8
holistic theology 126–8, 157
human dignity 12, 46, 58, 60, 79–80, 89–90, 109, 120, 127, 155, 157–8, 164–7, 191
human rights:
- absolute rights 159
- basis of 157–62, 166–7
- definitions 155–7
- origins of 153–5
- philosophy of 153–62
- theology of 157–62

Image of God 90, 105–6, 111–12, 114, 164–8, 206, 211
Imago Dei, see Image of God
imminence 30, 39–40, 129–31, 171, 199–202
imminent *see* imminence
individualism 46, 49–50, 86–7
Ingathering Programme 66–7, 211

Jenkins, Roy 159, 165

Kant, Immanuel 166, 169
Kellog, John Harvey 16, 59–64, 75
Kingdom of Glory 173–7, 180, 184–6, 211
Kingdom of God 4, 42–3, 48, 56, 87, 115, 130, 153, 167–86, 188, 197, 206, 211
Kingdom of Grace 173–7, 184–6
Kisekka, Babi Mululu 27–8, 211
Kubo, Sakae 109–10, 118, 189, 193, 199–206

Ladd, George Eldon 178
Land, Gary 149
LaRondalle, Hans 143
liberation 28, 70, 84, 87, 97, 109, 125, 137–8, 147, 150, 160, 191–3, 206, 212
Liberation Theology 137–8, 192
liberty 5, 14–6, 18, 20, 26, 38, 41–2, 47, 75–6, 133, 156–8, 161, 193, 208
Life Boat Mission 61, 210
Lochman 159–60, 162
Locke 49, 154, 158
Londis, James 111–13, 131, 133

MacCarty, Skip 113
Martin, Walter R. 139–41, 148
Medical Missionary and Benevolent Association 62–3, 210
Mennonites 135
millennium 11, 42–3, 174, 177, 184
Miller, William 11–12, 39, 43
MMBA, *see* Medical Missionary and Benevolent Association
Moltmann, Jürgen 153, 155, 157, 160–1, 165, 167, 171–2
moral law, *see* Ten Commandments

natural law 153
Nazism 179–9, 21, 36
Neall, Beatrice S. 113–7
new creation (humanity) 85, 167
New Theology 4, 137–50, 209–10

O'Mahony 157–8, 161, 198
ordination 97–100, 103–4, 109–10, 115–18, 121

Pagels, Elaine 161
parousia, see Second Coming
Paxton, Geoffrey 141–3
Pearson, Michael ix, 4–5, 11, 44–8, 103, 130–2
perfection 45, 87, 141–3, 147, 182, 190
personhood 127–8, 158, 164
political ethics 183
politics 47, 192

poverty 3, 6, 15, 53–6, 70–3, 126, 183, 209
pragmatic *see* pragmatism
pragmatism 3–5, 36, 48–9, 75–6, 79, 84, 90, 130, 132, 137, 174, 208
premillennialism 42–3, 174–5
present truth 137–8, 150, 154, 206, 208, 212
principles of interpretation 74, 118–21
prophetic role 7, 147, 194–8, 210

Questions on Doctrine 139–42, 174–7, 180

racism 6, 19, 80–2, 85–7, 90, 125–6, 209
radical discipleship 89, 134–6
Rauschenbusch, Walter 169
Raz, Jopseph 157
REACH International 68–9
Read, Walter E. 140
realised eschatology 170–1, 180, 211
Regional Conferences 79–81
religious liberty 13–7, 20, 38, 41–2, 47, 133, 208–9
remnant 5, 46–8, 89, 133–4, 145–7, 149, 175
Reynolds, Keld 64, 140
Rice, Richard 164–5, 167–8, 177–9, 191, 194, 199, 202
Ritschl, Albrecht 168–70
Robinson, John T. 199
Rock, Calvin 55, 81

Sabbath 4, 6–7, 12–14, 17, 27, 30, 38, 43–4, 55, 73, 94, 149, 164, 187, 189–94, 206, 210–12
Sabbathical year 15, 190, 193–4, 211
Sabbath Sunday issue 40–2
SAWS 27, 29, 57–8, 65–6, 128
Schwarz, Richard 61, 141
Scriven, Charles 135
SDA World Service, Inc., *see* SAWS
Second Advent, *see* Second Coming
Second Coming 4, 7, 11–12, 17, 39, 43, 55, 89, 129–31, 137, 149–50, 172–4, 176–7, 182, 187–8, 198–206, 210–12
Shaking of Adventism 142–3
Shelkov 21–22
Social Gospel 59, 169–70, 180, 211
Social Gospellers 169
Soviet Union Adventists 21–3, 25–6
Spectrum 5, 26–7, 29, 117, 142, 210
Standish, Colin 146–8
Standish, Russell 143, 146–8
Stirling, Betty 110
Stott, John 37, 71
supreme principle 159
Symposium at Camp Mohaven 98, 104

Teel, Charles Jr 5
Ten Commandments 44–5, 187–9, 194, 197–8, 211
Tenney, George C. 100–2

United Nations 1, 26, 154
Unruh, T. Edgar 140

Vlastos, Gregory 158
Volunteers International 28–9

Waldron, Jeremy 156–7
Walters, James 129–31, 133
Warren, Max 200
Weiss, Johannes 169–71, 173
Whidden, Woodrow 148
White, Ellen G. 6, 16, 41–2, 44, 46, 5, 53–8, 60–1, 64, 76–8, 82–4, 89, 92–4, 100, 102–5, 115, 128, 138, 141, 145, 147, 172–5, 184, 203
White, James 100–1, 138
Wilson, Neal 126
wholism, *see* holism
women, ordination of 97–100, 103–4, 110, 115–18, 121
women, role of 3, 5, 49, 92–121, 209